Library of
Davidson College

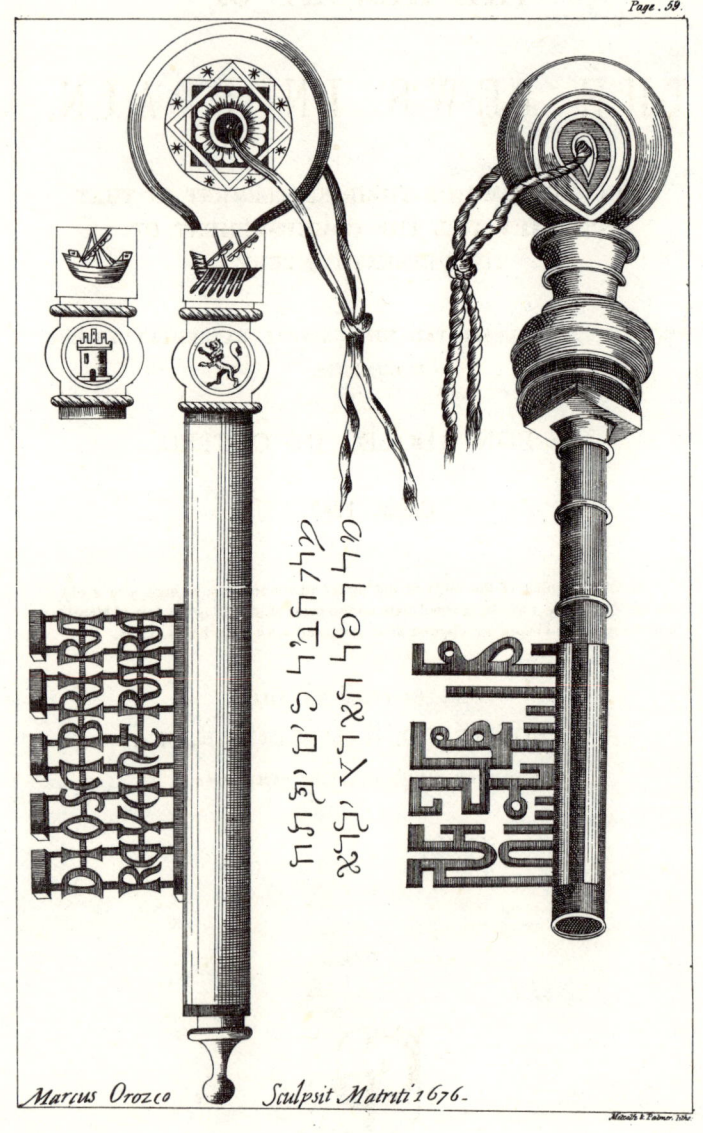

THE HISTORY OF
THE JEWS IN SPAIN,

FROM THE TIME OF THEIR SETTLEMENT IN THAT
COUNTRY TILL THE COMMENCEMENT OF
THE PRESENT CENTURY.

WRITTEN, AND ILLUSTRATED WITH DIVERS EXTREMELY SCARCE
DOCUMENTS,

By DON ADOLFO DE CASTRO.

CADIZ, 1847.

"At the beginning of the reign of the right Catholic spouses, so high a tone did the heresy assume, that the learned were on the point of preaching the law of Moses, and the unlearned could not disguise their Judaism."—ANDRES BERNALDES.

TRANSLATED BY THE
REV. EDWARD D. G. M. KIRWAN, M.A.,
FELLOW OF KING'S COLLEGE, CAMBRIDGE.

GREENWOOD PRESS, PUBLISHERS
WESTPORT, CONNECTICUT

The Library of Congress has catalogued this publication as follows:

Library of Congress Cataloging in Publication Data

Castro y Rossi, Adolfo de, 1823-1898.
  The history of the Jews in Spain.

  Translation of Historia de los judios en España.
  Reprint of the 1851 ed.
  1. Jews in Spain--History. I. Title.
DS135.S7C3513 1972   296'.0946   70-97273
ISBN 0-8371-2593-6

Originally published in 1851
by John Deighton, Cambridge, England

First Greenwood Reprinting 1972
Second Greenwood Reprinting 1973

Library of Congress Catalogue Card Number 70-97273

ISBN 0-8371-2593-6

Printed in the United States of America

TRANSLATOR'S PREFACE.

THERE is no nation under the sun whose history can be more interesting than that of the Jews, particularly that branch of them which, after the destruction of Jerusalem by Titus, emigrated to Spain, and for many centuries lived in that land, which they regarded as their adopted country.

In spite of the insults, the hardships, and the persecutions which they endured in Spain, the sons of Israel cultivated the arts and sciences, fed the lamp of literature, and kept it continually burning for a succession of ages, during which it may be justly said that "darkness covered the greater part of Europe, and gross darkness the people."

That the Jews of Spain were far more enlightened than the Christians and Mohammedans of that country will appear from the pages of this history. We cannot therefore be surprised that a man of such eminent literary attainments as Don Adolfo de Castro should devote himself to the task of writing it. *Task* I call it, for that it really was such must be obvious to any one who will give himself the trouble of looking at the numerous authorities (cited in the notes to this Translation) which the Author had to consult; and although this is but a brief history of the Spanish Jews, I make no doubt that its brevity is mainly owing to circumstances over which Don Adolfo had no controul, viz. want of books, records, and documents to throw a light upon it, some of which were in all probability burned, and some carried away from Spain by the Jews at the time of their expulsion from that kingdom by Ferdinand the Unprincipled, otherwise called the Catholic.

The Author of this work has been for some years advantageously known to his countrymen by his literary merits, and within the last twelve months a work of his, entituled " *The History of the Persecution of the Protestants by Philip the Second,*" has been translated into English by Mr. Parker; to which, perhaps, my translation of the " *History of the Jews in Spain*" may be regarded as a suitable accompaniment.

Don Adolfo de Castro, unable *to defend* Queen Isabella's conduct in establishing the Inquisition, endeavours *to palliate* it by saying that *she acted in compliance with her husband's wishes and the counsels of her confessor!*

But is such compliance as this to be accepted as an excuse for a gross violation of God's laws? Are we to be told that a woman, who, pandering to the avarice of a worthless husband and the fanaticism of an ignorant confessor, consents to the foundation of a tribunal calculated to deluge her native land with the blood of thousands of her innocent subjects, and to unjustly deprive the heirs of the unhappy victims of their property, is a person of *an amiable and gentle disposition?*

Vain is the attempt which English as well as Spanish and Portuguese writers have made to throw a false colouring upon this act of Queen Isabella! The false colouring has worn off and exposed to view the dirt and filth which lay beneath it. The damning act is written with an iron pen in indelible characters!

Does the youthful Queen who now sways the sceptre of the Spanish monarchy desire to transmit her name to posterity as that of the most upright sovereign who ever sat on the throne of a noble kingdom? Then, let it be her first act to make reparation to the Jews for the wrongs done to their race by her ancestors, and especially by her namesake: let her blot out from the statute-books of Spain every penal law that affects the Israelites: let her invite them back to the land which they still regard as the land of their adoption, and confer upon them greater privileges than they have ever enjoyed in any country since the time of their general dispersion.

In the Appendix is given a letter, purporting to have been written to Philip the Second by Arias Montano, entituled "Instruction for Princes," &c., which, as the reader will see by note 4 to page 262, is a forged one: although this will not affect the credit of the history, (inasmuch as no fact mentioned in it rests on the authority of the "Instruction," which was published for the purpose of confirming the Author's opinions about the Jesuits,) it is much to be regretted that he should have printed it. Were I to consult my own inclination I should suppress it, but it strikes me that, were I to do so, I should be disingenuous; and were I to publish it without stating it to be a forgery, I should be still more disingenuous.

The Author of this history has omitted, in general, to give the authorities from which his information is derived, a defect which I have endeavoured to supply; but owing to my having been obliged to grope my way in the dark, and to the difficulty of procuring Spanish books, my success, though greater than I had expected, has not been such as I could wish.

Wherever I have had access to the works *cited* by the Author, I have verified his quotations, *except in one instance*, (see note 59, page 151), in which he has, perhaps, inadvertently referred to a wrong authority.

In order to avoid the introduction of foreign idioms, as far as possible, into my translation, I placed my manuscript in the hands of a friend (one of the Fellows of Trinity College), not acquainted with the Spanish language, who has kindly read the greater part of it, and, at his suggestion, I have made many alterations, which are, I trust, improvements.

To another friend, W. G. Clark, Esq., Fellow of Trinity College, my best thanks are due for having procured me a copy of Don Adolfo de Castro's work.

King's College, Cambridge, July 5th, 1851.

ERRATA.

PAGE
2, note 1, for *Española* read *de España*.
6, substitute figure 4 for the asterisk.
8, note 10, for 30 read 15
8, note 16, the words after España *should be in brackets*.
19, note 27, last line, dele *Book*.
28, note 38, last line, for 1 read 2.
29, line 10, for *burying* read *buying*.
31, note 42, line 1, for *Pandilla* read *Padilla*.
39, line 14, dele *but*.
49, the last sentence of note 52 *should be in brackets*.
59, note 9, the words after 1677 *should be in brackets*.
70, note 24, last line, after *paragraph* insert *except that of* 1335 : *see following note*.
73, ninth line of the note, for *slain* read *mortally wounded*.
80. last line of the text, *dele* 22.
80, the last sentence of note 23, including the word *Translator*, should be in *rectangular* brackets.
100, note 61, line 3, *dele from*
120, line 9, for *Aragon* read *Arragon*.
140, note 43, line 2, for *his holiness* read *His Holiness*.
172, line 8, for *porutray* read *pourtray*.
207, line 11, for *however* read *how*
221, 8th line of the text and 2nd line of note 20, for *Teixera* read *Teixeira*.
224, line 11, *dele* 27.
255, line 16, for *affrontery* read *effrontery*.

SUMMARY OF BOOK THE FIRST.

INTRODUCTION.—Settlement of the Jews in Spain in Nebuchadnezzar's time, fabulous.—Apocryphal character of the letter said to have been sent to Jerusalem by the synagogue of Toledo, to protest against the execution of Jesus Christ.—Idle tales which grew out of this fiction.—Real settlement of the Jews in the Spanish peninsula.—Resolution against them by the fathers of the council of Elliberis.—Arrival of the Goths in Spain.—Liberty the Jews enjoyed there as long as the former continued to be Arians.—Recaredo is converted to Catholicism.—Decree of the third council of Toledo against the Jews.—Persecution of them in the days of king Sisebuto.—Decrees of the councils of Toledo in the reigns of Chintila, Recesvinto, and Ejica.—Protection said to have been afforded to the Jews by king Witiza, fabulous.— The Jews of Spain concert a plan with their brethren of Africa for the invasion and reduction of the peninsula by the Arabs.— Arrival of the latter and battle of the Guadalete, in which the flower of the Gothic nobility is cut off.—The Jews assist the Arabs in their enterprises; garrison the principal cities which were conquered by the latter; regain their liberty.

BOOK THE FIRST.

I AM about to treat of the chequered and almost-always-tragic fortunes of the Jews in Spain: a history replete, not with glorious conquests, signal feats of valor and lofty aims, but with calamities, conflicts, persecutions, riots, robberies, conflagrations, banishments, deaths by fire on public scaffolds, losses of caste,[1] imprisonments, degradations, and other extremely rigorous punishments.

Herein I shall demonstrate the unreasonableness of those writers who corrupted the truth, and described, and still describe, the ancient Spanish Jews as men utterly given up to usury and accustomed to hide in the bowels of the earth the fruit of their labours, their commerce, and their acquisitions; whereas it is to them that Spain owes the great advancement she made in medicine, philosophy, mathematics, and navigation. They were in the habit of being consulted by kings on the most critical affairs of state, and it was by the aid of their counsels and hard cash that the most difficult, the grandest, and the most hazardous enterprises were undertaken.

I shall also point out the great error as well as

---

[1] Literally, *infamies of lineages*. Persons descended, or supposed to be descended, from those who have in them any mixture of Jewish or Moorish blood, or descended, or supposed to be descended, from ancestors convicted by the tribunal of the Inquisition are, *to this day*, more or less looked down upon in Spain; but this illiberal prejudice is gradually wearing away. Pedro Salazar de Mendoza, in his Monarquía Española (lib. III. cap. 1), speaking of the council of the Inquisition (of which he was a member), and the persons connected with that tribunal, says: "they are all, from the Inquisitor General down to the porters and servants who attend and wait upon them, old Christians, pure and in no wise descended from Jews, Moors, or persons who have had penance imposed upon them by the same holy office." The original words are, "Son todos desde el Inquisidor General hasta los porteros y familiares que les sirven y acompanan, Cristianos viejos, limpios, sin raza ni descendencia de Judíos, Moros ó penitenciados por el mismo Santo Oficio."—*Translator.*

injustice which the Catholic Sovereigns[a] committed, when they ordered the Jews to be banished from the realms of Spain, and shall support my opinion by showing the extreme impolicy of a measure which must, necessarily, be attended with such fatal results, and exhibit the utter fruitlessness and futility of persecutions, punishments, and other severities for religion's sake: for monarchs may, indeed, by the arm of the law, coërce the bodies of their subjects, but they will find it an easier task to check the winds and turn back the courses of rivers, than to subdue the minds of men. I write this history dispassionately and impartially—passion and partiality belong not to me. I neither am a Jew, nor a descendant from Judaizers. My sole aim is to stand up for the truth—a rule by which every historian ought to be guided: and the truth cannot be endangered by my pen, as I am not in the habit of viewing things with prejudiced eyes: this is a practice quite inconsistent with my notions.

Some writers have mentioned the prosperity and adversity of the Spanish Jews, and there has been no want of great geniuses who have treated of the times of the expulsion of the latter; but, owing to their fear of the Catholic sovereigns, while these were living, and after their deaths, to their own hatred of every thing that concerned the Jewish nation—a hatred

---

[a] This expression is emphatically applied by Spaniards to Ferdinand and Isabella: in the original it is *Reyes Católicos, i. e.* Catholic *kings*, but as it means a *King and Queen*, I thought it would be better to render it as I have done.—*Translator.*

imbibed at their mothers' breasts—hardly any of them have cut out their stories according to the measure of truth.

Hence it was that men of high birth, and reputation for prudence, of singular virtue, and eminence in science, allowed themselves to be borne down the stream of a thousand follies and extravagances, arrived at a pitch of extreme blindness, and did irreparable damage to history and literature: from which it is evident that neither studies, nor brilliancy of talent, nor science suffice to create wisdom in man, but only serve to ransom his spirit from the dungeon in which it has been imprisoned from his childhood, purified from the corruption and poison of vulgar doctrines which it has imbibed, through the ignorance of his parents and teachers.

The information we have respecting the settlement of the Jews in Spain is infected with many great errors, since persons of great learning and historical credit have relied on fables told by the low and ignorant populace, and on documents forged, either from interested motives or from a vain desire to have both the documents and the lies contained in them believed.

It is related by some writers that Nebuchadnezzar, king of Babylon, after he had levelled proud Jerusalem's walls, and carried the Israelitish people into captivity, followed up his victorious enterprises with the destruction of Tyre and Egypt, and the towns situated on the African shores. After he had taken vengeance on the Phenicians, and had exacted satisfaction from them for succouring the Tyrians while he was hemming in the latter with an obstinate blockade, he invaded the Spanish territory, vanquished its inhabitants, and left there a large number of Jews, who travelled with his army, and laid the foundations of Toledo, Seville, and other very ancient cities.[3] Tertullian, Eusebius of Cesarea, St. Clement of Alexandria, as well as other authors, treat largely of the conquests made and marches undertaken by Nebuchadnezzar, through Libya and all Asia as far as Armenia; not one of whom speaks of his arrival in the Spanish peninsula, and his capture of it by fire and sword. And even if such forcible reasons and arguments could be adduced as should serve to prove clearly that he acquired these lands by force of arms and power, there exist much stronger reasons for believing that no Jews went thither with his army. The perpetual enmity and discord that existed between the Jews and Assyrians, especially in religious matters, are proved by the testimony of the grave and authentic historian Flavius Josephus. While they lived together, their minds were alienated from one another by blind rancour and hostility: the former were dissatisfied with the state of slavery and misery to which they were reduced; the latter were disgusted at the repeated injuries they suffered, without a murmur, at the hands of those very men whom they had burdened with the yoke of a wearisome captivity. It is, therefore, im-

[3] Garibay's Compendio Historial, lib. v. cap. 4; Mariana's Hist. Gen. de España, lib. I. cap. 17.—*Translator.*

possible to suppose that Nebuchadnezzar would take with his army, in his extremely bold march through Africa and Spain, such terrible and such troublesome enemies as these; and, still more so, that he would leave in their power the lands which he had acquired at the expense of the blood, sweat, and toils of his subjects.

Other historians assert that some Jews came to Spain about this time with Pyrrhus their captain,[4] and built towns in two places—one of them was Toledo, the other Lucina or Lucena. But all these accounts are many miles away from the truth. The best established and only true story is, that those who escaped death at the capture of Jerusalem, were brought in chains to Babylon. This is the account given in the books of Kings and Chronicles.

Those who have wished to prove the fact that the Jews settled in Spain after the latter were subdued by the arms of Nebuchadnezzar,* relate that they had synagogues in the most considerable cities of the Spanish peninsula, of which the head and first in dignity was the one at Toledo. They go on to state that when Jesus Christ commenced preaching at Jerusalem, the Scribes and Pharisees determined to destroy Him, and

---

[4] Strabo says that Nebuchadnezzar penetrated beyond the pillars of Hercules, and led an army from Spain into Thrace and Pontus (book xv.). Josephus also states that he (Nebuchadnezzar) conquered τὴν Ἰβηρίαν, or, as it is in the Latin version, which is of equal authority, *bonam partem Hispaniæ*. (Antiquities, book x. chap. 11.) For this story of Pyrrhus, &c., see Garibay's Compendio Historial, lib. v. cap. 4.—*Translator*.

that (as in matters of the greatest difficulty they were accustomed to consult with all the synagogues in the world in order to ask their advice and consent,) they dispatched to the chief of the synagogue of Toledo letters from the chiefs and priests by the hand of their messenger, one Samuel. The Jews of Toledo met in council and in the names of the other synagogues in Spain, from which they had received full powers, after hearing read to them the letters of one Eleazar, a priest of their own country and a man of holy life, who had gone on business of his own to Jerusalem, and had been witness to, and had a high esteem for, the life and miraculous acts of Jesus, answered, that the Spanish Jews could not allow their brethren of Jerusalem to take away the life of Jesus Christ. The answer, they say, was afterwards found at Toledo, when Don Alfonso the Sixth rescued this city from the power of the Moors; it was written in the Hebrew tongue, and afterwards translated into Arabic by order of a wise Moorish king, named Galifre: the former monarch ordered it to be put into the Castilian language of the day, and it was preserved till the year 1494 in the archives of Toledo, whence it was carried off by the Jews when they were expelled from Spain.

This fiction, for such I consider it to be, has obtained credit with many very good writers who were deceived by the forger of the document, as for instance, Don Fray Prudencio de Sandoval,[5] Arias Montano,[6]

[5] Historia de los Reyes de Castilla y de Leon, &c.
[6] Commentaria in XII. Prophetas.

Dr. Juan de Vergara,[7] Dr. Francisco Pisa,[8] Fray Juan de Pineda,[9] Quintana Dueñas,[10] Rodrigo Caro,[11] Tamayo de Vargas,[12] Francisco de Padilla,[13] Don José de Pellicer,[14] Don Diego de Castejon,[15] Rodrigo Mendez de Silva,[16] and many others whom, to avoid prolixity, I omit. For the credit of Spanish literature, I must say that several distinguished writers, including the Marquis of Mondejar and the very learned Nicolas Antonio, as well as other excellent critics, have regarded the story as apocryphal. Here follows what people would have us believe to be the translation of the letter in the language of the day in Don Alfonso the Sixth's time.

"*Levi, chief of the synagogue* (archisinagogo), *and Samuel, and Joseph, good men of the Aljama of Toledo, to Eleazar, great High-Priest, and Samuel Canut y Anás, and Caiaphas, good men of the Al-*

[7] Historia de Toledo publicada por Pedro Alcocer.
[8] Historia de Toledo. 1ª parte [cap. 23. Pisa thinks that Nebuchadnezzar marched into Spain, but that he did not take any Hebrews thither. He is of opinion, however, that some of that race settled in the neighbourhood of Toledo many years before our Saviour's passion.—*Translator.*]
[9] Monarquía Eclesiastica, &c.
[10] Santos de Toledo, siglo 1º de la ley de gracia. [cap. 1. In the second chapter he gives his opinion of this letter, and quotes the chronicle of Julian the archpriest, mentioned below at page 30.—*Translator.*]
[11] Antiguëdades, &c. de Sevilla.
[12] Novedades antiguas.
[13] Historia Eclesiástica de España. [vol I. fol. 16.—*Translator.*]
[14] Lecciones solemnes á las obras de Góngora.
[15] Primacia de la Santa Iglesia de Toledo.
[16] Poblacion General de España, fols. 10, 11.—*Translator.*

jama of the Holy Land, salvation through the God of Israel.

"The letters that ye sent us, wherein ye informed us how matters stood with the prophet of Nazareth, were brought to us by your man Azarias, a doctor of law, who saith that the prophet worketh many miracles. One Samuel, son of Amasias, passed through this city not long since, and gave us an account of many kind acts done by this man, who, according to his statement, is a humble and meek person, and talketh to the afflicted: he doeth good to every body; and when they do wrong to him, he wrongeth not any one: he dealeth boldly with proud and evil men, and ye are so wicked as to bear ill-will to him, because he told you your misdeeds to your faces. Now, as ye bore this ill-will towards him, we enquired of the former man in what year, month, or day he [the prophet] was born, and he told us. We found that it was on the day of His nativity that three suns were seen in these parts, which gradually became but one sun; and when our fathers observed the miracle, they, on consideration, proclaimed that the Messiah was soon about to be born, nay, that He was, perhaps, already born. Reflect, brethren, whether He have already come, and been rejected by you. The aforesaid man likewise informed us, on his father's authority, that certain magi, men of great wisdom, arrived in the Holy Land at the time of His nativity, and enquired for the place where the holy Child was born, and that your king Herod considered with himself, and assembled the wise men of his city, and asked where the Infant should be born, for whom the magi were enquiring, and they answered him, *In Bethlehem of Judæa*, according to the prophecy of Micah de Perginó, and that those magi declared that they had been led from afar to the Holy Land by a star of exceeding brightness. Consider whether it be not the fulfilment of this prophecy, *Kings shall sing and walk in the brightness of His birth*. Take heed, moreover, that ye do not persecute Him whom ye are bound to honour highly and to receive with good will, but be well advised. We tell you that we cannot, either by counsel or will, consent to His death, for were we to do so, then to us would the prophecy apply, which saith, *They shall assemble with one consent against the Lord and against His Messiah*. And we advise you, wise though ye be, that, in so weighty a matter as this, ye proceed with caution, lest the God of Israel, in His wrath with you, should destroy the second house of your second temple; for be ye well assured that it will soon be destroyed, and this was the reason why our ancestors who came out of the captivity in Babylon (under the guidance of Pyrrhus their captain, who was sent by king Cyrus, and who brought them out with great riches which he carried away from Babylon, in the sixty-ninth year of the captivity, and they received protection from the pagans of Toledo), built a large Aljama, and would not return again to Jerusalem.—Toledo, fourteenth day of the month Nisan; era of Cesar, eighteen, and of Augustus Octavianus, seventy-one."[17]

The following are the grounds on which I support my opinion that this letter is an entire fiction, namely, on the fact that at the time of Jesus Christ's death there were no Jews living in Spain; on the improbability and absurdity of the supposition that the Jews of Jerusalem should hold a conference with their brethren who were scattered throughout the world; and lastly, on the assertion of all who believe in the genuineness of the document, that it was translated into Spanish at the time when Toledo was conquered by Alfonso the Sixth, for in this age all documents were written in Latin. In addition to this, the translation of this document is written in a barbarous language, a confused medley of ancient and modern Castilian, with a smattering of Portuguese and Gallician.[18]

There cannot be the slightest doubt that this letter originated in the desire to make the Jews appear less odious than they were in the eyes of the people and even of the nobility, and the wish to mitigate the cruel persecutions they suffered in modern times by the tri-

[17] This letter is published by Sandoval in his *Historia de los Reyes*, &c. (see reign of Alonso the Sixth), but he says that he does not know what amount of credit to attach to it.—*Translator*.

[18] Let those who wish to have their ears tickled with the sound of this beautiful jargon, go to Vigo or Tuy, both of them towns in Gallicia, for a few days, and they will have a fine opportunity of putting the delicacy of their auricular organs to the test. I speak from experience.—*Translator*.

bunal of the Holy Office. I formed this opinion after reading the accounts of several authors who assert that the descendants of those Jews of the synagogue of Toledo who raised their voices against the execution of Jesus Christ, deserved to be rewarded and esteemed as good men.

Father Juan de Pineda, in his *Monarquía Eclesiástica*, writes as follows: "The Jews who lived at Toledo were not at Jerusalem at the time of our Redeemer's passion, nor did they consent to it. Such being the case, they may boast of the highest lineage in the world; for nobility of blood depends on the personal excellence of parentage, as well as on privileges and honours conferred by princes. And the founders of the house of Israel, to wit, Abraham, Isaac, and Jacob, were very eminent men and more highly honoured by God than any who have been born into the world. Therefore, as many persons of Jewish descent as shall prove that their ancestors in no wise consented to the Redeemer's death (on the score of which they forfeited their nobility (hidalguia)), and believed in Him, like Nicodemus, Gamaliel, and some others, must, without question, equally with those ancestors, be of the highest lineage in the world."[19]

Father Quintana Dueñas, in his *Singularia*, a posthumous work, launches out still further in his account of the merits of all that proved descent from the Jews

---

[19] Francisco de Padilla, in his Historia Eclesiástica, vol. i. fol. 2, speaks of Pineda and refers to this passage, of which he quotes the substance, though not the exact words.—*Translator*.

who opposed the death of Jesus; for he says they ought to be honoured with admission to the military orders, and be preferred to ecclesiastical dignities. As his words are very quaint, I give a translation of them from their original Latin:[20] " I shall not forbear to remark that if any one shall prove his descent from that family of the Hebrews which in no wise consented to Christ's death, and it shall appear that the said family did oppose it, and after the publication of the law of grace did not relapse to Judaism, he may be admitted to ecclesiastical orders and dignities, and not only religious, but military ones, even though by the statutes of both, persons of Hebrew extraction are excluded from admission to them."

There is nothing extraordinary in the supposition that after the Jews were expelled from Spain, those who reluctantly received baptism and remained under the disguise of Christians, on seeing the contempt in which such were holden as were descended from the converts, should forge this document and should spread these notices to exalt their pedigree, by thus flattering the affections of the vulgar, the learned, and even their very persecutors and enemies.

[20] Singularia moralis Theologiæ ad quinque præcepta ecclesiæ necnon ad ecclesiasticas censuras et pœnas; opus· posthumum. Madrid, 1652.

Tandem non desinam hic adnotare quod si aliquis probaret se ex ea Hebræorum familia descendere quæ nullo modo morti Christi assensum præbuisset, immo et contradixisse constaret, nec etiam post promulgatam gratiæ legem in Judaismum incidisset, posset quidem admitti ad ordines ac dignitates ecclesiasticas, necnon ad religiones quascunque etiam militares, quantumvis illæ à suo gremio expelli omnes ex sanguine Hebræorum procreatos statuerint.

The words of these authors prove the weakness and blindness of human reason, and its readiness to twist and turn the tempers of mortals in such a manner as to make them hate what they most love, and love what they most abhor. For, as men's opinions are almost always swayed by the force of passions, they experience more changes than the sea or the moon; and as they dash to the ground whatever accords not exactly with their own sentiments, so do they praise up to the skies whatever agrees with their natural disposition and temper. Thus they who once abhorred all that observed the law of Moses and refused the descendants of the latter admission to ecclesiastical dignities and military orders, would now throw the door wide open to them, owing to a mere fiction that was pleasing in their eyes. Such is the effect of a notice which carries with it the appearance of truth, and has the good fortune to obtain credit with persons of illustrious birth, established fame, and eminence in the literary world!

By means of the credit given [by such persons] to the letter which stated that the Spanish Hebrews, and particularly those of the kingdom of Toledo, though earnestly solicited by their brethren of Jerusalem, refused to lend their vote and consent to Christ's death, other lies were invented which met with an equally favourable reception. One of these was the assertion that, in the year 33, the Jews sent to Jerusalem two messengers, named Athanasius and Joseph, to make a verbal protest in the name of the Toledan and all other Jews in Spain, with the intent to obstruct the designs of the Scribes and Pharisees. It is also falsely asserted that, after Christ's crucifixion, the chief of the synagogue (*archisinagoga*) of Toledo sent a second embassy to Jerusalem with letters to most holy Mary and St. Peter, desiring them to instruct the bearers of them in the Christian faith; which letters were brought by Saints Indalecio and Eufrasio. Then, say they, Eleazar, who held the office of president of the Spanish synagogue and people in Sion, wrote to the brethren of Toledo to inform them of the death of Jesus, which was caused by the machinations of Annas and Caiaphas, and that a holy man named James, son of Zebedee, was coming to preach the law of grace in Spain.

In the lying chronicle, printed as the work of Julian, high-priest of Santa Justa, is inserted the following apocryphal letter, of which a translation from the Latin is here given for the amusement of the curious.

LETTER FROM ELEAZAR TO THE SYNAGOGUE OF TOLEDO.[21]

"*Eleazar, president of the Spanish synagogue and people at Jerusalem, and the elders of his council, to Levi, president of the council of Toledo, and to the elders Samuel and Joseph, salvation through the God of Israel.*

"Know, my brethren, that a just man, named *Jesus of Nazareth*, preacheth in this city of Jerusalem, worketh many miracles, raiseth the dead,

[21] Santos de Toledo por Quintana Dueñas, siglo 1° de la ley de gracia, cap. 1°.—*Translator.*

healeth lepers, giveth sight to the blind, feet to the lame, use of limbs to the paralytic: He is a universal benefactor, a man that is humble, compassionate, grave, fairer than the children of men, affable, mighty in deeds, and in all His actions superior to the rest of the human race: many venerate Him as the Messiah. John, the son of Zachariah, pointed Him out to us with his finger, and said, *This is the Lamb of God.* We have refused to give our consent to His death, which was compassed by Annas and Caiaphas and the chief-priests, and give you this intimation, in order that neither ye nor any of the twelve tribes who chance to live in Spain, may approve of so sacrilegious an act. Remember how Haman gave command that not only our ancestors, but many other Hebrews also who were scattered about in divers places, should suffer death ignominiously on the gallows, and how God finally ordered it that the man himself should be hanged on the one he had prepared for our father Mordecai. Our fathers received letters from Artaxerxes, by which they learnt at once that the weeks of Daniel were very soon to be accomplished, in which the Holy One should die, if He were not already dead! Remember, too, how our fathers were warned by Daniel when he was in Babylon (whence by his order and arrangement they came to Spain), and how he foretold to them the death of the Holy One, on account of which the temple of Jerusalem was to be destroyed, and how ill an opinion Jeremiah and other prophets entertained of the Jews that remained at Jerusalem, and would not go down to Egypt with Jeremiah himself;[22] while they speak favourably of the good Jews whom God sent to Spain. In short, I beg of you, should certain Jews of Jerusalem, now about to proceed to Spain, arrive there with letters, not to receive such persons; or, if ye receive any one, let that one be James the son of Zebedee, and none other: he is a good man and a disciple of Christ crucified, Who, according to His disciples, hath already risen again. Receive this man kindly, as well as the other disciples of the Apostles. God preserve you.—Jerusalem, fifth of the month Nisan."

Many writers enlarge so much upon this apocryphal letter as to relate other equally extraordinary falsehoods and events, which, to avoid tarnishing my history with the account of additional errors, I pass over in silence.

As I am now about to enter upon matters which have been more clearly established by the writings of learned men, I affirm that the Israelites, during the Roman supremacy in Spain, had very little information respecting the countries of the west, or what went on in them: for as they neither lived on the sea-coast, nor were in the habit of making voyages from one place to another for the purpose of selling their merchandise,

---

[22] It is strange that the forgers of this letter should make Jeremiah and other prophets state *precisely the reverse* of what we read in their prophecies respecting such as should go down to Egypt.—*Translator*.

nor fatigued themselves with pilgrimages all over the world for the sake of seeing new regions, new people, or new customs, they were only acquainted with such kingdoms as bordered on their own; and this acquaintance arose partly from the proximity of those kingdoms, and partly from wars and cruel discords originating in conflicting interests.

When the Jews were informed of the achievements of the Romans, and found that the latter had discovered in the heart of Spain so many and such large gold and silver mines, they sent messengers[23] to congratulate them on their victories and prosperity, and at the same time to make a friendly league with such valiant folks. They did not come to Spain, but went direct to Rome, and took with them commendatory letters addressed to the kings of Asia and Europe, through whose territories they would have to travel in order to execute their mission. And though, on this occasion, the Jews made a treaty of amity with Rome, there is no record to prove that any of them remained and lived in that city, which was then the mistress of the world. So say Flavius Josephus and Justin.[24]

Nor, in those days, were the Jews in the habit of travelling to Greece, though this country was so near to them; for there is no writer of that time who says a word about the acts of the Hebrews.

[23] First Book of Maccabees, ch. viii.—*Translator.*
[24] " A Demetrio cum descivissent" (Judæi), *amicitia Romanorum petita*, &c.—*Justin*, lib. xxxvi. cap. 3.
See 1 Maccabees viii., and Josephus' Antiquities, lib. xii. chap. 17. --*Translator.*

When, by means of the dissensions existing between Aristobulus and Hyrcanus, Pompey the Great[25] obtained possession of Jerusalem and made Judea tributary (this was sixty-three years before the birth of Christ), some Israelites went to Rome, and many others were afterwards carried thither by Gabinius and Crassus:[26] this accounts for the large number of them in that city,[27] and for the service which they rendered Pompey in his wars with Julius Cesar.

The emperor Augustus showed them much kindness, inasmuch as he allowed them to live in a quarter separated from Rome by the opposite bank of the Tiber—the first settlement they ever acquired in Europe. But, owing to the bad use they made of this privilege, in the time of Tiberius Cesar they were expelled from the city, and the consuls raised four thousand soldiers out of them to be sent to Sardinia. And those who, from religious or other motives, disobeyed the rigorous com-

---

[25] Joseph. Antiq. lib. xiv. cap. 8; Tacit. Hist. lib. v. cap. 9; Flor. Rer. Roman. lib. iii. cap. 5; Epit. lib. deperd. Liv. cii.—*Translator.*

[26] I think the word *Craso*, in the original, is a misprint for *Casio*. Crassus marched direct from Jerusalem to Parthia, where he perished with all his army. I do not find it expressly stated, either by Josephus or the Roman authors, that Gabinius or Cassius brought any Jews with them to Rome; the Jewish historian, however, asserts that, "upon the capture of Taricheæ by Cassius," that general "carried thirty thousand Jews into slavery," but does not mention *whither they were taken.* (*Jewish War Book,* lib. i. cap. 6.)—*Translator.*

[27] It appears from the oration *pro Flacco,* that in the time of Cicero, who was murdered B.C. 43, there was a flourishing community of Jews in Italy, " cum *aurum, Judæorum nomine* quotannis *ex Italiâ... Hierosolymam exportari soleret,* &c." (Cicero, *pro L. Flacco,* cap. 28.) —*Translator.*

mands of the emperor, and refused to enter upon military service, were punished with death.[28]

There are no records to prove the existence of any Jews in Spain in those times. Strabo, speaking of the dispersion of the Jews in different parts of the world, gives a detailed account of the provinces which they inhabited, but makes no mention of Spain: neither does Agrippa in the letter he wrote to the emperor Caius Caligula in behalf of the Hebrews, although he takes particular notice in it of all the places where they were settled.

It was in the seventieth year of the Christian era, after the destruction of Jerusalem by the emperor Titus, son of Vespasian, that the Jews spread themselves all over the world, and consequently came to swell the population of Spain: here they neither founded cities nor gave names to them, as some have asserted, without sufficient reason. They came, like conquered persons, to receive protection from others, not to build ramparts for themselves. In the cities which they were allowed to enter, they lived for many years mingled with the natives and other inhabitants; and after that, by dint of hard labour, they had amassed riches, they made separate barriers that they might the better enjoy the comforts of life, and hold congregations

---

[28] Suetonius says they were ordered to quit the city under the penalty of *perpetual bondage*, in case of disobedience: his words are, "Judæorum juventutem, per speciem sacramenti, in provincias gravioris cœli distribuit: reliquos gentis ejusdem vel similia sectantes urbe submovit, sub pœna *perpetuæ servitutis*, nisi obtemperassent." (Suet. in Vita Tib. Cæs. cap. xxxvi.)—*Translator*.

in their synagogues with the more perfect freedom. The majority of the Jews who went to Spain lost their own language, and were very easily reconciled to the vernacular tongue of the country; and this is the reason why, according to Dr. Bernardo Aldrete,[29] so few Hebrew words have been engrafted on our language, for we should, unquestionably, have had more of them had the Jews continued to use their own, and transmitted it to their descendants and the inhabitants of the cities in which they lived.

A very short time elapsed ere the peace of the Jews was disturbed. In the year 303, the bishops, assembled in council at Elliberis,[30] forbad communication, dealings or contracts with them, as far as possible, alleging as a reason that the Jews were striving with most active and urgent importunities to bring over the people to the law of Moses. Moreover, they (the bishops) thundered anathemas against all who should eat in company with the Israelites, and all who should allow the latter to bless the fruits which the lands of the Christians yielded spontaneously.

In the opinion of some, these canons afford a strong argument to prove that the number of the Jews then living in Spain was exceedingly large; but in the laws of the Visigoths, the collection of which is called *Fuero Juzgo*, I find a still stronger

---

[29] See Antigüedades de España, &c., por Bernardo Aldrete, lib. II. cap. 8.—*Translator*.

[30] See 49th and 50th canons as given in Francisco Padilla's Historia Eclesiástica.—*Translator*.

one for holding the contrary opinion. In these statutes we learn how they divided the Peninsula: the Goths took two-thirds of it for themselves, and left one-third to the Romans; for by this name were the Spaniards of that time known to them. One of the statutes alluded to runs thus: "The partition of the mountain lands made between the Goths and the Romans must not, in any wise, be broken, provided the boundary can be proved. The Romans must not take nor lay claim to any portion of the two-thirds belonging to the Goths, nor the Goths to the remaining third which belongs to the Romans."[31] Whereby we see how small was the number of Jews then dwelling in Spain, when no notice of them is taken in this partition—a silence which could not have been observed had they been many in number.

Let not persons who hold the opposite opinion try to weaken this argument by saying that the Goths looked down upon the Hebrews with supreme contempt and disdain, nor ask why the former should apportion lands to folks in such little esteem with them as the latter, as being persons who were gaining a more comfortable subsistence by trading, whereas they could not reap the fruits of the land without much persevering toil and labour: such reasoning as this is built on a weak foundation, and is easily overthrown.

It was from pure ambition that the barbarians of the north quitted their own houses, and it was by pure courage that they made themselves masters of other

[31] Lib. x. tit. 2. ley 8ª.—*Translator.*

people's. All the forces which vainly attempted to dispute their passage made about as much show of resistance as a slight cloud of dust offers to a strong and impetuous wind. It was by good government that they succeeded in retaining possession of the conquered lands and dominions they had usurped, and exalted their power to the skies, laying its foundations on the real obedience and love of the natives, and not turning to account the animosities and party interests which, however much they may uphold empires for a time, eventually overturn them, resembling in this respect the foundation-stone of an old building which keeps gradually mouldering away: its ravages escape detection, till after it has crumbled to pieces, and caused the fabric it was supporting to tumble down, when it is too late for either art or industry to prevent its fall.

Now, as the Goths were not influenced in their actions by catholic intolerance, but by the desire of firmly maintaining their conquests, we can hardly suppose that when they made the division of Spain, they would have allowed the Hebrews to be forgotten had there been a large number of the latter living in their cities.

'Tis certain that the Gothic kingdoms were replete with fraternal hatreds, insults, and calamities of every description. Like rude barbarians, they were completely under the influence of their passions, especially of ambition, and rushed with furious rapidity into the commission of every crime that their unbridled wills suggested to them. Subjects ousted kings, and deprived them by violence of their thrones and lives, sometimes by the agency of poison, sometimes by the sword; and not only were such things done by subjects, but brothers received like treatment from brothers, and children from parents. So fearful is the effect produced by the ambitious thirst of power! much more is this the case when this desire is combined with hardness of heart, ferocity of disposition, and ignorance of right! But in this age, in which crimes, and even those most repugnant to nature, had risen to such a height, the Spaniards had but few grievances to complain of. Subjugated as they were and unable to shake off the yoke of oppression from their shoulders, but at the same time living under a good government, they never took part with the factions that rose up for the purpose of wresting the sceptre from the hands of those who, in previous tumults, had received the regal dignity from the army and the people. These quarrels were confined to the Goths, and resembled those of two beasts, which, after helping one another in the struggle for a prize and succeeding in getting it, engage furiously together, each with the view of making it his own.

From the time that Ataulphus and his powerful host invaded the Spanish peninsula with fire and sword, and reduced it to obedience, with scarcely any opposition (which, according to conjectures more or less probable, happened in the year 415), till the year 586, when Recaredo the First began to reign, and, abjuring Arianism, embraced the Catholic religion,[32] the Jews lived

[32] See Francisco Pisa's Historia de Toledo, lib. II. cap. 17.—*Translator.*

in peace and had a regular trade and intercourse[33] with both Goths and Spaniards. They were neither despised nor oppressed.

Recaredo, after repudiating the doctrines of Arius and bringing over a large number of the Arian party to Catholicism, was the individual who opened the door to the persecutions of the Hebrew people. In the council assembled at Toledo in the year 589,[34] it was decreed that the Jews should not hold public offices, or have Christian mistresses or Christian slaves: that all children of the latter, born in captivity, should be manumitted, and brought over to the Catholic religion by the waters of baptism.

St. Gregory[35] bestows much praise upon king Recaredo for not allowing himself to be blinded by covetousness when the Jews offered him a large sum of money to abrogate these laws, which, it is said, were passed to hinder them from seducing their domestic slaves, whether male or female, from Christianity to conformity with the Mosaic law.

I have no doubt that they were then attempting to make great numbers of proselytes to their religion—a mischievous design which the fathers of the council were anxious to prevent: at the same time, I am fully

---

[33] The word *comercio*, in its primary sense, signifies *trade* or *commerce*; in its secondary, *intercourse*. I think the author intends to use it in *both*, and have therefore *given* both in the text.—*Translator*.

[34] See the Crónica General de España, por Ambrosio Morales, lib. XII. vol. VI. p. 18.—*Translator*.

[35] See the same work and volume, p. 31, 32, and Padilla's Hist. Eclesiást. vol. II. fol. 124.—*Translator*.

persuaded that the measures which they took to check the advance which Judaism was making in Spain, were precisely the reverse of those which they should have taken. The Hebrews were now numerous, and, owing to their wealth, powerful; and, driven by outrage and persecution, committed riots and disturbances in the kingdom. To close the door against such evils was the aim of Sisebuto, a man described to us as magnanimous, valiant in war, rigidly just in peace, always compassionate, and, above all, a great zealot in the Christian cause, on which account (his great piety not allowing him to have subjects that were not Catholics) he ordered all Jews who would not receive baptism to be banished from Spain. Many of them fled to France[36] in order to escape giving up their law; but those (about thirty thousand) who remained to preserve their estates and dwellings, finding themselves forced into it by tortures and other extremely rigorous punishments, and threatened with death into the bargain, were baptized; continuing, however, to be Jews in heart, though Christians in name, as appeared by subsequent events. St. Isidore, a man who had no partiality for the customs of the Israelites, excuses the king's zeal, which he calls a good, a rational, and a justly directed one, but finds fault with the means of which the king availed himself; for he says that the truth of the Christian faith should have made its way to the minds of the Jews, not by force, fear, or power, but by means of soft and persuasive words.

[36] Ambrosio Morales, vol. vi. p. 70. 71.—*Translator.*

We are assured by good authors that king Sisebuto was urged on to this obstinate and cruel persecution of the Hebrews by a letter he received from the emperor Heraclius, who had given himself up to the study of judicial astrology and the desire of prying into futurity by means of curious arts, and had become a great diviner and very attentive to prognostics: by one of these he learnt that he was to be dethroned and murdered by circumcised people, and thought to prevent his dethronement and murder by bringing over the Jews that lived in his dominions to the Christian religion, by means fair or foul, and not only them, but all the Jews dispersed throughout the globe: in which enterprise he strove to engage all kings who were in friendship or alliance with him.

There is no reason to disbelieve that this was the cause of the persecution of the Jews in Spain by Sisebuto, and, after him, by Dagobert, king of France, in his lands and seigniories; but before the times of the emperor Heraclius and his auguries and prognostics,[37] Recaredo had already begun to oppress and harass these people, whence I conclude that this Gothic monarch was rather influenced by some reason of state, than led by the persuasions of others, to check the evils occasioned to Christianity by the excess of liberty enjoyed by the Hebrews who lived in his dominions.

[37] This is the opinion of the historian Mariana, who says with a sneer, that Sisebuto would have done well to apply the prediction to the Moors and Saracens instead of the Jews. This writer in many passages of his history ridicules the astrologers and their science. See his Historia General de España, lib. vi. cap. 1.—*Translator.*

A short time only elapsed ere Sisebuto discovered how little had been the success resulting from his measures. He saw that the calamities which had befallen his kingdoms owing to his constraining the Jews to turn Christians, were on the increase; and, like a barbarian and ignoramus, instead of attributing them to his own error in the choice of means to arrest their progress, adopted other methods,—I will not say equally, but even more cruel than the former. He took care that the complaints of the Hebrews should come to his ears—as the complaints of all subjects, how grievous soever they be, do come to the knowledge of kings— in an extenuated form. And, in concurrence with the bishops and nobles in the Cortes and council of Toledo, A.D. 633, he resolved that all who had received baptism should be compelled to observe the ceremonies of the Christian religion: that they should not be allowed to educate their young children, but that the latter should be entrusted to the care of old [38] Christians: and, finally, they were from that moment forbidden, under pain of perpetual slavery, to have any dealings with persons who had not come over to the faith. In addition to this, the fathers of the council threatened to excommunicate all who should disobey these orders; for the Jews were, at this time, winning over to their side the minds, not only of the powerful, but of some bishops

---

[38] Good, according to Morales. The word *old* has no reference whatever to the actual *age* of the persons thus described. It is the boast of many a Spaniard that he is a *Cristiano viejo, rancio y sin mancha*, that is, *an old Christian, a rank one and without stain*. See the note to page 1.—*Translator.*

and priests, both by means of the friendly intercourse which was maintained by their industrial and commercial pursuits, as well as by their riches—keys, with which, in the most calamitous times, they used to lock the doors through which misfortunes entered. Sisebuto was not satisfied with issuing such strict orders as these; and so for the purpose of oppressing the Hebrew *converts* still more, by the twelfth, thirteenth, and fourteenth laws of the *Fuero Juzgo*, second title, [book twelfth,] he prohibited them from burying Christian slaves, or obliging any of those whom they then possessed to be circumcised or to judaize, and further compelled them to manumit these in conformity with the Roman law.

It will surely appear strange to some, that, after so many persecutions, the Jews should not only persevere in an obstinate adherence to their creed, but communicate it to others, with a view to its general adoption in Spain. But, from what has been said, it will be acknowledged that these men were reduced to a depth of extreme oppression, and to the lowest and most miserable condition, and also that they were under the necessity of procuring a mitigation or termination of it at once, or else of continuing in it, or something worse than it, for the remainder of their lives. They found their hopes nipped in the bud; for the rigorous laws against the Hebrews were revived with additions to them, in the Cortes and council of Toledo, in the reign of king Chintila,[39] A.D. 638.

[39] Lucas Tudensis, in his *Chronicon mundi*, lib. 3, says Chintila was *persecutor et malleus hæreticorum* (*the scourge and hammer of heretics*),

King Flavio Recesvinto, too, was desirous of applying a remedy to the evils continually and secretly brought on the countries over which his rule extended, by Jews who wore the cloak of Christians; but in this undertaking he did not choose to strike out into a new path, and would only tread in the steps of his predecessors.[40] In the Council holden at Toledo, in the year 655, he called on the prelates to make careful provision for closing the avenues to those malpractices of which the Jews were daily guilty, in spite of so many laws and penalties. They, in the mean time, knowing what objects of suspicion they were to the king, and taught by past experience not to expect any favour from their opponents, addressed letters to Recesvinto (which may be seen in the *Fuero Juzgo*),[41] in which they acknowledged that they had hitherto obstinately adhered to Judaism, but were now become real Christians, and would no longer observe any of the ceremonies of their law, and thus give clear proof of the complete renunciation of their errors.

This frank declaration [only] served to put a stop to the severities and cruelties practised upon the Jews, and so the whole fury which the Council had directed

and the good Bishop evidently thinks that, *as such*, this monarch was entitled to some commendation. See Schott's *Hispania illustrata*, vol. iv. p. 51: also 9th Canon of Toledan Council, A.D. 638, in Padilla's *Historia Eclesiástica de España*, fol. 224, and Morales, vol. vi. page 116.—*Translator*.

[40] Morales, vol. vi. fols. 167, 168.—*Translator*.

[41] Lib. xii. tit. ii. leyes 2—11, 15—17. See also Padilla's Hist. Ecles. vol. ii. fols. 261 and 262.—*Translator*.

against them was limited to a renewal of the ancient laws, and an order to the judges to carry them out with the greatest rigor. But it was all in vain. They persevered in adhering to their law and communicating it to others, and the bishops and nobles continued to follow the mistaken and toilsome road they had chosen to effect the extirpation of Judaism in Spain.

In the Councils and Cortes holden at Toledo in the years 656 and 681, they again revived the old laws and added new ones to them. King Ejica, in the Council which was also holden at Toledo in the year 693,[42] asked the prelates to devise a scheme for the seemly decoration of the temples, and for maintaining the small churches in good repair, and for having them well ornamented and properly served: for his great piety had been dreadfully shocked at a report which reached his ears of the great and frequent ridicule bestowed upon them by the Jews, who said, *They have taken away from us good synagogues, and keep for themselves such temples as these!* He likewise requested that they might be forbidden to frequent or carry on negotiations at the *catablo*,[43] a word of Greek origin, according to

---

[42] For these councils, see Pandilla's *Historia eclesiástica de España*, chap. 43, 57, and 69, vol. ii., fols. 264, &c., 298, &c., 322, &c.; and for the last of the three see also Morales' *Crónica General de España*, chap. 49, vol. vi. p. 341.—*Translator.*

[43] I apprehend that Morales is right in his conjecture. καταβάλλειν, according to Liddell and Scott, sometimes means "*to bring, carry down,* especially *to the sea-coast,* καταβάλλειν σιτία, Hdt. 7, 25, where others take it *to lay in stores* or *depôts.*" If this definition of καταβάλλειν by the two learned lexicographers be correct, may not the noun καταβολή (or *catablo*) signify the *port*, or place to which

Ambrosio Morales, which, by a species of circumlocution, comes to signify *the port*. It is said that this step was taken with the view to excite in the minds of the Christians an eager desire to apply themselves to commerce and traffic with the maritime cities of the Levant, where ships, laden with merchandize brought from foreign kingdoms, used to anchor: these ships were first purchased by the Hebrews, the only or at any rate the principal traders of those days in Spain; for the majority of the Goths, and a considerable number of the Spaniards, who were now united to them by the ties of consanguinity and friendship, were wholly occupied in involving the kingdom in civil wars, and in electing and dethroning kings.

The medicines applied to the complaints bore a much stronger resemblance to poisons and deleterious drugs than to cures. The Jews were freemen in the eye of the law, though treated as harshly as slaves, and not only as slaves, but worse than the most destructive and ferocious animals. The children of their slaves were taken from them as soon as born, while the Christians kept the children of their own slaves in the same servitude as their parents. The Jews were prohibited from offering themselves candidates for public offices: the wings of their free trade were clipped: they had a religion forced upon them, which did not accord with the principles instilled into them in their childhood:

goods are *brought, carried down,* or in which *stores are laid?*—See Morales and Padilla, in places referred to in the last note.—*Translator.*

they were forbidden to abstain from articles of food, of which, up to that time, their laws had not allowed them to partake, and to which they had long entertained a feeling of repugnance, as they were not accustomed to them. On completing their seventh year, the children lost, if not the love, at least the kindness and fond caresses of their mothers: for they were taken from them to be educated in the Christian faith, by persons not attached to them by the ties of blood or friendship. What else could they learn from such teachers but contempt for and hatred of those very persons to whom they owed their being? The complaints of the latter were not listened to. Listened to, do I say? they were not even allowed to be made. In their way to obtain redress for the outrages inflicted upon them by all classes of people, mountains of difficulties were raised; while, in order to punish them for the slightest faults, crags and precipices, down which to hurl them with greater facility, presented themselves to the eyes of the judges. They lived without hopes of deriving any benefit from existing laws, and in constant dread of future ones still more severe; for all laws were framed with the design to make their condition worse and still more and more miserable. The act of speaking to a person not reputed to be a true Christian entailed upon them the loss of liberty and perpetual bondage. Their wives, their children, and their estates were exposed to the cupidity and hatred of their persecutors. Laws favourable to them were forgotten when they were put on their trial, and unfavourable ones were interpreted in a sense still more unfavourable to them. Whithersoever they turned their eyes, they only met with enemies. Miscreants, unawed by fear or shame, robbed them at their pleasure; for who was to succour them in their perils, when the magistrates denied justice to their suits? In this manner did they live, incapacitated from attending to the honest care of their estates and their houses, their children and their wives. These were in continual fear for the lives and liberties of their husbands, who, as well as they, passed the best days of their life without seeing their children, in the greatest bitterness, and in expectation of still greater affliction in store for the days of their old age, without the warm affection and protection of their sons: in defiance of law, they were daily insulted and aggrieved, and, while they found none to redress their wrongs, were unable to revenge them with their own hands: they were persecuted by kings, bishops, and nobles, as well as plebeians: they experienced the same hardships as slaves, or even worse: they suffered the whole weight of adversity, while they looked not for the blessings of prosperity: they found no ears open to their complaints, no countenance given to their speculations, no consolation in their troubles, no reparation or compensation for their losses: lastly, they were, always, and in all places, and by all classes of people, oppressed, despised, hated, and even reviled.

In order to shake off their necks the intolerable yoke under which they were groaning, the Jews made a plot to murder king Ejica, and all the nobles and prelates opposed to themselves, and make themselves masters of the Spanish territories: an enterprise which they intended to execute with the help of their brethren that were settled in the African cities. In spite of the precautions they took to prevent the discovery of their secret before the time for action was ripe, the traps they were laying for the destruction of the king became known to him: and in the seventeenth council of Toledo, the last holden in that city, he acquainted the prelates and nobles of the realm, who were assembled in parliament, with this so serious and important a matter, and at the same time declared what he had discovered by clear proofs and the confession of some of the conspirators: it amounted to this—that the Spanish Jews had carried on a correspondence with their brethren of Africa, with the view to concert measures for rising against the Christians and destroying them.[45]

The minds of the latter were not much terror-stricken by the account of such machinations: on the contrary, they resolved that all Jews implicated in so atrocious an act of treason should incur the penalty of perpetual bondage; which was to affect them, their wives, and children, together with confiscation of property and dispersion throughout the kingdom, a barrier of intervening land separating one party of them from another, by which means they would be left in so low and miserable a condition as to be disabled from doing any hurt either to the king or to the Christians.[45]

[45] Padilla's *Hist. Ecl. de España*, vol. ii. fols. 328 & 330.—*Translator.*

Great were the acts of violence and cruelty practised upon the Jews by those whose duty it was to discharge such rigorous orders. These men proceeded according to their own free will, and brought in whomsoever they would accomplices in this treasonable plot: they confiscated property without listening to any pleas which the accused might put forward in their defence, and, in short, allowed all their steps to be guided, if not by hatred to the Hebrews, by the desire of possessing their goods.

Some think that these persecutions of the Jews were mitigated in the reign of Witiza, a monarch pourtrayed to us by the historians of his day as a model of virtue, and by those nearest to ours as a monster of iniquity in all its forms. I neither intend to extol nor blacken this king's memory. Intemperate vituperations of it are to be met with in our historians: there is also a very good defence of his acts in a little work by a fine writer (*The Glory of Spain*, Don Gregorio Mayans y Siscar), which is highly prized by the learned, and bears this title, *Defence of King Witiza*.[46]

Archbishop Roderic, in his Latin history of Spanish affairs, says that this monarch " having violated the rights of the Churches, raised the Jews to their former

[46] Rodericus Sanctius (Hist. Hisp. pars ii. cap. xxxv.), Alfonsus à Carthagena (*Regum Hispan. Anacephalæosis*, cap. xlii.), Lucius Marineus Siculus (*De Rebus Hispaniæ*, lib. vi.), Franciscus Tarapha (*De Rebus Hispaniæ*, anno 698,) and Joannes Vasæus (*Hispaniæ Chronicon*, p. 574), give this king a very bad character. I have not had an opportunity of consulting the work by Mayans y Siscar.—*Translator.*

condition, and honoured them with privileges of greater immunity than he granted to the Churches."[47] Ambrosio Morales says the same thing, and so do Juan Mariana and other equally grave authors who have written histories of Spain. Not a word about the protection given to the Jews by king Witiza is to be found in the works of any Gothic writer. Isidore, Bishop of Badajoz, and therefore called El Pacense,[48] while lauding the virtues and notable acts of this monarch, says, that after the death of his father Ejica, he had no sooner begun to reign with unshackled power over the inhabitants of Spain, than he published a general amnesty of the offences of which several nobles had been accused in the preceding reign, and after restoring them their property which had been unjustly confiscated, he not only gave them permission to return to the Peninsula, but also to reside at his court, and even in his palace, and to be about his person.

The first writer who spread the report of king Witiza's giving orders for the return of the absent and persecuted Jews to Spain, was Don Lucas, Bishop of Tuy; he composed a Chronicle in the year 1235, in the execution of which he did not adopt the opinion of any Gothic author, but took hold, no doubt, of the popular fables or the false accounts of Arabic writers,

[47] Rodericus Toletanus, *De rebus Hispaniæ*, lib. iii. cap. xvi. See Morales, *Corónica General de España*, lib. xii. cap. lxv. sect. 8; Mariana, *Historia general de España*, lib. vi. cap. xix.—*Translator*.

[48] Mr. Ford, speaking of Badajoz, says, "The name was corrupted by the Moors from *Pax Augusta*." See Murray's Handbook of Spain, vol. i. p. 521, ed. 1845.—*Translator*.

and employed them for his pole-star on his road, and thus caused Archbishop Roderic and Don Alonso the learned (on the credit of his authority) to palm off the same fiction in their narratives of the events that had occurred in the Peninsula, up to the times in which they lived.[49]

It is an undoubted fact that the Spanish Jews, during the long reign of Witiza, were kept in the most intolerable captivity, and did not advance a single step in their design to put an end to the rigorous oppression and state of misery, to which they had been reduced by former monarchs. However, a short time only elapsed ere their hopes were raised in the quarter where they had been so long buried. King Roderic, by usurping the throne in violation of the rights of Witiza's children, without having been called to it by the people, and, in violation of reason, law, and justice, receiving the royal investiture solely from the Senate, caused the kingdom to be divided into two factions; and then the Jews beheld the opportunity draw near for bursting open the gates through which they were to escape from the bitter captivity in which they were living.

These party dissensions were so many sparks which served to inflame the minds of these men and encourage them with such hopes of liberty and vengeance, that they began to devise a plan for exterminating their

[49] Lucas of Tuy is better known by the name Lucas Tudensis: his Chronicle is published in the fourth volume of Schott's *Hispania Illustrata*. For Witiza's character as given by the Bishop of Tuy, see lib. xii. of his *chronicon mundi*, 69th page of volume referred to.— *Translator.*

oppressors by fire and sword. As a river, when stopped for a time by flood-gates to prevent its inundating the country, returns and rushes against them with redoubled force, bursts them and spreads itself over the fields with increased violence, and commits greater havoc and destruction; so the oppressed Hebrews, after so often miscarrying in their attempts to break their chains, did at last find means to avenge themselves on their enemies, and did clearly prove to kings and individuals entrusted with the government of large states, that there are diseases which usually require mild remedies, and that, oftentimes, violent cures and cruel operations only give a sudden check to the progress of the malady, and even then for but a space of time of more or less brief duration, and serve not to prevent them from attacking the body again more dreadfully than before, and bringing upon it pains more acute, more distressing, more dangerous, and even death itself.

When governors imagine that, to gain their point, everything, how contrary soever to order, law, and custom, is fair, and carry their decrees at the point of the sword; the people, overruled by necessity, yield to the force of arms, while they ever retain in their hearts the desire to shake off the yoke and avenge their captivity. This fire, though latent, needs but a breath of air to fan it into a flame; and so, in their outbreaks or rebellions, particularly when they have been oppressed without cause, the people follow the worst examples, besides availing themselves of the most wicked, the most daring, the most bloody, and the most ferocious means.

I do not mean to say that the Jews who conspired against the lives of the kings and the state to which they were in subjection, should have been allowed to escape with impunity; but there are times when, if lenity cannot be adopted, at least the extreme of severity should be avoided. It is not in fair weather that the dexterity of pilots is discovered, but when the vessel is tossed by the fury of the billows, at one moment lifted up to the clouds, at another pitched down into the depths of the sea and in danger of being dashed to pieces against the rocks. It is a maxim of great politicians that the monarch who is the object of universal dread, is compelled, for the preservation of his life and throne, to be in fear of all.

Up to the present time the majority of historians, in treating of the loss of Spain, have attributed it to Count Julian's vengeance on king Roderic for an illicit amour with his daughter, when the Count incited the Arabs to the conquest of the Peninsula, and exerted in their behalf all the interest he had through his relatives, his kindred, his friends, and his partisans. Others attribute it to the Divine wrath, which was moved by Roderic having broken the doors of an enchanted cave near Toledo, on one of the banks of the deep-flowing Tagus. But both these events are fictitious, resting, as they do, on no other foundation than the small talk and fabulous accounts of the vulgar, and the popular ballads and romances invented by Moors and Christians to while away their leisure hours.[50]

It is positively certain that the sons of Witiza and other nobles, disgusted at Roderic's usurpation of the Gothic throne, at his cruel government, and the wickedness of his life, went to Africa for the purpose of earnestly soliciting Muza to send Arab troops into Spain. This daring and renowned warrior listened to their statements, but before he engaged his word and his people in this enterprise, he began to make secret enquiries through the medium of the Jews settled in Africa, who carried on a constant correspondence with their Spanish brethren. The latter answered that Spain was destitute of strength and vigour, the kingdom was divided into factions, the castles were dismantled, many nobles were disgusted with the tyrannical yoke of their monarch who was given up to vice, the plebeians were oppressed with misery, the treasury was exhausted by reason of the supplies it had been compelled to furnish for so many long civil wars, the sea was without vessels, the land without troops, and, finally, that there was a want of the two principal nerves which keep the bodies of states together, that is to say, agriculture and commerce. The Jews likewise offered to render all the assistance in their power towards the capture of Spain, provided that, after its conquest, permission were granted to them, their wives, and children, to live

[50] I find the same opinion expressed in a note to the eighth chapter of Conde's *Historia de la dominacion de los Árabes en España.*—*Translator.*

according to the law of Moses, and the Arabs not allowed to molest or afflict them with punishments or other severities.

This answer fired the mind of Muza and encouraged him to try and obtain so easy a prize: and so, having the Caliph's permission, he ordered the chieftain Taric to land with some picked cavalry on the opposite coasts of Andalusia. He passed the straits of Hercules with five hundred Arab cavalry in four large barques, and made a successful descent upon the Spanish shores. The Moslems made incursions and carried off some cattle and people, while no one went out to encounter them. With this prize and good fortune Taric returned to Tangier, where he was well received. Muza then raised a powerful army and placed it under the command of the same chieftain. These troops passed the strait, and jumped on shore at the place where Algeciras is now situated. The Spaniards made an ineffectual attempt to hem them in and defend the pass against them, and after some slight skirmishes, took to flight. Taric commanded his ships to be burnt, in order to deprive his army of any certain means of escape from death, in the event of its experiencing a reverse of fortune; an action which was imitated nine centuries later at the conquest of New Spain by Hernan Cortés, and which has been so highly eulogized by the historians of that enterprise.

The Spanish chieftain who made face against the Arabs was named Tadmir: he it was who wrote to inform the king of the arrival of the people from

Africa, and made mention of his own exertions to maintain the pass against them, when he was unexpectedly attacked and obliged to yield to superior numbers: he added that the enemy was encamped in the country and beginning to make incursions; that the king must send to his relief all the men he could muster; and, in conclusion, that such was the necessity and strait he was in, that, unless the king himself took the field with all the forces of his realm, its loss was inevitable.

Roderic was alarmed at the news, and assembling his council, and the principal gentlemen that resided at his court, and his personal attendants, harangued them thus: "A horde of African savages have invaded our territories, laid waste the country, carried off cattle, and taken many into captivity: all who offered resistance to them have been scattered with the same rapidity that an eagle scares away a flight of pigeons. Make ready your arms and horses; hands on your swords; off to the Arab camp; down with their squadrons; make a terrible and frightful slaughter of them. And if fortune look upon our enemies with smiling and cheerful countenance, and snatch away from us the laurels of victory, at least we shall be slaying them while we die ourselves. Ye are the descendants of those Goths who were the terror of Rome: ye are the descendants of those Goths who were the dread and the admiration of the world: in a word, ye are the flower and glory of Spain. On, on! let not your delay allow their God time to come and help them:

our God hath put weapons into our hands and courage into our hearts. Freemen are we, and freemen will we be, though the Arabs threaten us with chains; for our courage will wrest these from their hands for us soon to fasten them on their own untamed necks. But if fortune overset our designs, then let the world behold our corpses rather than see us enslaved to the Arabs; and ere we are killed or vanquished, let us give them additional proofs of the valour we inherit, the courage we possess, and the powerful resistance we can make."

Roderic raised an army of ninety thousand men and arrived with them at the plains of Xerez. All the nobility of his kingdom had received a summons to take part in this expedition. Some went armed with coats of mail and quilted underwaistcoats; some only with lances, shields, and swords; some with bows, arrows, and slings; some with axes, clubs, and mowing scythes. The Arab chieftains collected their cavalry, which was, at the time, disbanded and employed in making incursions. When his squadrons were drawn up, Taric made them a speech to the following effect: " Moslems, see ye that powerful army, under the feet of which the earth trembles and quakes, and hear ye how it makes the air resound with the clashing of arms, the noise of drums and trumpets, and with what shouts it animates itself for the combat? Do ye observe how far superior in numbers it is to our own? Well then, turn your eyes in the other direction, and what do ye behold? a sea which will cut off your retreat, if fortune should deal hardly with us, and bring upon us an unhappy reverse. To this quarter, then, let us not look for refuge or shelter, but death; and were it death alone, that is a thing which ye are accustomed to look at with firmness of foot and serenity of countenance: but infamy as well as death await us. Turn your eyes the other way. If ye fall by the hands of that army, ye will die an honourable and glorious death. If ye disperse it, those lands and all the riches ye find upon them will be your own. God and our intrepidity can alone save us. Remember your past victories, by which ye did honour to our country and your own name. Do not by disgraceful and inconsiderate fear forfeit that which hath cost you so much fatigue, nor give our enemies occasion to doubt the fact of our being those Moslems so famed in the world for their courage and firmness in battle—those Moslems to whom so many a valiant nation hath bent the neck in order to receive chains imposed by our hands."

The morning had no sooner appeared than the two armies engaged with the fury of enemies, and during the whole of that day the victory remained doubtful. The shades of night parted the combatants, and put a stop to the bloody carnage. When the rays of the sun shot forth, they engaged again with like success: fortune was neither favourable nor unfavourable to either party. On the third day of the fearful encounter, Taric seeing that the spirits of the Moslem troops began to decline, stood up in his stirrups, and, encouraging his horse, raised his voice and said: "Brave Moslems, ever victorious, never vanquished; what blind madness inspires you to give up the field and the victory to this Gothic enemy? Where is your intrepidity? Where are your past victories? Where is your constancy? Follow me, then. Our honour is in the power of that army. Let us wrest it out of their hands, and let all who compose it, fall by ours. It is not meet that any one should ever have cause to tell the world that vile fear had more influence on your hearts than the memory of the heroic exploits achieved by your ancestors, and the deeds which have made us so famous and so terrible, so respected and so powerful." And, giving reins to his spirited horse, he dashed into the midst of the Gothic army, trampling down and wounding all who vainly attempted to arrest his progress.

The Moslems attacked the enemy, who considered the victory as all but won, with like spirit. Both sides fought with unexampled fury, foot to foot: they also wounded and slew each other with pikes and swords. The cavalry, as the ground was level, hurled their lances at random, rushing into the midst of the enemies' ranks and retreating from them at half speed; and though both they and their horses were covered with wounds, this did not prevent them from fighting like valiant warriors. When the struggle was most obstinate, the infantry showed redoubled courage; though wounded over and over again, they did not care to bind up their wounds,—in fact they could not stop to do so, as the valor of the enemy gave them no other alternative than to fight or die. At this time Taric came up with the war-chariot in which Roderic was riding, boldly attacked him and pierced the king's breast through with a dart of his lance. The unfortunate king fell down dead, and Taric cut off his head and sent it to Muza, to give him a proof of the success which had attended his arms. On the death of the king and many of the great men of the Gothic nobility, the survivors began to slacken the fight and retreat. The Moslems followed up their advantage on horseback; for when they had once obtained the victory, their wounds gave them no more pain, nor did hunger and thirst fatigue them, nor did they appear to have undergone any hardships or troubles.

The valor and spirit of the Gothic troops became known by the fact that nearly all of them covered with their dead bodies the posts they had defended while living: and the dying exhibited their wonted look of ferocity. The Arabs did not obtain this victory without loss; for the most courageous of them either fell or were very severely wounded in the battle. All over the field lamentation was variously mixed with joy, pleasure with pain. The air resounded with the music of the drums and trumpets which proclaimed the success of Taric's arms, and with these were mingled the cries of the wounded and dying. They who went to strip the corpses and seize the stores, ammunition, and the rest of the booty, found by the side of an enemy's corpse that of a relation, brother, or parent—in short, that of the person who was most loved or most hated by him. This frightful encounter took place in the year 711.

Such of the Gothic nobility as had found means to

escape with their lives, withdrew to the principal cities and commenced putting them into such a posture of defence as the furious activity of the enemy in pouring its warlike hosts into all parts of Spain would allow. The Arab army was but small in comparison with the arduousness of the enterprise; but after so important a victory, nothing could check the rapidity with which it followed up its conquests. The news of the disastrous rout of the Gothic army on the banks of the Guadalete travelled before their enemies, carrying with it terror to the natives and pourtraying the fierceness and power of the Arabs in the most vivid colours which consternation at so serious and grievous a calamity could invent; for misfortunes are usually more terrible in imagination than in reality.[51]

The Spanish Jews now saw that the time to break their chains was drawing nigh, and began to recover their breath, just as persons do who travel with a heavy weight on their shoulders, and who, when they have laid down their burden, think no more of their past labours nor of their present rest from them, and only derive satisfaction from the pleasure that arises from their hearts respiring with perfect freedom.

Into each of the large cities that Taric won, whether by fire and sword or by capitulations that were honourable and advantageous to the vanquished, he placed a

---

[51] For this and the eight preceding paragraphs, see Conde's *Historia de la dominacion de los Árabes en España*, cap. 8, 9, and 10; It seems singular that, in them, Conde should not make mention of the Jews.—*Translator.*

garrison of Arabs, in whose charge he left them, while he relied for their main security on the multitude of Jews, into whose hands he had placed arms, in order to obtain assistance from them in this expedition for the reduction of the Spanish peninsula, and at the same time to help them to escape from their captivity and destroy those who had, for so many years, oppressed the descendants of the ancient Jewish nation.

With these and with a small part of his army he defended the cities of Seville, Córdova, Toledo, and others:[52] Granada was entrusted to the Jews alone, and for this reason it came to be known, at the commencement of the Arab dominion in Spain, by the name of *Jews' Town*.[53]

I think the smallness of the number of Christians who sided with the Moslems when Spain was lost, is

[52] Archbishop Roderic, speaking in his history of Taric, says, "Ipse autem captam Hispalim de Judæis et Arabibus populavit." And in another place, " Judæos autem qui inibi morabantur cum suis Arabibus ad populationem et custodiam Cordubæ dimiserunt." And further on, " Taric autem ex Arabibus quos secum duxerat et Judæis quos Toleti invenerat, munivit Toletum." And elsewhere, " Exercitus autem qui Malacam iverat, coepit eam, et Christiani qui inibi habitabant, ad montium ardua confugerunt. Alius exercitus Granatam diutius impugnatam victoria simili occupavit, et Judæis ibidem morantibus et Arabibus stabilivit." The first, third, and fourth quotations are from lib. iii. cap. 23, the second is from cap. 22 of the same book.—*Translator.*

[53] In the history ascribed to Rasis the Moor, we find these words, "The other is the castle of Granada, called JEWS' TOWN : 'tis the most ancient town in the district of Elibera, and was peopled by the Jews." [For accounts of the invasion of the Peninsula by the Arabs, I would refer the classical reader to the works of Rodericus Sanctius,

clearly shown by the fact that there were not enough of them to fortify the populous cities, unless it be said that the Arabs, seeing that the friendship of the Goths was based on party spirit and ambition (very weak foundations, which are wont to give way unexpectedly with the buildings that rest upon them), were unwilling to commit the keeping of their conquests to the hands of such good-for-nothing rascals as scrupled not at surrendering their own power in Spain, and sacrificing the liberty of their countrymen, merely to gratify their desire of revenge. Nevertheless, it is most rational to suppose that the Christians who incited and encouraged the Arabs to this contest were but few in number, and that these few pointed out the way to master the forces of those who attempted to dispute the passage of the Arab army.

The Jews, on the other hand, were numerous, and all of them well affected to the conquerors for two reasons: first, because the latter had accepted the invitation sent them to accomplish the capture and reduction of the Spanish peninsula; and secondly, because it was owing to the assistance of the Arabs that they had freed themselves from the oppression in which they had lived so unhappily and so miserably for so long a period.

These were the fruits which the Goths reaped of the

Rodericus Toletanus, Lucius Marineus Siculus, Alphonsus á Carthagena, Joannes Vasæus, and others: they will be found in a volume published at Frankfort in 1579, entituled *Rerum Hispanicarum Scriptores.—Translator.*

horribly cruel persecutions they had raised against the Jews, without reflecting that injuries must call down the vengeance of the injured parties, and that men are more easily led by reason and conviction than force; for no one finds any difficulty in travelling on a road strewed with flowers, while all men shrink form clambering up rugged mountains covered with thorns and caltrops, and surrounded with crags and precipices. It is certain that things may happen which it is difficult to believe. It is to this class, therefore, that we must refer the extremely bold determination of the oppressed Hebrews to shake off their shoulders the yoke which galled them, and recover their liberty for ever. But in serious undertakings men ought to calculate, ere they engage in them, the amount of evil or danger which is likely to ensue from them. And though human foresight cannot always point out the effect of causes, it cannot be doubted that the manner in which they are directed has much to do with their turning out well or ill.

By their rash and fierce persecution of the Hebrews, the Goths acted like a horse that is frightened in a storm by the flashes of lightning discharged from the clouds, and wildly scampers away for safety, without seeing whither he is going until he is compelled by his very speed to dash into a deep-flowing river,[54] which

[54] I have seen the beds of rivers in Spain completely dried up in *summer*, so that the epithet "deep-flowing," used in the text, is by no means superfluous. The diligence from Málaga to Granada, owing to the narrowness of the streets in the former town, cannot get out of it except by the usually dry bed of the river.—*Translator.*

happens at the time to be swollen by continual rains, and has become much more rapid than usual, and is about to lose its waters with its name in the sea. Not considering the results of things is the same as attempting to fly from an uncertain danger, not to a greater one, but to one beyond the reach of human skill or remedies, in which case we must leave to time the cure of the damage it may occasion.

SUMMARY OF BOOK THE SECOND.

RABBINICAL Academy of Córdova founded.—First men who adorn it.—Decree of Ferdinand the First in the Cortes and Council of Coyanza (now called Valencia[1] de Don Juan).—Notice of some learned Rabbins.—Conquest of Seville by St. Ferdinand.—Jewry in this city.—Laws of Don Alfonso[2] the learned against the Jews.—Protection granted them by king Pedro.—They found a new synagogue at Toledo.—Complaints of Rabí Don Santo.—Ordinances of King Henry the Second.—Trap laid by the Jews for Don Juzaf Pichon.—Preachings of the Archdeacon of Écija.—Popular insurrection against the Hebrews.—Sacking and burning of the Jewries at Seville, Valencia, and other cities.—Conversion of numerous Jews to Christianity.—Famous dispute at Tortosa between many of the most learned Spanish Jews and Jerónimo de Santa Fé, in presence of the Antipope, Pedro de Luna (Benedict the thirteenth).—Nearly all who went to hear the dispute were baptized.—Bull of Pedro de Luna against the unconverted Jews.—Assessment made upon the Jews in the year 1474.

BOOK THE SECOND.

How far do they wander from the truth who think that force is the only means of bringing to the true faith all those who are either ignorant of it, or, to their

---

[1] As there are several towns in Spain called Valencia, it may, perhaps, be as well to state that the one mentioned in the text is in the province of Leon.—*Translator.*

[2] Sometimes called Alonso.—*Translator.*

own injury, disregard it! Of this they may find examples as they go through the chequered narrative of this history; first, from the bitter fruits which the Gothic monarchs reaped of the cruel persecutions they inflicted upon the Jews, in order to impress the truth of the Christian religion upon the minds of the latter; and secondly, from the number of Hebrews who forsook the law of Moses when they met with no persecutions from the kings of Spain, when they enjoyed the blessings of free commerce, when they lived in the quiet of domestic life, and when they could, with perfect tranquillity of mind, leisurely apply themselves to the study of literature.

The Arab conquerors of Spain, indebted as they were to the highly favourable reception they met with at the hands of the Jews, while they were engaged in the conquest of these lands, as soon as they had reduced them to obedience and had begun to reap the fruits of peace, kept the small remnant of the Goths, out of pure spite, shut up in a corner of the Peninsula, while they allowed the Hebrews full liberty to live according to the Mosaic law: and thus the latter laid the foundations of numerous synagogues in the larger and more considerable towns.

The barbarous persecutions raised against the Jews in the East by the Caliph Cader, of the dynasty of the Fatimites, forced many of them to seek in Spain the termination of their misfortunes. And as the Hebrews who lived in the East were men of much learning, it resulted that the greater part of the new comers to these lands began to adorn them with their writings and to found academies, in order to diffuse among the people their own remarkable knowledge in every branch of art and science. The first, and undoubtedly the most celebrated of these academies was established in the year of the world, 4708,[3] and of the Christian era 948, at Córdova: its founders and first masters were Rabbi Moseh and his son Rabbi Hanoc, the most eminent of the sages who came from Pombeditá and Mehasia in Persia. Induced thereto by the fame of these men's learning, the Spanish Jews commenced sending their sons to be instructed at the academy there: the consequence of which was that, in course of time, there was a large number of Hebrews in the Peninsula, learned in every branch of science.

Rabbi Izchaq Bar Baruq, a Cordovese, who succeeded Moseh in the presidency of the academy of his country, wrote a work entituled *Gaveta de Mercaderes*, (*Mercers' drawer*). The Barcelonese Jehudah Ben Levi Barzili, an eminent lawyer, composed an *Ordenamiento de los contratos* (law of contracts) and other books. Selomoh Ben Gabirol, a native of Málaga, and resident of Zaragoza, wrote several poetical works, and some on moral philosophy. In those times the following persons were also in high repute: Abraham Ben

---

[3] According to the most generally received system of chronology, the Creation of the world took place 4004 years before the Christian era: the Spanish Jews, whom the author has followed, place the date of that event 244 years later. Crónicas del Rey Don Pedro, &c. por Lopez de Ayala, *passim.—Translator*.

Mija Hanasi, a great astronomer, Rabbi Izchaq, a noted physician and author of a curious book on fevers, and Moseh Aben Hezra Ben Izchaq, a celebrated poet and musician. And while the Arabs left all the numerous Jews who lived in their dominions at full liberty to observe the law of Moses, the kings of Castile, in those days, saw the necessity of allowing this people to dwell undisturbed in their lands and seigniories; though it was a source of constant annoyance to them, as they had not yet become tutored by experience of the fruits which the Gothic monarchs reaped of their cruel persecutions. Hence it was that, in the Cortes and Council of Coyanza (now called Valencia de don Juan), convoked by the order of Ferdinand the First, king of Castile and Leon, an ordinance was passed by the Bishops and nobles in the year 1050, that no Christian should live in the same house or eat in company with Jews; and it threatened all who should disobey this injunction with the penalty of performing open penance for the space of seven days,[4] and in case of a repetition of the offence they were to be punished with excommunication for the period of a year, if nobles, and with a hundred lashes, if plebeians. Whence it appears that the hatred of kings, bishops, and nobles was not yet extinct, and that the permission given to the Jews to live according to their ancient law, sprang

---

[4] See Coleccion de Cortes de los reinos de Leon y de Castilla por la Academia Española, 6th canon of the Council of Coyanza: the canons are in Spanish and Latin; the former version says nine, the latter seven days.—*Translator.*

from the well-grounded suspicion and fear of their migrating with their possessions 'and riches to the neighbouring lands of the infidels, and thereby diminishing the population and revenues in the territories of the Christians, to the great injury of all.

But there were not wanting in those times illustrious Jews, who received baptism from conviction. One of these was Rabbi Moseh,[5] born in the city of Huesca, in the year 1062, who, when 44 years old, was baptized in the church of his native place, and received the names of Pedro Alfonso: he was named Pedro, because the ceremony was performed on the day that the Church celebrates the martyrdom of the Apostle St. Peter; and Alfonso, because Don Alfonso, the sixth of Leon and the first of Castile, was his godfather.

Several Jews of the Cordovese academy continued to enlighten Spain with their works on every description of science; as for example, Abraham Aben Hezra, a philosopher, astronomer, physician, poet, grammarian, cabalist, the most learned of his persuasion in the interpretation of the sacred books, and, finally, the inventor of the method of dividing the celestial globe into two equal parts, by means of the equator: Jehudah Levi Ben Saul, a fine poet of Córdova, and many others, whose names and works are given in the first volume of the *Biblioteca Española*,[6]

[5] See Garibay's Compendio Historial, vol. ii. p. 65, column 2nd. Barcelona edition of 1628.—*Translator*.

[6] This is an exceedingly interesting book, and, I should think, particularly useful to the Hebrew scholar.—*Translator*.

(Spanish library), got up by Don José Rodriguez de Castro, to which volume we refer those readers who are anxious to obtain further literary notices of the Spanish Rabbins of those days.

Out of respect for the learning of the Spanish Hebrews, Alfonso the Eighth, sirnamed the Good, granted them, in the charter of Cuenca, the rights (such as they were in those days) of citizenship, and placed them on perfect equality with the Christians. From the protection given to the Jews by this monarch arose the indecent and lying story respecting his amours with one Rachel, a beautiful Hebrew woman, which amours were the scandal of Spain.[7] But although the learned king, Alfonso the Tenth, has, in his general chronicle of Spain, printed these with other popular fictions that disfigure a work of so elevated a style and of such great merit, they are, for all that, fabrications forged by the common people.

St. Ferdinand followed the example of his predecessor[8] in the throne of Castile, and did in no wise oppress the Hebrews; and when he had made himself master of the principal cities of Andalusia, he allowed the Rabbins who held their academy at Córdova to transfer it to Toledo, because this city is in the heart of

---

[7] See Crónica del Rey Don Alfonso VIII. por Cerdá y Rico, cap. XXIII. p. 67-69; also work with same title, by García de Avellaneda, cap. XVI.; also Anales de Sevilla por Diego Ortiz de Zúñiga, p. 37, 2nd column.—*Translator*.

[8] Not *immediate* predecessor: many sovereigns intervened between Alonso or Alfonso the Eighth and St. Ferdinand.—*Translator*.

Spain, and because the knowledge of those learned men who were the ornaments of those schools could, from this latter place, be diffused all over his realms with greater facility.

When this pious king reduced the city of Seville to subjection, the Jews, who had synagogues in it, went out to receive him, and, as a proof of submission and respect, put into his hands a silver key, with spaces in it alternately plain and gilt, with a Hebrew inscription upon it, of which the following are the words:

THE KING OF KINGS SHALL OPEN: THE KING OF ALL THE EARTH SHALL ENTER.[9]

St. Ferdinand left the Jews in possession of the great Jewry which they had in the city of Seville, on con-

---

[9] A drawing of this key may be seen in the *Anales de Sevilla* by Don Diego Ortiz de Zúñiga, Madrid, 1677. The author omits to state that the words

GOD SHALL OPEN—KING SHALL ENTER

are carved on the wards of the key. Zúñiga interprets the two passages thus: " By the miraculous way which God should open for him, and by that way only, could the holy king enter, who was worthy to reign over the whole earth, and *that way* the King of kings *had opened* or *would open* for him." He also informs us that another key, said to have been presented at the same time to St. Ferdinand by the Moors, and inscribed with Arabic characters of similar import to those engraved on the key delivered to that monarch by the Jews, was, when he wrote (viz. about 1677), in the possession of Don Antonio Lope de Mesa, an inhabitant of Seville. The former of these keys was *then* (and I believe *now both* of them are) in the safe keeping of the dean and chapter of Seville. As this author has favoured us with drawings of both the keys, I have had a facsimile of them prepared for the readers of this work. The key represented on the left side of the plate is the one given by the Jews. See Zúñiga's *Anales de Sevilla*, p. 17, 18.—*Translator.*

dition that they paid him the same tributes as they used to render to the Moorish kings. The Archbishop, together with the dean and chapter of Seville, were appointed collectors of the tribute, the sum of which was to be applied to the maintenance of the ornaments and the divine service of the holy church: but it is an undoubted fact that they bore this burden with a heavy heart, inasmuch as, by deferring the times of its payment, they gave occasion to the turbulent clergy to make a complaint of them to king Alfonso the Eleventh, in the year 1327. The Jews, in exculpation of themselves, said that the chapter, influenced by excessive cupidity, was setting up a claim to more money than what they were bound to pay in the name of tribute. At last the king gave a commission to Fernando Martinez de Valladolid, his chief notary in the realms of Castile, to investigate this matter, and as this man gave judgment the same year in favour of the claims of the Archbishop, dean, and chapter of the holy church of Seville, the Jews had no other means of escaping the penalties with which they were threatened, than by satisfying the claim of three maravedis a year per head, a tax due from the moment of their birth till the completion of their sixteenth year (a maravedi was, at that time, equivalent to tenpence), making a total of thirty pence annually, for which they were made liable from the moment that St. Ferdinand rescued the city of Seville from the Moors.[10]

[10] Zúñiga, *Anales de Sevilla*, p. 184, &c.—*Translator*.

His son, Alfonso the Tenth, to whom fame justly awards the name of *Learned*, in the composition of his *Tables*, availed himself of the knowledge of the most learned among the Jews and Arabs. In the preface of a very ancient manuscript copy of the *Alfonsine Tables*, the following curious words occur: " The king ordered meetings of the undermentioned individuals to be holden, to wit, Aben Rajel and Alquibicio, his Toledan masters, Aben Musio and Mahomet of Seville, and *Josef Aben Alí* and *Jacobo Abvena* of Córdova, and more than fifty others whom he brought from Gascony and Paris, at high salaries, and directed them to translate the Quadripartite of Ptolemy and compare it with the books of Mentesam and Algazel. *Samuel* and *Jehudá* (the converted alfaquí[11] of Toledo) were charged to see that the meetings took place in the alcázar of Galiana, and to hold disputations on the motion of the firmament and stars. When the king was not present, Aben Rajel and Alquibicio acted as presidents. There were frequent disputations among them from the year 1258 to 1262, and at last they made some famous Tables, as every one knows; and after this work was completed by them, and they had received many rewards from the king, he sent them back well-pleased to their own countries, and gave them privileges, and granted to them and their descendants exemption from the payment of taxes, duties, and contributions; respecting which there are letters extant at Toledo, bear-

---

[11] An alfaquí was a Mussulman doctor.—*Translator*.

ing the date of the 12th of May, in the era 1300.[12] King Alfonso the Tenth, out of gratitude, no doubt,

[12] The Marquis of Mondejar, in his *Noticias Históricas del rey Don Alonso el Sabio*, makes mention of this manuscript, and cites from it the above extract. To make the Spanish era agree with the Christian, thirty-eight years must always be subtracted from the former, so that the *era* 1300 corresponds to A.D. 1262. An account of the *Alfonsine Tables* is given in the *Penny Cyclopædia* (vol. I. p. 37). It is obvious that the *Alquibicio* in our author's text and the *Al Cabit* of the Cyclopædists are the same person. As some important matters given in the Cyclopædia are not mentioned in the manuscript just cited, I shall transcribe the whole article of the former on this interesting subject: " Alonsine or Alphonsine Tables, an astronomical work, which appeared in the year 1252, under the patronage of Alonso X., in the first year of his reign. They contain the places of the fixed stars, and all the methods then in use for the computation of the places of the planets: but they are not made from original observations, nor is there any material difference between the astronomy contained in them and that of Ptolemy, except in two points. The length of the year is supposed to be 365 days, 5 hours, 49 minutes, and 16 seconds; which is a more correct value than had been given before, being only 26 seconds over the best modern determinations. The mean precession of the equinoxes is stated at half its real amount, being such as would carry the equinoctial points round the circumference of the globe in 49,000 years. An inequality, however, is supposed, having a period of 7000 years, by which the mean precession is alternately augmented and retarded 18 degrees. It is difficult to say whence a theory so at variance with the phænomena could be derived. The general opinion is, that these tables were constructed by Isaac Ben Said, a Jew, but others suppose that Al Cabit and Aben Ragel, the preceptors of Alonso, were the real superintendents. The numbers above cited, in speaking of the precession, have been supposed, from their connexion with the number 7, and the difficulty of accounting for them otherwise, to have been the ideas of a Jew. These tables are constructed for the meridian of Toledo, and the epoch 1256. They were not held in much esteem by succeeding astronomers. Regiomontanus says, ' beware lest you trust too much to blind calculation and Alphonsine dreams.' And Tycho Brahé, who reports that 400,000 ducats had been spent upon them, laments

for the great labour which these most learned rabbins had, together with himself, undergone, for the sake of the advancement of literature and learning in his kingdom, confirmed the Jews in their ancient rights and privileges, by the imposition of heavy penalties upon all who should infringe upon the same. Since, however, in his time the Hebrews became possessed of too much liberty and committed divers crimes, he forbad them in one of his laws of Partidas,[13] on pain of death, to preach to or attempt to convert any Christian.[14] He likewise commanded them all to wear a

---

that this sum had not been employed in actual observation of the heavens. A full account of their contents may be seen in Delambre, *Hist. de l' Ast. du Moyen Age*, p. 248. Till the time of Copernicus and Tycho Brahé, they continued in general use, being, in truth, with some modifications, a body of Ptolemæan astronomy. They were first printed in 1483 by the celebrated Ratdolt of Venice. A copy of this *editio princeps* is in the Royal Library at Paris. Subsequent editions appeared in 1488, 1492, 1517, 1521, 1545, 1553."—*Translator.*

[13] " His enemies have endeavoured to deprive this learned prince of the merit of having been the author or compiler of Las Partidas, pretending that this code was written by his father. It is, however, worthy of remark that every one of the Partidas begins with one letter of his name, forming the following acrostic:

   1st A l servicio, &c.
   2nd L a fé católica, &c.
   3rd F izo nuestro Señor, &c.
   4th O nras señaladas, &c.
   5th N ascen entre, &c.
   6th S esudamente, &c.
   7 h O lvidanza y atrevimiento, &c."

Penny Cyclopædia.—*Translator.*

[14] Partida 7ª, tit. 24, ley 2ª: "Moreover, they must take special care not to preach to nor attempt to convert any Christian to Ju-

badge of red cloth on their left shoulder, that they might be known to be Jews, according to the injunction issued by Gregory the Eleventh to the bishop of Córdova, and the direction of the Lateran Council, and threatened all who should disregard this law with the penalty of ten gold maravedis, and, in default of payment, with ten lashes, to be inflicted on them in public:[15] this king also spoke of the *many improper and outrageous doings between Christian men and Jewesses, and also between Jews and Christian women, for* (says he) *in the country houses they live and dwell together.* He ordained that the Christians should not receive medicine[16] from the hands of the Hebrews, nor eat with them, nor drink wine made by them, nor would he allow of their getting into the same bath together.[17] At the same time, in the second law of the twenty-fourth title, in the seventh partida, he made the fol-

daism, either by eulogizing their law or reviling ours. Whoever shall offend in this particular, will render himself liable to capital punishment and confiscation of property."

[15] Same partida and title, law eleventh: "If any Jew shall neglect to wear that badge, we order him to pay ten gold maravedis every time that he shall be discovered without it; and if he cannot pay the money, then let him receive ten lashes in public."

[16] Same partida and title, law eighth: "Let no Christian accept medicines or purges prepared by the hands of Jews; but he may take them by the advice of a Jewish physician, provided only that they be prepared by a Christian who knows and understands the nature of their ingredients."

[17] Same partida and title, law eighth: "Let no Christian man or woman invite a Jew or Jewess, nor accept an invitation from one of them to eat and drink together, nor drink wine prepared by them. We further command that no Jew have the audacity to bathe in the same bath with Christians."

lowing ordinance: "*Because we have heard say* that in some places the Jews have commemorated and do still commemorate the passion of our Lord Jesus Christ on Good Friday in a scoffing manner, stealing children and crucifying them, and making waxen images and crucifying them when they cannot procure children; we order that, in case a report of any such thing having been done shall henceforth arise, *if it can be proved*, all engaged in such act be *taken, seized, and brought before the king, and whensoever he shall be convinced of its truth*, it shall be his business to issue his warrant for putting them to an ignominious death, how many soever they be. We moreover forbid all Jews from quitting their barrier on Good Friday, and enjoin them to remain in it, and keep close till the Saturday morning; and if they act in defiance of this law, we declare them no longer entitled to any compensation for damages or for insults then offered them by the Christians."

The framing of this law by Alfonso the Tenth for the punishment of those Jews who crucified children in commemoration of the death and passion of Jesus Christ, was owing to the idle tales which ran upon the tongues of a gossiping and superstitious people. Even the monarch himself who ordered this law to be written, was not sure that the observers of the Mosaic ritual were guilty of such atrocities: this may be proved by a mere glance at those words *because we have heard say*, and also by his excluding the magistrates from the hearing of charges brought against the authors of this crime; for the accused were to be brought into the immediate presence of the king, in order that *he,* after satisfying *himself of the truth of the charges,* might condemn them to an ignominious death. If Alfonso the Learned had been sure that such deeds were perpetrated, he would have spoken of them in the same way as of any other crimes, and not have declared in his law that he acted upon hearsay evidence, nor would he have declined committing the investigation of such causes to others, reserving the hearing of them to himself and his successors in the crowns of Castile and Leon.

These crucifixions of innocent children by the Jews were mere fables, invented by ignorant old women, in order to frighten into good behaviour those naughty children that try to obtain whatever they want by crying for it. As the vulgar are pleased with every thing that is odd and strange, they hit upon the expedient of giving out that so barbarous an amusement as this was commonly practised by the Jews; and hence it was, no doubt, that these lying stories came to be reported to king Alfonso the Learned, who, unwilling to let persons guilty of such offences (if peradventure such persons existed) escape the punishment they deserved, spoke of the authors of those crimes in the manner and form briefly described above.

If this be not the case, then let those who still strive to defend as truths the words which passed from mouth to mouth among the blind and ignorant vulgar respecting such acts of the Jews, tell us what object the latter could have in perpetrating such barbarities? Was it written in the books of their law that all who observed the Mosaic ritual were under any obligation to commemorate in so brutal a way, on Good Fridays, the death to which their ancestors put Jesus Christ?

The story is a fiction made to pass current among the people by reason of the frivolity of the Spanish Christians, as well as by reason of their hatred and contempt for all the Hebrews, and is just like that now current among the vulgar that the Jews have tails: for as the learned in their law were called *rabis*,[18] whence the name rabbins, the people, doubtless, for the purpose of ridiculing them, or else because they really believed the truth of such an absurdity, began to circulate this story, which has no more truth[19] in it than the one told of persons employing themselves in crucifying children in commemoration of our Saviour's passion.

Let not those who differ from me imagine that they upset my arguments by saying that this story is mentioned in the laws; for all know that legislators are men, and

[18] *Rabo* is the Spanish for a *tail.—Translator.*

[19] One cannot help being struck with the gravity with which the author concludes this paragraph. Truly, Spaniards are very odd people, and Spain is a very odd country. I cannot resist the temptation to give an extract, in this place, from a book lately published by my friend, Mr. Clark. "Some sceptic present interposed with a doubt as to whether Jews had tails really or not. The majority held that it was unquestionable; but as one or two still questioned it, the dispute was referred to Señor Vazquez, a travelled man. He quietly decided the matter in the affirmative; 'for,' said he, 'when I was in London, I saw Baron Rothschild, who is a Jew of a very high caste, and he had a tail as long as my arm.' So the sceptics were silenced, and smoked the cigar of acquiescence." (Gazpacho; or, Summer Months in Spain.)—*Translator.*

consequently liable, in all respects, to human infirmities, and apt to be guided in their decisions by the deceptions of false counsels or by error of judgment. In Alfonso the Learned, I admire the most eminent man of his age and the monarch who used his utmost endeavours to have his subjects instructed in every branch of art and science; but, with all his knowledge, there were many things of which he was unable to take a dispassionate view, and in many things that he did, he could not help being dragged along by that ignorance which was so common in those days, and even for some centuries afterwards. In the same laws, in which he determines the punishment to be inflicted upon the Jews who should be proved to have crucified children, he speaks of the penalties to which all were to be liable who should hold compact with the devil, or be wizzards or witches.[20]

[20] The first Spanish writer who ridiculed those that believed in witches was the learned physician of Segovia, Andrés Laguna. In his translation and illustration of the work of Pedacio Dioscórides Anazarbeo, he gives a list of the ingredients, of which the unguents made to be applied to various parts of the body by the people called witches, were composed. As his words are very quaint, I take them down for the amusement of the curious. Speaking of some wizzards taken at Nancy in 1545, he says, " Among other things found in the cave of those wizzards was a jar half full of a certain green unguent, similar to poplar ointment, with which they used to anoint themselves; the strength and offensiveness of its smell showed it to be a composition of herbs of the most chilling and soporific qualities, such as *hemlock, night-shade, henbane, mandrakes*. Through the medium of the alguazil, who was a friend of mine, I contrived to get a box of it made, and, afterwards, when in the city of Metz, I had the executioner's wife smeared over with it from head to foot: this woman had, through jealousy of her husband, entirely lost the power of

THE JEWS IN SPAIN.

Besides the laws already cited, which were made to the prejudice of the Jews by Don Alfonso, and placed among those contained in the Seven Partidas, he ordained in those of the Fuero Real[21] that the children

sleeping, and become, as it were, half frenzied. I had this done to her because she was a very fit subject to try such experiments upon, and also because she had made trial of innumerable remedies without effect, and, besides, I thought it was a very proper remedy and one which, judging from the smell and colour of it, could not fail of doing her good. The woman, all on a sudden, while being anointed, and with her eyes open like a rabbit and presenting the appearance of a boiled hare, fell into such a sound sleep that I never expected I should be able to awake her. However, by means of strong ligatures and friction of the extremities, washings of oil, costus and spurge, fumes and vapours applied to the nostrils, and, finally, by the use of cupping-glasses, I made such dispatch with her that, at the expiration of six-and-thirty hours, I restored her to her reason and memory, though the first words she uttered were, ' *Why in evil hour have ye awaked me, for I was surrounded with the greatest conceivable pleasure and delight?*' And with her eyes turned towards her husband, she said to him, smiling at the time, ' *Rascal, I let thee know that I have put on my horns for thee, and with a younger and finer gallant than thee.*' After saying many other extraordinary things, she pressed us to leave her alone and let her fall again into her sweet sleep: from which we gradually diverted her, but she always had her head filled with some vain fancies. *From which we may conjecture that whatever the unfortunate witches say or do is a mere dream produced by very chilling beverages and unctions, which have such a destructive effect upon the memory and imagination as to make the poor timid creatures fancy and firmly believe they have done, while awake, what they have dreamed in their sleep: which results cannot proceed from any other cause than the excessive coldness of the ointment, which is absorbed into their system and gets to their very marrow.*" ANDRÉS LAGUNA.—Pedacio Dioscórides Anazarbeo, on materia medica, translated from the Greek into the vulgar Castilian, and illustrated with clear and substantial notes. Antwerp, 1555; Salamanca, 1570.

[21] Lib. IV. tit. ii. law 4. The first, second, third, fifth, and sixth laws of the same book and title are also aimed at the Jews. For these laws, see Opúsculos Legales de Alfonso X., publicados por la Acad. Esp.—*Translator.*

of Christians should not be suckled by Jewesses, nor the children of Jews by Christian women.

His successors, kings Sancho the Brave, Ferdinand the Fourth, and Alfonso the Eleventh, renewed the above-mentioned statutes against the Jews: this was done by the first of the three in the Cortes holden at Valladolid in the year 1293: by the second, in the Cortes holden at the same place in 1295, and in those holden at Medina del Campo in 1303: and by the third, in 1310,[22] in the collection of Leyes de Estilo,[23] and afterwards in the Ordenamiento de Alcalá.[23]

In the council of Zamora in 1313, in that of Valladolid in 1322,[24] and in that of Salamanca in the year 1335, several statutes against the Jews were passed: and though Pedro the First, of Castile, commanded the said ordinance which his father had made at Alcalá, to

[22] There is either an error in these figures or in the name of the sovereign to whom this act is ascribed, for Alfonso the Eleventh did not come to the throne *till the year* 1312.—*Translator.*

[23] The *Leyes de Estilo* have been published with the *Opúsculos Legales* of Alfonso X., because, in a manuscript book which contains the *Fuero Real*, they come immediately after it, but are not considered by the editor to be the works of that monarch, though, possibly, they may have been composed by Alfonso XI.: this collection contains some severe laws against the Jews, and so does the *Ordenamiento de Alcalá*, published also by the Royal Academy in the *Coleccion de Cortes de Leon y de Castilla*. For the Ordenamiento de Alcalá, see also Semanario Erudito, vol. II., from page 65 to page 128.—*Translator.*

[24] The editor of the *Coleccion de Cortes*, &c., says he thinks this council took place in the year 1325, and that the chroniclers are wrong in supposing 1322 to be the true date. I cannot discover anything with regard to the other councils mentioned in this paragraph.—*Translator.*

be observed and complied with, he continued for their benefit (though in opposition to the general wish of the states assembled in the Cortes at Valladolid) the jurisdiction of an ordinary judge,[25] who was to *hear them and deliver their pleas in civil causes,* alleging, as a reason for this appointment, that the Jews *were poor and miserable, helpless, and in need of protection.*[26]

This protection and countenance given to the Jews by Don Pedro, was very gratefully acknowledged by them, inasmuch as, in all the enterprises which this ill-fated monarch undertook against his rebellious brothers who embroiled the kingdom in civil wars, they assisted him with money, and, in some instances, even with arms. In 1355, several gentlemen of the faction of Don Fadrique,[27] Master of Santiago, and

[25] *Juez ordinario,* a term thus explained in the dictionary of the Royal Spanish Academy: " the judge who takes cognizance of causes and suits in the *first instance."* This expression *first instance* is a legal term; in Spain there are judges of the first, the second, and the third instance. For the council of 1335 (or, as some think, 1336), see the *Semanario Erudito,* vol. XVI., from page 2 to 230, but particularly page 178. See also Aguirre's *Notitia Conciliorum Hispaniæ.—Translator.*

[26] It is gratifying to find an example of benevolence displayed by a prince, to whom the epithet of *Cruel* was, not without reason, given by his subjects. I think it might have been, with equal if not greater justice, applied to his brother, Henry the Second, who murdered and then succeeded him.—*Translator.*

[27] This Don Fadrique was treacherously murdered by his brother Pedro, as will be shown by the accounts given by the historians Mariana and Lopez de Ayala: the latter I have abridged.

" At the commencement of the year 1358, Don Fadrique, Master of Santiago, took Jumilla by force of arms and rescued it from the power of the Arragonese. When he had done this, the Master came to Seville, and on entering the Alcázar, was cruelly murdered by

Don Enrique, Earl of Trastamara,[28] carrying these lords with them and placing them at their head, ap-

some of the king's macebearers, by the command and before the eyes of the king his brother. This was the reward and favour conferred upon him for the service he had just rendered the king. It is certain, however, that Fadrique was not pacifically inclined, and was at this time thinking of going over to the side of Arragon: I suspect that this must have come to the knowledge of the king, and that for this reason his death was accelerated." (Mariana, *Historia General de España*, lib. xvii. cap. 2.) According to Ayala, Pedro *wrote several letters to the Master of Santiago requesting the latter to come to him at Seville*, and when Fadrique made his appearance, the king, who was playing at some game (expressed in Spanish by *Las tablas*, probably backgammon, draughts, or chess), received him *with apparent kindness*, and told him to go to his lodgings and return presently: the Master withdrew from the king's presence and went into another apartment of the Alcázar, which was occupied by María de Padilla and her daughters, whom he wished to see, and while there, discovered by the sad expression on María's countenance that all was not right: on this he went out into the courtyard, the doors of which he found locked, and discovered that his mules had been taken away: while he was hesitating as to what he should do, he was summoned by two gentlemen into the king's presence: in this dilemma he thought it best to obey, and entered the palace with no other attendants than the Master of Calatrava (who knew nothing of the plot) and two other gentlemen, for the persons who had charge over the gates had given directions to the porters not to admit any more. When they got to the iron palace in which the king then was, they found the door locked, and after they had waited a considerable time, during which they were joined by Pero Lopez de Padilla, chief macebearer to the king, a secret door or postern (*postigo*) was opened in the palace, and Don Pedro appeared and said to Pero Lopez de Padilla, "arrest the master:" Pero Lopez enquired, "which of them shall I arrest?" the king replied, "the Master of Santiago." Pero Lopez de Padilla immediately laid hold of the master, Don Fadrique, and said to him, "surrender yourself." The master became much frightened and offered no resistance; and then the king said to some of his macebearers who were present, "Macebearers, kill the Master of Santiago." This was more than they durst do at proached the walls of Toledo which had declared for the king; and as a friend whom they had inside the

first; but one of the king's chamberlains, named Rui Gonzalez de Atienza, who was in the secret, cried lustily to the macebearers, "Traitors, what are ye about? don't ye see that the king commands you to kill the master?" Then the macebearers, seeing that the king had given the command, began to lift up their maces to strike Don Fadrique. The master, observing this, shook off Pedro Lopez de Padilla, bounded into the courtyard (*corral*), and attempted, though ineffectually, to draw his sword, for the hilt of it got entangled in his dress, and after a desperate struggle he was slain by the macebearers. The king, after this, went out of the Alcázar, in hopes of being able to lay hold of some of Fadrique's attendants, but they were too quick for him, and all of them escaped, save one who had taken refuge in María de Padilla's apartment, into which the king entered and found the man there, and, with the assistance of a gentleman, dispatched him. The king then went to the spot where the master lay, and, finding him all but dead, drew a dirk from his belt, and put it into the hands of a young chamberlain who gave the finishing stroke to the dying man. After this (humanity shudders at the recital!) *the King sat down to dinner in the chamber where the master's corpse lay:* this was called the room of the azulejos (*encaustic tiles*). See Lopez de Ayala's Crónica del rey Don Pedro, año 1358, cap. 3. In Dunham's history of Spain and Portugal, this murder is said to have taken place *in a corridor:* I think this is incorrect, for at the time of his death the master was in the *corral,* which signifies *a courtyard* and *not a corridor;* at least no such interpretation of it is given in the dictionary of the Royal Spanish Academy. Besides this, from the words dó el rey estaba (*where the king was*), the writer appears anxious to show that Pedro was not in his usual apartment at the time he issued the order for his brother's murder; and I cannot but think that this room was on the ground-floor: its being called the room of the *azulejos* will not, I think, help to prove anything with *regard to its position*, for, if my memory fail me not, there are *several rooms* in the Alcázar of Seville (*some upstairs and some on the ground-floor*) paved with these tiles.—*Translator.*

[28] According to Mariana, this Enrique, in the year 1369, had been victorious over his brother Pedro in a battle fought in the neighbourhood of Montiel, and the king was compelled to shut himself up in

city, opened a gate to them with the greatest secrecy, and without being observed by the party within, those ragamuffins threw themselves into the streets of Toledo, got possession of the Alcázar and the Jewry called Alcaná, where they put to death all the Jews who dwelt therein, (these were about 1200, men and women included), intending, no doubt, to plunder them of their property.[29] Thence they proceeded to the Grand Jewry,

the castle of that town, which he was afterwards induced to quit by hopes of effecting his escape with the assistance of Bertrand Duguesclin, to whom he had offered a large sum of money as well as considerable estates in Spain, on condition of his compliance with his (the king's) wishes; but the fellow who had promised to do as he had been asked, played a double part and betrayed him, one night, to his brother. "When Pedro had entered Bertrand's tent, the former said it was time that they should both be off. Enrique then entered it in armour: when he saw Pedro, he kept quiet for a little while, and was apparently alarmed: either the enormity of the crime he was about to commit had paralyzed and unnerved him, or, owing to the number of years that had elapsed since they had met, he did not recognize his brother. The bystanders vacillated between fear and hope quite as much as he did. At length a French gentleman said to Enrique, pointing out Pedro to him with his hand, ' *See, there is your enemy.*' Pedro answered with his natural ferocity, *I am, I am.* On this, Enrique drew his dagger and wounded Pedro in the face with it: they immediately closed with each other and both of them fell to the ground: it is said that Enrique was undermost, and that, with the aid of Bertrand (according to Froissart and Ayala, one Rocaberti) *who turned them round and placed him uppermost,*" he was enabled to give his brother repeated stabs, with which he at last succeeded in killing him." (Historia General de España, lib. xvii. cap. 13.) Ayala's account is too long for insertion in this place, but those who like to consult it I refer to the Crónica del rey Don Pedro, año 1369, cap. viii.—*Translator.*

[29] See Lopez de Ayala's Crónica del rey Don Pedro, año 1355, cap. 7, and Mariana's Historia general de España, lib. xvi. cap. 21. The latter writer says they slew more than a thousand Jews, and plundered the mercers' shops in the Alcaná.—*Translator.*

but did not meet with like success; for the party within, apprized of their intention, placed themselves in a posture of defence, displaying great courage; and presently, with the assistance of a body of gentlemen who were on the king's side, made those who took part with the master retire.

As a reward for this action, Don Pedro gave the Jews of Toledo permission to rebuild their synagogue, in which they placed a long inscription in the Hebrew tongue, which, for the sake of its curiosity, and because of its agreement with what I have said, I have transcribed and insert in this place: I follow the translation given in one of the works of Frey Francisco de Rades y Andrada.[30]

"*Behold the sanctuary which was hallowed in Israel, and the house which Samuel built, and the wooden tower, where are read the written law, and the statutes, ordained by God and composed for the purpose of enlightening the minds of those that seek perfection.*

"*This is the fortress of perfect literature, and these are the words they spoke and the deeds which they did to Godward, to assemble the people who come before the gates to hear the law of God in this house.*

"'These are the mercies which God was pleased to show us, in raising up among us judges and princes to deliver us from our enemies and oppressors; for after Israel's last captivity (which came of God, and was the third captivity from which God delivered us),

---

[30] Crónica de las tres órdenes y caballerías de Santiago, Calatrava y Alcántara. Toledo, 1572.

as there was no king in Israel to protect us, we dispersed ourselves, some going to this country, some to that, where they are yearning for their country and we for ours. And we of this land have built this house with strong arm and power upraised. The day on which it was built was a great and a pleasant one to the Jews, who hearing of it, came from the ends of the earth to see if there were any means of raising some lord over us, who should be to us a tower of strength and have perfection of understanding, in order to rule our commonwealth. Such a thing was not to be found among us who are settled in these parts: but Samuel [31] rose up among us and came to our help, and God was with him and us, and he found grace and mercy for us. He was a man of war and peace, of great influence with all people, and a famous architect. This took place in the days of king Pedro. May God be his helper, may He enlarge his dominions, grant him prosperity, exalt him and raise his throne above that of all princes! God be with him and all his house, and let every man bow down before him; let the great and powerful in the land acknowledge him, and let all who shall hear his name rejoice to hear it, and let it be manifest that he is become the protector and defender of Israel!

"Under his protection and with his authority, we determined to build this temple. Peace be with him

---

[1] The person here alluded to is Samuel or Simuel Leví, treasurer to Pedro the Cruel. He was arrested by this king's order, in the year 1360, and put to the torture in order to make him declare what treasures he had, and died under it. (Lopez de Ayala).—*Translator*.

and all of his descendants, and comfort in all their troubles. Now hath God ransomed us from the power of our captivity: we have never had such a deliverance as this. With the advice of our learned men we erected this fabric. Great was the mercy of God to usward. Don Rabí Myer enlightened and guided us, blessed be his memory! This man was born to be a treasure to our people, for, before his time, our countrymen used to have daily quarrels at the gate. This holy man gave such discharge and relief to the poor as was not done in the first days nor in ancient times. He was no other than a prophet sent of God; a just man, and one that walked uprightly. He was one of those who feared God and had respect unto His holy name. Besides all this, he desired to build this house of prayer for the name and fame of the God of Israel. This is the feasting-house for those who desire to know our law and to enquire after God. It was God who commenced building this house and abode for Himself, and completed it in a happy year for Israel. It was God that increased the number of His servants by eleven hundred, after that this house was built for His service: these persons were men of rank and might, by whose instrumentality this house was to be supported with the strong arm and upraised power. Previously to this, there was not known in all the regions of the world a more feeble people than ourselves. But, O Lord our God, as Thy name is strong and powerful, thou wouldest that we should complete this house in good days and fair years, in order that Thy name might dwell therein, and the fame of the builders might be sounded in all the world, and that it might be said—

THIS IS THE HOUSE WHICH THY SERVANTS BUILT TO INVOKE THEREIN THE NAME OF GOD THEIR REDEEMER."

We learn from this inscription that king Pedro, by the advice of his intimate friend Samuel Leví, allowed the Jews to erect a new synagogue at Toledo—a thing they could not have done without the consent of the king of Castile, as they were forbidden to build such edifices, and were only allowed to keep their old ones in sufficient repair to prevent them from tumbling down. A striking proof of the special favor shown to the Jews by king Pedro appears in the following words of the inscription just cited: *May God be his helper, may He enlarge his dominions, grant him prosperity, exalt him and raise his throne above that of all princes! God be with him and all his house, and let every man bow down before him; let the great and powerful in the land acknowledge him, and let all who shall hear his name rejoice to hear it, and let it be manifest that he is become the protector and defender of Israel.*

In the times of king Pedro, the learned Jew Rabí Don Santo flourished in Spain; he was surnamed Carrion, because he was born at Carrion de los Condes, a town in old Castile. Some say he abjured Judaism and was afterwards a good Christian; but this is questioned by others who cite the first strophe of his book, entituled, *Consejos y documentos del Judio Rabbi Don Santo al Rey Don Pedro* (Counsels, &c. of the Jew

Rabbí Don Santo to king Pedro), which he composed in his old age:—

> "Noble lord, both high and mighty,
> Listen to this sermón,
> Which Don Santo doth indite'ee,
> The Jew of Carrión."

This genius seems not to have met with much favor at king Pedro's hands, as appears from the following verses taken from his work just cited:—

> "The rose is not of little worth,
> Which from the briar takes its birth.
> Nor less valued is good wine,
> Because the grape springs from the vine.
> The gosshawk's lowly place of rest
> Is good as any other nest.
> A moral also may be true
> Although 'tis taught you by a Jew.[32]
>
> * * * * *
>
> I'm good as others of my race,
> Who from the king have got a place."

But it is a fact placed beyond all doubt, that Rabí Don Santo was converted to the Christian faith, for he has introduced a Christian doctrine into a poem, at the commencement of which we find these lines:—

> "The Virgin's praises shalt thou sing,
> And her a handsome off'ring bring;
> For she, God's holy mother, alway
> For us poor mortals deigns to pray."

Rabí Don Santo was likewise author of a poem entituled *La Danza general de la muerte, en que entran*

---

[32] There are some variations between the lines here given and those cited by Don José Rodriguez de Castro.—*Translator.*

todos los estados de gentes, (The general dance of death, in which all classes join): this, as well as the above-cited works of his, are extant in manuscript, in the library of the Escurial.

In the Cortes of Toro, in the year 1371, king Henry the Second issued a decree, which compelled the Jews to wear a badge by which they might be known,[33] and also prohibited all observers of the Mosaic law from using such names as were then borne by Christians. He also declared that evidence given by the former, in courts of law, against the latter, should be null and void.

John the First likewise took measures to arrest the progress of that excess of liberty to which the Jews living in his territories were then aspiring, and, besides carrying out the laws enacted against them in the Cortes of Soria[34] and Briviesça[35] by his predecessors; in those of Valladolid[22] holden in the year 1388,[36] he

[33] Don Pablo de Santa María, in his *Scrutinium*, [part 2nd,] chapter the tenth, says, "Consequenter etiam rex Henricus secundus, bonæ memoriæ, frater ejus, qui regnum fratris habuit, multas cædes seu strages, antequam regnasset, in Judæis fecit, tam in urbe Toletana, quam in quibusdam aliis villis et castris in confinibus regni Castellæ existentibus. Et cum hujusmodi rex Henricus secundus regnavit, regno accepto à fratre suo Petro, ipse instituit in curiis generalibus, quod Judæi portarent signum distinctionis in suis vestibus, prout jura canonica volunt; quod tamen nunquam fuit auditum in Hispania, sed indistincte cum fidelibus conversabantur: ex quo multa enormia et divinæ legis deformia sequebantur." (See also Lopez de Ayala's Crónica del Rey Don Enrique II., año 1371, cap. vii., and Coleccion de Cortes, &c.)—*Translator.*
[34] A.D. 1380, see *Coleccion de Cortes*, &c.—*Translator.*
[35] A.D. 1387, see *Coleccion de Cortes*, &c.—*Translator.*
[36] A.D. 1385, according to the editor of the *Coleccion de Cortes*, &c.—*Translator.*

ordered that certain imprecations, conjurations, blasphemies, and curses upon the Christians and Christianity should be erased from the Talmud, and that all who uttered them in future should be punished with the utmost rigour of the law.

In these times there lived a courtier, by some called *Don Juzaf Pichon*, by others *Don Jucaf Picho:* he was regarded as a thoroughly honourable man, and, in consequence of his many good services, was appointed collector of the revenues and chief accomptant to Henry the Second. It is said that some envious persons bore ill-will to him, in consequence, no doubt, of his exalted position and the favour shown him by that monarch: and those who owed him a grudge (a large number of the principal Jews of the Aljamas), determining to put an end to the confidence which Don Juzaf enjoyed with the prince, accused him to the king of Castile, of certain crimes—an accusation which, though false, was entertained, and Henry was compelled to administer justice[37] at the expense of the affection which the long-tried loyalty of this honourable Jew had kindled in his heart. Thus, after a struggle with himself between gratitude and the justice which was expected of him and dreaded by him, he ordered Don Juzaf to be arrested; and as the offences of which this Jew was accused called for a rigorous punishment, the king fined him forty thou-

---

[37] There is, at this day, no word in his language so hateful to a Spaniard as justicia (*justice*); the very sound of it makes him tremble from head to foot: the odious *escribano* (or low, pettifogging attorney) is the only person in Spain who does not shrug his shoulders when he hears it pronounced.—*Translator.*

sand doblas,[38] to be paid to the crown, which were liquidated at the expiration of twenty days.

As soon as Don Juzaf recovered his liberty, he began to complain of those who, with such perverse disposition, had brought these unjust accusations against him before the king, and had thereby destroyed the credit he had earned by so many good services rendered to Henry the Second's person. "How long," said he, "shall truth be banished from the courts and palaces of kings? How long shall it cease to go hand-in-hand with virtue, to guide the steps of mortals, and to be their constant rule in the most important as well as the most trivial of their actions? How long must honourable reward be exposed to the poisoned tongues of the wicked—those hidden asps that wear the guise of men—those hungry wolves and sly foxes—those tigers that are ever ready to devour the reputation of the good? How long will people listen to their words which are more deceitful than the crocodile's cry or the siren's song? But woe is me! In evil hour was I born! How can the dishonest bestow honour, and how can the people discriminate between truth and falsehood, when the former cannot give what they do not possess, and the latter throw open the doors of their understanding to the belief of all that is deceitful and wicked, and close them when they see the light of truth appear? Oh, how blind and weak is human reason, how open to deception and villainy, how unfavourable to justice!

---

[38] See Lopez de Ayala's *Crónica del Rey Don Juan I.*, año 1379, cap. 3, and Zuñiga's *Anales de Sevilla*, p. 242, column 1.

Whithersoever I turn my eyes, I only meet with enemies, and am even scared by the shadow of my own body. If as an innocent man I suffer thus, what would have become of me had my heart been polluted with sin? Then, perhaps, I should have been more esteemed by the people, and if I had not entirely escaped envy, should have, at least, met with less persecution from her. Yet will I not invoke upon the wicked their deserts; for even were I wicked, and were the people not to envy or persecute me, I should then reproach myself inwardly for my actions, be my own bitterest enemy, and have to endure the torment of knowing that this new reprover of my crooked steps was telling me the truth, while among my adversaries I now see nothing but deceit and the rancour of envy. And so, of two misfortunes, I would rather [choose the least and] have others for my enemies than myself."

The punishment inflicted upon Don Juzaf Pichon by king Henry the Second did not mitigate the hatred of the Jews to him: immediately on the death of this monarch they went to his son and successor to the crown, John the First of Castile, who was at Burgos with the states assembled in parliament, and requested him to issue letters-patent (*albalá*) addressed to Fernan Martin, the alguazil, ordering the latter to put to death the person pointed out to him as an evil-speaker (*malsin*). When they proffered their petition to the king, they adduced arguments to show that it was a custom generally received among the Jews to put to death certain men of little worth and of ill condition among them: these were the *malsines*, who disturbed the peace of the community with their tongues, excited ill-feeling and animosity amongst one another, and gave occasion to many disasters and constant inquietude. John the First heard this verbal petition of the Jews, and as he was busily engaged in acquainting himself with matters of state and the proceedings of the Cortes, and it being, in short, the beginning[39] of his reign, he did not give due consideration to what he had been asked to do, and, without being aware of what he was about, issued the albalá (*letters-patent*) to his alguazil, directing him to see that the parties accused of being *malsines* were put to death.

When those who had obtained this permission were provided with the king's letters, they applied for others from the Jewish rulers and governors of the Aljamas of the kingdom, to authorize the alguazil, Fernan Martin, to put Don Juzaf Pichon to death.[39] The news of his

---

[39] Lopez de Ayala, in his *Crónica del Rey Don Juan I.*, gives the following account of Don Juzaf's death: "The Jews took the alguazil with them, and went to the abode of Don Juzaf Pichon, and had him called up, for it was very early in the morning and before the people of the house were up, and he was yet lying in bed when they came; and they got into the house, and said that some men wanted to take away his mules for claims which they had upon him for money that he owed them. This was a mere invention for the purpose of getting him to come down from his chamber. He immediately went down to one of the doors of the house, where those Jews who pretended that they wanted to take his mules were waiting for him. Here stood the king's alguazil who went with the Jews to execute the king's albalá, which was shown to Juzaf, and no sooner did he see the Jews and the alguazil than he was taken by them and decapitated in his own

THE JEWS IN SPAIN.

execution (which took place on the 21st of August, 1379)[40] reached the king's ears, together with the complaints of all the gentry in the kingdom, who were astonished and incensed at the commission of so gross an act of injustice; for the virtue and integrity of Don Juzaf Pichon were universally known: he was a Jew in high esteem, even with the Christians, for the many good services he had performed during the lifetime of Henry the Second.

The wickedness of the Jews who were engaged in this infamous act had the effect of stirring up the wrath of king John the First: he commanded that Don Zulema and Don Zag, who had given the order to put Don Juzaf Pichon to death, should themselves be publicly executed, and he would have subjected the alguazil[40] to a similar punishment, had not the grandees

---

house, without a word having been said to him." [año primero, cap. 3. Ayala informs us that the king's coronation-festival, at which Juzaf Pichon was present, had not concluded when the Jews applied for the albalá.—*Translator*.]

[40] Lopez de Ayala says it was suspected that the king had issued the albalá in compliance with the advice of some persons in his confidence *who had been bribed by the Jews*. Mariana, too, declares that, from the promptness with which the *Royal Executioner* (as he calls Fernan Martin) obeyed his orders, there was good reason to suspect *him also of having received a bribe*. Neither of these writers mentions the month or day on which Juzaf Pichon was judicially murdered, nor does Zúñiga. Eugenio Amirola, in his notes on Ayala, states that, in the *Compendio*, the date given is *Sunday* the 21st of August, which however, he adds, could not be, for the 21st of August 1379 was a *Tuesday*: what book he means by the *Compendio*, I am at a loss to know; for, on referring to Garibay's work, I do not find the month or day of Juzaf Pichon's death given; neither does he refer to Ayala's abridgement, because this he calls the Abreviatura. See *Crónica de*

of the realm interceded in his behalf, and represented to the king that the man had merely done his duty and complied with the order contained in the *albalá*, which the king himself had issued; that he had been deceived by the Jews, and that no blame could attach to him for fulfilling the commands he had received. These reasons had some weight with John, who ordered the execution of Fernan Martin to be respited, and commuted his punishment to the loss of a hand, which was publicly cut off by the executioner. The Jews who applied for the king's *albalá*, and craftily withheld the name of the person to whose injury it was about to be issued, were also put to death, and the like punishment was inflicted upon a *merino* of the Jewry of Burgos, for being concerned in the tragical fate of Don Juzaf.[41]

This, however, did not abate the king's wrath against the persons who had so villainously deceived him, and he took away from them the power of life and death over persons of their persuasion—a privilege hitherto enjoyed by the aljamas of the kingdoms of Leon and Castile.[41]

* * * * * * * *

[*The author here interrupts his narrative with accounts of Jewish poets, with specimens of whose poetry he fills*

Don Juan I., año 1379, cap. III., with Amirola's notes to the same; Mariana, lib. XVIII. cap. 3.; Garibay's *Compendio Historial*, lib. xv. cap. 20; Zúñiga's *Anales de Sevilla*, año 1379, page 242.—*Translator*.

[41] For these two paragraphs, see the same authors and chapters given in last note. The word *merino* signifies a *shepherd*, and also *a judge* or *inspector of sheepwalks*; in which sense the author uses it I know not; the reader can take which he pleases.—*Translator*.

several pages: these effusions would be very tiresome, and even offensive, in some instances, to the English reader.]

At this time a large number of Jews abjured Judaism: this abjuration, however, did not result from their conviction of the truth of Christianity, but rather from their fear of the common people who, under the cloak of devotion and piety, raised tumults in the Jewries for the purpose of murdering the inhabitants thereof, and making prizes of their goods and property. This violent conduct of the populace, which was attended with such dreadful consequences to the unhappy Jews, was brought about by the sermons preached at Seville by Don Fernando Martinez, Archdeacon of Écija, in which he dwelt upon the usurious rate of interest they received on loans and goods sold on credit, to the great injury of the Christians: so vivid, in short, were the colours he employed to describe the wickedness of those who observed the Mosaic ritual, that many of the lower orders (always fickle,) regarding their destruction as an act of piety and service done to their crucified Lord, slew them in the open streets, without fear or shame and without the slightest opposition. The news of these disasters reached the ears of John the First, who saw no other mode of checking the seditious rabble than sending to the dean and chapter of the holy church letters, in which he strongly urged upon them the necessity of muzzling Archdeacon Fernando Martinez, owing to whose expressions, devoid alike of reason and moderation, these calamities and troubles had arisen;

For though his zeal is good and holy and worthy of admiration, I shall order him to beware how he attempts to stir up the people against the Jews by his sermons and harangues; for though the Jews are wicked and perverse persons, they live under my royal protection and authority, and must not be outraged: but whensoever they shall offend, they shall be punished according to law, and I shall command this to be done.[42]

No sooner had John the First expired (in the year 1390) and his son and successor, Henry the Third, ascended the throne of Castile, than the archdeacon of Écija, freed from the irksome restraint he was under during the lifetime of the former king,[43] and unawed by respect for that monarch's memory, recommenced preaching against the Jews: he delivered his harangues in the most public and most frequented places of Seville, and inflamed the minds of the lower orders, setting before their eyes their own poverty and the riches of those who observed the law of Moses, to whose covetousness he attributed the misfortunes which the Christians endured, and is said to have addressed to them discourses of the following character: " Unhappy and everlastingly wretched people, who can relieve your misfortunes and calami-

---

[42] The king's words in the letter which he wrote to the dean and chapter of Seville about this affair in 1388.—*Anales de Sevilla por Zúñiga,* [año 1388.—*Translator.*]

[43] The archdeacon appears to have taken advantage of the king's youth and the unsettled state of the kingdom during his minority; for when John the First died, Henry the Third was only eleven years old. See Zúñiga's *Anales de Sevilla,* page 252, and Lopez de Ayala's *Crónica del Rey Don Enrique* III., año 1391, caps. v. and xx.—*Translator.*

ties? Do ye see with what a cruel famine yourselves, your wives, and your children are afflicted? Never shall there be a mitigation of it; never shall ye break the chains which bind⁴⁴ you to misery; never shall ye taste those sweets which inconstant fortune is wont to offer mortals! Woe to thee, thou race born to misfortune alone! Famine attacks thee, and thou canst not procure money to relieve thee from it, for the few pieces which would enable thee to go through the bitterness of life with less toil, are buried for ever in those secret chests of iron in possession of the Jews. These men are the constant foes to the name of Christ—they think to blot it out from the face of the earth, and strive, by every means which presents itself to their eyes, to destroy the Christian people. Unhappy generation! thou art about to disappear from the face of the earth, and to leave thy children in bondage to those who did not scruple at crucifying their Lord! What love, what pity, what good offices can they expect from such cruel executioners as these? Cursed be the moment that we allowed these birds of prey to build their nests nigh our dwellings; for this very proximity affords them greater facilities for hiding from our eyes all that they rob us of! Let those ill-advised shepherds who allow wolves to live among the sheep, be awakened. Let the barkings of the faithful dogs be heard, now that the flock is on the point of being devoured and of getting beyond the reach of help. But how are they to be awakened who have fallen into the profound sleep of a blind con-

⁴⁴ Literally, *moor.—Translator.*

fidence? The butchering wolves cannot be scared by stones dexterously hurled from the slings, because the hands of the shepherds are cast down to the ground. The bowstrings are broken, the steeled barbs of the arrows wear a coating of rust: the dogs that watch over the flocks are few in comparison with the number of the wild beasts. Alas, unhappy lambs! what will become of you, unless ye derive strength from weakness, and endeavour to defend yourselves against your watchful and savage enemies?"

Thus, urged on by the sermons of archdeacon Fernando Martinez, the fulness of the people's animosity burst upon the Jews, and they began publicly to upbraid such of them as had the reputation of being great misers, or of having attained power by means of their wealth. Don Alvar Perez de Guzman, chief alguazil[45] of Seville, Ruy Perez de Esquivel, and Fernan Arias de Quadros, the two alcaldes, determined to punish these excesses of the people, and therefore arrested several of the ringleaders in those disorders, and sentenced two of them to be publicly whipped on Ash-Wednesday, the 15th of March, 1391. But the mob, enraged at this just act of severity, tumultuously assembled, with the fixed determination to prevent the execution of it at all hazards. The chief alguazil[45] and Count Niebla in vain strove to appease the tumult by addressing the people and employing the strongest arguments they could think of: meanwhile the rabble,

[45] The office of alguazil mayor or chief alguazil answers, I think, nearly to that of our *high constable.—Translator.*

II.]   THE JEWS IN SPAIN.   91

now grown more insolent in their demands, stoned those who had charge of the delinquents, rescued the latter out of their hands, and put them into the cathedral. They then turned their fury upon the Jewries, where they commenced wounding and slaying every man, woman, or child they met, besides others who had concealed themselves; they made prizes of the jewels and money which they found in the houses, and, finally, dashed to pieces everything belonging to the Jews. The authorities of Seville, assisted by the nobility, came to the help of the poor Hebrews, and succeeded in saving most of their lives and rescuing a portion of the large spoil which the licentious and savage mob had gotten into their clutches.

When the tumult was appeased, the chief alcaldes concluded that, were they to punish the numerous delinquents concerned in those acts of inhumanity, the malcontents and others who yet coveted the estates of the unfortunate Jews would again be exasperated, and the city reduced to a strait still more dreadful than the last.

They determined, therefore, on proclaiming the pardon of the authors of these offences, while the hapless Jews, intimidated by the late popular outbreak, had not yet dared to go out into the streets, and were now thinking of professing Christianity, in order to secure their lives and properties from the hatred and covetousness[46] of the people."[47]

[46] Literally, *ambition*.—*Translator*.
[47] See *Anales de Sevilla por Zúñiga*, p. 252, and Lopez de Ayala's *Crónica del Rey Don Enrique* III., año 1391, cap. v.—*Translator*.

The Archdeacon, elated with the success of his oratory, and observing the insolent carriage of the plebeian folks after the impunity which followed their late attempt, is reported to have preached again on Sunday the 9th of July, in the same year, against the Jews; to have pourtrayed their avarice in the most vivid colours, and to have set forth in high-flown language the calamities that threatened the Christians, while they suffered these foes to the name of Christ to live with perfect freedom, according to their law, within the cities of Castile.

The people—animated on the one hand with the desire of getting possession of the estates of the Jews, and, on the other, regarding the latter as brambles, nettles, and caltrops which grow amidst the cornfields and draw off all the substance of their mother earth, thus leaving them without the slightest nutriment, and rendering them liable to be wasted and burned up by the rays of the sun, and to be deprived of strength and power to resist the violence of the stormy winds—created a fresh tumult and ran to the Jewries, with intent to exterminate all the Israelites born or dwelling in them.

These barbarians, unworthy to bear the name of Christians, caused four thousand Jews to perish by the edge of the sword. Those that escaped unhurt or with but slight wounds from the terrible tumult raised by that unbridled rabble, fearful of the people's wrath, and awed by the last two insurrections, professed Christianity at once.[48] Such was the method employed by

[48] See *Anales de Sevilla por Zúñiga*, p. 252, and Lopez de Ayala's *Crónica del Rey Don Enrique*, III. año 1391, cap. xx.—*Translator.*

a set of wicked Christians to make the truth of religion take root in the minds of the Jews; and as this was the effect of constraint and fear, but a short time elapsed ere they began to prevaricate, as was natural enough: for I do not believe any one can love the truth when, in order to bring it home to him, his adversaries have recourse to arms and intimidation, fire and sword. These means, of which the tyrants of this world avail themselves for the purpose of maintaining their power, or obtaining, with lightning-like rapidity, the ends which they have in view, are attended with evil consequences to the people for a time; but they are afterwards converted into arms, to be employed in the destruction and extermination of the tyrants themselves who have used them—a truth of which abundant instances occur in history.

When intelligence of what the people of Seville had done reached Córdova, Toledo, Zaragoza, Valencia, Barcelona, and Lérida, risings in these and many other cities took place. Henry the Third dispatched letters to the alcaldes of all these cities, directing them on no account to allow those wicked proceedings, of such pernicious consequences to the unhappy Jews, to go on; but neither cities, towns, nor gentry, cared a fig for the king's mandamus. The people, above listening to any admonition, became exceedingly haughty in their demeanour, in consequence of the success which had attended their rebellions, seditions, and massacres.[49]

[49] Lopez de Ayala, Crónica del Rey Don Enrique III., año 1391, cap. xx.—*Translator.*

From 1391 to 1395, in the latter of which years Henry determined to go down from Segovia to Andalusia to punish the authors of the past riots, he disguised the resentment which he felt at seeing his commands disobeyed. He entered Seville on the 13th of December, and on the same day ordered Fernando Martinez, archdeacon of Écija, to be arrested, for having, by means of his harangues, caused the seditious movements of the people against the Jews.[50]

Master Gil Gonzalez de Ávila,[51] speaking of the Archdeacon, says that the king *punished him in order that no one might, in future, attempt, under the cloak of piety, to stir up the people.* We are unable to gather from any of the historians what punishment this fellow suffered. Zúñiga asserts that he died some years after,[52] with a *strong odour of sanctity.*

The object of these popular outbreaks against the Jews is declared in the Chronicle of Henry the Third, composed by that illustrious gentleman Pero Lopez de Ayala, in these words, *all this was love of pillage and plunder rather than devotion.*[53]

In those days lived a famous Jew in Spain, named Jehosuah Halorqi, who was born at Huesca, in the year 1350, as is supposed; he was a noted Talmudist

---

[50] Anales de Sevilla por Zúñiga, p. 257.—*Translator.*

[51] Historia de la vida y hechos del Rey Don Henrique III. de Castilla. [The passage from this writer, given in the text, is quoted by Zúñiga. Anales de Sevilla, p. 257.—*Translator.*]

[52] Namely, in 1404. See his Anales de Sevilla, pp. 257 and 275.—*Translator.*

[53] Año 1391, cap. xx.—*Translator.*

and one of the principal masters of the law of Moses, and had studied medicine with great success. He abjured Judaism, and, on professing Christianity, took the name of Jerónimo de Santa Fé, which the Spanish Jews could not patiently endure, but were much displeased and shocked at seeing a man so well acquainted with the Holy Scriptures as he was, declare their rites to be vain; and for this reason they used scoffingly to call him Halorqi the *Blasphemer*.[54]

It has been said that the conversion of this Jew was effected by the preaching of San Vicente Ferrer, who used, about that time, to travel about the cities of Spain and overturn the law of Moses, not by discourses which incited the people to attack the unhappy Jews, as was the practice of the Archdeacon of Écija, but by leading them into the way of truth through the medium of kind words, forcible and conclusive reasonings, and evangelical discourses.[55]

Owing to the reputation which Jerónimo de Santa Fé enjoyed in all[56] these kingdoms as well as in foreign states, and to the credit and estimation in which he was holden for his deep acquaintance with the occult sciences, he obtained the honour of an invitation to the

[54] José Rodriguez de Castro, in his Biblioteca de los Rabines Españoles, says that the Jews formed a Hebrew word, which signifies *Blasphemer*, out of the initials of his name Jerónimo de Santa Fé: this was the unkindest cut of all.—*Translator.*

[55] See the same work.—*Translator.*

[56] Modern Spain consists of several kingdoms, formerly separate. While I write these lines, I have before me a two-cuartos piece of the year 1845, which bears on its reverse the inscription *Reyna de las Españas*, (*Queen of the Spains*).—*Translator.*

Court of the Spanish Antipope, Pedro de Luna, who was anxious to have him near his person, in order that he might cure him when suffering from any of those numerous infirmities which so obstinately beset our mortal bodies. This was that Pedro de Luna who wished to rule the church from his residence at Avignon by the title of Benedict the thirteenth.

About this time an event occurred which served to increase the applause so deservedly and so universally bestowed upon the convert Jerónimo de Santa Fé, for his great learning. Jerónimo de Zurita, in his *Anales de Aragon,* relates that in the year 1413, owing to the obstinacy of the Jews in refusing to be converted to the law of grace, new methods were tried to overcome those objections raised by them, which prevented their admitting the light of truth into their minds. "By the Pope's command, the principal Doctors and Rabbins of all the Aljamas in the kingdom assembled in the city of Tortosa, for the purpose of being publicly admonished, in his presence and in that of his whole Court, to acknowledge the error and blindness in which they walked. The principal Rabbins were Rabí Ferrer, Master Salomon Isaac, Rabí Astruch el Leví of Alcañiz, Rabí Joseph Albo, Rabí Matatías of Zaragoza, Master Todroz, Benastruc Desmaestre of Girona, and Rabí Moisés Abenabez: and though there were many distinguished Masters and Doctors of Divinity at the Pope's Court, who were men of learning and great divines, the Pope was, nevertheless, anxious that in the questions and disputations propounded, the care of instructing and teaching those Rabbins should be more especially and particularly entrusted to Jerónimo de Santa Fé, his physician, inasmuch as the latter was well read and grounded in the Old Testament, together with the glosses upon it, and all the treatises of the Rabbins, as well as their Talmud; by the authorities and sentences of which it was the Pope's intention that they should be convinced and led to see the blindness and unsoundness of their doctrine, the obstinacy of their errors and lives, their rash and perverse interpretation of their law. The first assembly was holden on the 7th of February last year (1413); and, in the presence of the Pope, his College, and all his Court, the questions and articles to be discussed and argued were propounded: the Pope attended other meetings besides this, and deputed the Minister General of the order of Preachers and the Master of the Sacred Palace to supply his place as President, during his absence. Of this learned assemblage was one Garcí Álvarez de Alarcon, a man well acquainted with the Hebrew, Chaldaic, and Latin tongues. Andrés Beltran, Doctor of Divinity, and almoner to the Pope, a man well read in Hebrew and Chaldaic literature, and originally of Jewish persuasion, materially helped to convince and bring over many of the principal families in the kingdom: he was a native of Valencia, and it was out of respect for his piety and learning that the Pope conferred the church of Barcelona upon him, by whose arguments the doubts respecting the translations of the Bible, which the Rabbins twisted as it suited their purpose, were resolved."[57]

This is Jerónimo de Zurita's account. The Jews who went to Tortosa, in order to take part in the famous disputation carried on there, were the following: six from Zaragoza, named, Zarachías Levita, Vidael Benvenista, M. Mathatías Izahari, Macaltiob (the nasi or chief of the Spanish Jews), Samuel Levita, and M. Moisés; one from Huesca, named Todros; two from Alcoy, whose names were Joseph, son of Aderet, and Meir Galigon; one from Daroca, named Astruch Levita; one from Monreal, called Joseph Albo; two from Monzon, named Joseph Levita and M. Jomtob Carcosa; one from Montalban, called Abuganda; three from Blesa, named Joseph Abbalegh, Bongosa, and M. Todros, son to Jecht of Gerona.[58]

On their arrival at Tortosa, they elected as their spokesman at the congress Vidael Benvenista, one of the most learned in their law, and immediately went to the Palace and presented themselves before Benedict the Thirteenth, who received them with great affability, and gave orders that they should be most comfortably lodged and entertained, and treated with the greatest kindness: he promised them also that they should meet with no molestation whatever, inasmuch as they had come in order to be convinced, or not, (as the case

---

[57] Anales de Aragon por Jerónimo de Zurita, lib. xii. cap. 45.—*Translator.*

[58] See Rodriguez de Castro's Biblioteca de los Rabinos Españoles, vol. I. p. 207, column 2, fol. edition, Madrid 1781.—*Translator.*

might be) of the erroneousness of their doctrines, and not to be vexed or harassed in any way.[59]

On the day after their arrival at Tortosa, the Jews attended again at Benedict's palace, and found the hall in which the assembly was to take place crowded with persons high in authority and rank. Sixty chairs were occupied by Cardinals, Bishops, and other dignitaries.[59]

When the congress met and silence was obtained, Benedict the Thirteenth briefly addressed the Jews,[60] and then Jerónimo de Santa Fé commenced an harangue, in which he set forth with clearness of argument and gracefulness of language the fulfilment of the prophecies relating to the Messiah's advent, an event still looked for by the Jews. In answer to this harangue, Vidael Benvenista delivered another, the design of which was to show, by arguments taken from the Talmud, that the Messiah had not yet come. I should observe that both these discourses were expressed in very elegant Latin; for both the disputants were men of general learning. Next day, another harangue, in

[59] See the last note and pages which follow the passage referred to.—*Translator.*

[60] Vos Hebræorum sapientissimi scitote, me non hîc adesse neque vos advocasse ad disputandum nostra-ne an vestra vera sit religio. Certo certius mihi est, religionem meam verissimam esse. Vestra quidem lex olim vera fuit, at abrogata ea nunc est. Non alio auctore huc accersiti estis nisi Hieronymo, qui Messiam jampridem venisse, se demonstraturum dixit, ex Talmude vestro : quem magistri vestri, vobis longe sapientiores, olim condiderunt : proinde aliud disputare cavete.—*Speech of Pedro de Luna (Benedict the Thirteenth) to the Jews assembled at Tortosa.* [Rodriguez de Castro's Biblioteca de los Rab. Esp., p. 205, col. 2nd.—*Translator.*]

support of what Vidael Benvenista had said, was delivered by Zarachías Levita the Jew; and on the third day of their assembly, that famous disputation commenced, which lasted from the 7th of February, 1413,[61] till the 12th of November, 1414,[61] the result of which was that all the Jews who were present at the debate, and took an active part in it, (either by speechifying, or by throwing such light as their wisdom suggested on those points for which they so pertinaciously contended), were converted to the faith. Rabí Ferrer and Joseph Albo were the only persons among them who contumaciously adhered to their original opinions.

Rabí Astruch then presented to Benedict the Thirteenth a confession in his own name and in the name of the other Jews, wherein they declared themselves to have had the worst of the argument, and in consequence abjured the errors of their ancient law, and sincerely embraced the Christian faith. When this confession[62] had been read before Benedict and the

---

[61] These dates are taken from a manuscript in the Escurial, cited by Rodriguez de Castro in his Biblioteca de los Rabines Españoles, vol. I., see from pages 206 and 207.—*Translator.*

[62] Et ego Astruch Levi cum debitâ humilitate, subjectione et reverentiâ Reverendissimæ Paternitatis et Dominationis Domini Cardinalis, aliorumque Reverendorum Patrum et Dominorum hîc præsentium respondeo, dicens: Quod licet auctoritates Talmudicæ contra Talmud tam per Reverendissimum meum Dominum Eleemosynarium, quàm per honorabilem Magistrum Hieronymum allegatæ, sicut ad literam jacent, malè sonent; partim quia primâ facie videntur hæreticæ, partim contra bonos mores, partim quia sunt erroneæ; et quamvis per traditionem meorum Magistrorum habuerim quod illæ habeant vel possint alium sensum habere: fateor tamen illum me

Cardinals, dignitaries, and other persons in whose presence the converts were, the Antipope ordered the new decrees (which from that moment he enforced upon all Jews who persisted in adhering to their ancient law,) to be read. These decrees were then inserted in the bull which Benedict published in the city of Valencia on the 11th of May, 1415. The substance of them is contained in the following heads, taken from the *Biblioteca de los Rabines Españoles* (Library of Spanish Rabbins), arranged and prepared by Don José Rodriguez de Castro.

" First. All people in general, without respect of persons, are forbidden to hear, read, or teach the doctrine of the Talmud, publicly or privately; and within the space of one month all copies of the Talmud, glosses upon it, summaries, compendiums, and other writings whatsoever, bearing directly or indirectly upon the said doctrine, that can be found, are to be deposited in the Cathedral church of each diocese; and diocesans and inquisitors must look to the due observance of this decree, and visit in person or by procuration (once

---

ignorare. Ideo dictis auctoritatibus nullam fidem adhibeo, nec auctoritatem aliqualem, nec illis credo, nec ea quidem defendere intendo, et quamcunque responsionem per me superius datam huic meæ ultimæ responsioni obviantem, illam revoco, et pro non dictâ habeo in eo solum in quo huic contradicit. Omnibus Judæis et Rabbinis totius congregationis ibidem præsentibus (Rabbí Ferrer et Rabbí Joseph Albo duntaxat exceptis) magnâ voce clamantibus et dicentibus : Et nos in dictâ cedulâ concordamus et illi adhæremus.— *Schedule of Rabí Astruch, presented in his own name and in the name of the other Jews converted at the assembly of Tortosa.* [This passage is extracted from the manuscript spoken of in the last note].—*Translator.*

every two years at least) all those places within the limits of their jurisdiction in which there are any Jews living, and punish all offenders with the utmost rigor."

"Secondly. No Jew may have, read, or hear read, the book entituled MAR MAR JESU (because it is full of blasphemies against our Redeemer Jesus Christ)' nor any other book or writing which is injurious to Christians, or contradicts any of their doctrines, or any of the rites of the Church, in what language soever it be written: every person who violates this decree is to be punished as a blasphemer.

"Thirdly. No Jew may, under any pretence whatever, restore, mend, or even have in his house, crosses, chalices or sacred vessels, or bind books for Christians, in which the names of Jesus Christ or the Most Holy Virgin appear: and every Christian, whatever be his motive, that shall put any of these things into the hands of Jews, is to be excommunicated.

"Fourthly. No Jew can be allowed to hold the office of a judge, even in lawsuits that may occur among Jews themselves.

"Fifthly. All synagogues built or repaired in modern times are to be shut up, except in places where there is but one, which may in such cases remain open, provided such building be not excessively costly; and where there are two or more of them, the smallest only may continue open: but should it be proved that any one of the said synagogues was formerly a church, it must be closed immediately.

"Sixthly. No Jew may be a physician, surgeon,

shopkeeper, druggist, purveyor, marriage-maker (*casamentero*), or hold any public employment which shall make him acquainted with the affairs of Christians: nor may Jewesses be midwives or have Christian wet-nurses: nor may Jews employ Christians, or sell to them or buy of them meats for daily consumption, or be present with them at any banquet, or bathe in the same bath with them, or be stewards or agents in business for them, or learn any science, craft, or trade in the Christian schools.

"Seventhly. In every city, town, or village where there are Jews, separate quarters must be appointed for them to dwell in, apart from the Christians.

"Eighthly. All Jews and Jewesses must wear on their dress a certain device in red and yellow, of the size and form specified in the bull: the men must wear it on their outer garment on the breast, the women in front.[63]

"Ninthly. In order to guard against the tricks which the Jews are in the habit of playing, and the usurious interest they are accustomed to exact, no Jew may have dealings, or make any contract, with Christians.

---

[63] In the *Epítome de la Crónica de Don Juan II.*, by José Martinez de la Puente (Madrid, 1678), we find these words: "By the advice of San Vicente Ferrer, it was ordained that, in these kingdoms, the Jews should wear *tabards* (a kind of ancient Castilian cloaks) with a vermilion badge, and that the Moors should wear green capuces with a bright moon." [These *capuces* were old-fashioned cloaks, used as a holiday dress. See the dictionary of the Royal Academy,—*Translator.*]

"Tenthly. All Jews and Jewesses converted to the faith, and all Christians related to unconverted Jews, may be heirs to the latter, even though excluded from inheriting their property by testaments, codicils, last wills, or donations to people still living.

"Lastly. In all cities, towns, or villages, in which there is, in the judgment of the diocesan, a sufficient number of Jews, three sermons are to be preached annually, on three several days: one on the second Sunday in Advent; another on Easter-day; the third, on the day in which that portion of the Gospel *Cum appropinquasset Jesus Jerosolymam, videns civitatem, flevit super eam* is chanted. All Jews more than twelve years old must be present at the preaching of these three sermons, of which the following are to be the subjects: in the first of them, the Messiah's advent is to be demonstrated from those passages of the Scriptures and the Talmud which have been controverted in the assembly at Tortosa; in the second, the Jews are to have the errors and absurdities contained in the Talmud pointed out to them; and in the third, the destruction of the city and temple of Jerusalem, and the perpetuity of their captivity, according to the words of Jesus Christ and the holy prophets, are to be explained to them. At the conclusion of each sermon, this bull is to be read, in order that offenders against it may not plead ignorance."

After the famous dispute between Jerónimo de Santa Fé and the learned Rabbis of the Spanish Aljamas, many Jews were converted to the Christian faith: at

Zaragoza, Calatayud, and Alcañiz, the number of converts was more than two hundred: at Daroca, Fraga, and Barbastro, about a hundred and twenty families: at Caspe and Maella, five hundred persons: besides all the natives of the towns of Tamarit and Alcolea.[64]

Rabí Selomoh Halevi, who lived in Spain, was converted in the year 1390: he was a Jew, born in the city of Burgos, where he was baptized by the name of Pablo de Santa María. He afterwards went to the University of Paris to study divinity, and there he took his Doctor's degree, and, owing to his universal reputation for learning and virtue, he obtained the dignities of Archdeacon of Treviño, Bishop of Cartagena, and afterwards of Burgos, and, in addition to this, became high-chancellor in the kingdoms of Leon and Castile. He wrote several works for the conversion of the Jews and Moors to the Christian faith, among which is one entituled *Scrutinium Sacrarum Scripturarum*.[65]

Here follows Estéban de Garibay's account of the life and acts of Pablo de Santa María. "The excellent Dr. Pablo, Bishop of Cartagena, was a very notable prelate: though a Jew, not only by lineage, but by persuasion also, he received the waters of holy baptism and renounced Judaism. This notable prelate had, before his conversion, holden many discussions about

---

[64] Zurita. Anales de Aragon. [Lib. XII. cap. 45, vol. III.—*Translator.*]

[65] Printed at Burgos in 1591. [There is a copy of this work in the Cambridge University Library.—*Translator.*]

the Jewish law with several learned catholic doctors, whose arguments (owing to that obduracy which he inherited from his ancestors,) had not the immediate effect of withdrawing him from Judaism: but it chanced, one day, that a doctor who was averse from contending with him on other than scriptural grounds, gave him the learned treatise written by the glorious St. Thomas Aquinas, called *De Legibus*,......in which that holy doctor argues so admirably against the law of the Jews. Don Pablo read this treatise with much care and attention, and finding in it many secrets appertaining to Judaism, with which he (though the most learned Rabbi in these kingdoms) was unacquainted, he was enlightened by the Holy Spirit, and said in his heart that the law of the Christians was, undoubtedly, the law of salvation to the world. He, afterwards, went to the Roman Pontiff, and at his persuasion, publicly declared and confessed that since this holy doctor[66] (though better acquainted than himself with the secrets of the Jewish law,) professed the Evangelical law of Christ, the Christian was the true law and the way of salvation: and so he received holy baptism, and of his own accord ceased to continue in his former obduracy. Thus did Don Pablo become a Christian by means of St. Thomas's teaching.

"This eminent man was, in course of time, and very deservedly, appointed to the see of Cartagena, and thence translated to Burgos, his native city. He was an excellent prelate, a great philosopher and divine,

[66] Viz. Thomas Aquinas.—*Translator.*

a fine preacher, and at the same time a wonderfully reserved and prudent man. He wrote many works, particularly the book entituled *Scrutinium Sacrarum Scripturarum*, which is of large size, the additions to Nicolao de Lyra's Postil on the Bible, a treatise on the Lord's Supper, and other works. He was not only a learned clerk himself, but, having married before his conversion to Christianity, he had three sons, learned clerks also: the most distinguished of these was Alfonso de Cartagena, dean of Segovia, immediate successor to his father in the see of Burgos, and author of the *Genealogia de los Reyes de Castilla y Leon*, which has been sometimes cited. The next son was Gonzalo, bishop of Palencia, a prelate of great learning. The third was Alvar García de Santa María, who is said to have written the Chronicle of King Henry,[67] which I have not seen, and part of the Chronicle of King John the Second. This notable prelate Pablo, from having been born at Burgos, is called by theologians *El Burgense:* he it was who, on his conversion, advised King Henry (for good reasons, no doubt) not to admit any Jew or Jewish convert into the service of his royal household, to his counsels, or any other of the royal or public offices in his kingdoms, nor suffer him to administer the royal patrimony. It is a remarkable thing that, though he himself was one of them, this clever prelate should have entertained such an opinion of his countrymen."[68]

[67] Henry the Third.—*Translator*.
[68] Compendio Historial, 2nd vol. pp. 400 and 401 in the Barcelona edition of 1628.—*Translator*.

Such is Estéban de Garibay's account. But, notwithstanding that the number of Jews converted to the faith was considerable, the majority of them still adhered to their former erroneous opinions. The townspeople, on their part, whether ruled in their actions by a feeling of devotion both barbarous and cruel, or by the desire of taking from the Jews, contrary to all reason, law, and right, the estates which the latter had inherited from their ancestors, and afterwards considerably improved and augmented by their own labour, ceased not to molest them. In the year 1473 they again disturbed the kingdom with tumults, when the Jews, who had turned Christians, became the objects of their attacks; they masked their design of ill-treating and plundering them, under the plea that they were Judaizers. Miguel Lucas, constable of Castile, defended the unfortunate Hebrews of Jaen with all his might and dispersed the rebellious crowds, just as the sun bursts through and dispels the clouds which prevent him from darting his rays upon the earth. While the minds of the populace were exasperated at their ill-success and filled with resentment and hatred[69] against Miguel Lucas, they determined on putting him to death without mercy, out of revenge for his having prevented the destruction of the Jews dwelling in that city, who wore sheep's clothing and the cloak of Christians: accordingly, on the 21st of March in the year aforesaid, while the constable was hearing mass at the principal church of Jaen, a body of peasants, regardless

[69] Literally, *were full of gall and poison.—Translator.*

alike of the sanctity of the place and the dignity of his person, ran him through the breast with numerous stabs. No sooner did he drop down dead than the people fell upon the Jews, and commenced burning and pillaging some of the houses in which the persons of most consideration and in highest repute for wealth among the natives of that kingdom[70] dwelt. The mischievous example thus set was soon followed by a portion of the rabble in several cities of Andalusia, as for instance Andújar, Córdova, and other places also, where the Jews, after being severely wounded and after suffering other insults in their own persons and in the persons of their wives, did not obtain the slightest redress of their grievances; for justice became deaf to their complaints, and, rather than punish the guilty, chose to let the wound remain open, and thus, by allowing so pernicious an example as this to go unpunished, caused the authors of the above crimes to become more inflated with pride and more covetous of fresh riches, after having once tasted the sweets of plunder. It is certain, too, that in the calamitous times of Henry the Fourth's reign there was a want of concert in every thing; for the king had not sufficient power or vigour to keep in order the towns and people [nominally] subject to his obedience.[71]

Although a Jew could not legally hold the office of

[70] In the time of the Arab dominion in Spain, the province of Andalusia contained four kingdoms: these were Jaen, Granada, Seville, and Córdova, and even in these days we often hear them thus spoken of.—*Translator.*

[71] See Garibay's Compendio Historial, vol. II. p. 572.—*Translator.*

judge,[72] still, notwithstanding the prohibition, in Henry the Fourth's reign this dignity was filled by several of the most considerable persons, who (in spite of the many persecutions and popular tumults raised against them and their property) observed the Mosaic ritual. In 1474 was made the assessment of the amount which each of the aljamas in the kingdom was to pay annually for *service* and *half service* to the crown of Castile. The assessor was a Jew, named Jacob Aben Nuñez, Henry the Fourth's physician and chief judge: the assessment made upon each aljama is given below:

The Aljamas in the diocese of	mrs.
Burgos	30.800
Calahorra	31.100
Palencia	54.500
Osma	19.500
Sigüenza	15.600
Segovia	19.500
Avila	39.590
Salamanca and Ciudad Rodrigo	12.700
Zamora	9.600
Leon and Astorga	31.700
Archbishopric of Toledo	64.400
Diocese of Plasencia	56.900
Andalusia	59.800
* *Item or items omitted by the author*[73]	5.310
Total	451.000[74]

[72] Ordenanzas Reales, lib. VIII., tit. III., leyes 4 and 14.—*Translator*.

[73] The sum of the items given by the author is 445.690, and not 451.000, as he makes it to be: and as the next paragraph shows that there is no misprint in the figures of the latter number, I have taken the liberty to supply in the text the sum wanting to make up the deficiency.—*Translator*.

[74] " King Henry, it seems, increased the silver mark of 1250 mara-

The assessor, Jacob Aben Nuñez, had a thousand of these maravedis for his fees, and the four hundred and fifty thousand that remained passed into the treasury of the crown, which was much exhausted by continual wars and popular outbreaks. Spain was then in a very weak state: after her commerce was destroyed, the cultivation of the soil was sufficiently attended to, but from the general poverty that existed, this yielded to the farmer rather a paltry pittance than a good income. It is melancholy to see so powerful a kingdom afflicted with the greatest poverty in the times of that unhappy monarch Henry the Third,[75] and reduced to such extremities that men were obliged to part with their goods at scarcely remunerating prices.

vedis, and ordered it to be raised to 2250; hence every real contains 34 maravedis, and the said silver mark is now 66 reals and 6 maravedis: a maravedi was then worth a trifle more than it is at present." Sebastian Gonzalez de Castro, *Declaracion del valor de la plata ley y peso de las monedas antiguas de plata ligada de Castilla y Aragon.* Madrid, 1658.

[75] In 1406 this king issued a decree that provisions should be assessed, because they were becoming scarcer and scarcer every day. This strange document commences thus: " Forasmuch as we are bound to govern for the weal and benefit of our subjects and for the safety and preservation of our kingdoms and seigniories, we ordain and command that the price of wheat be fifteen maravedis a faneague throughout the realm in general, and eighteen at the court; barley, ten; rye, twelve old maravedis; oats, six: a pound of mutton, two maravedis; a pound of beef, one; a pound of butter, four; a pound of hog's lard, three old maravedis: hucksters must sell a partridge for five maravedis; a hare for three; a rabbit for two; a fowl for four; a pullet for two; a fat goose for six; a sucking-pig for eight; a pigeon for two old maravedis: an ox, Guadiana-bred and born, may be sold for two hundred maravedis; an ordinary ox for a hundred and eighty. [*Demostracion Histórica del verdadero valor de todas las monedas que corrian en Castilla durante el reinado del Señor Don Enrique III.*, nota vig^a cuarta.—*Translator.*]

Meanwhile, the Jews, from fear of the lower orders, concealed their riches, the most powerful declaring themselves to be only tolerably well off, while the middle classes said that they were in very reduced circumstances: they, therefore, looked upon commercial transactions with supreme contempt, and only trafficked in things of little value, whence scarcely any profit could be realized. All this arose from the well-founded suspicion that their reputation for wealth was calculated to bring upon them new persecutions and to excite that barbarous and covetous set of men to fresh disturbances. To such a pitch of misery were these kingdoms reduced by the alarm of the Jews and the care taken by them to bury their treasures in the bowels of the earth, that the circulation of gold and silver became very limited. The coin was all secreted in the coffers of the Hebrews, and what passed from hand to hand was bought at the houses of dealers, exchangers, or bankers: these persons were either converted Jews or Christians who traded with the money which the unconverted Jews had supplied them for the occasion, with the view of dividing the profits with them.[76] The stoppage of the traffic of the

[76] Bachelor Juan de Valverde Arrieta, in his work entituled *Despertador que trata*, &c., (Madrid, 1581), says, "Three hundred years before we had money from the Indies, the want of provisions and other things began to be felt; money lost its value, and tariffs were fixed, and this occurred more than once . . . . ; and before money came from the Indies for the prosecution of wars in Italy, Africa, and Granada, which was conquered by the Catholic king . . . . . ., there were ducats, half ducats, pieces of two, four, ten, and a hundred, doblas zahenas, Castilian florins and half florins, in such quantities,

Jews caused the ruin of all the commerce that formerly existed in the realms of Castile. All kinds of merchandise were reduced to the lowest figure. A yard of Chillon cloth was worth seventy maravedis, a yard of Lombai and Brussels fifty old maravedis, a yard of Ghent scarlet sixty, a yard of Ypres scarlet a hundred and ten, the cloths of Montpelier, London, and Valencia sold at sixty old maravedis per yard.

Everything else went on in the same way. The kingdom was weak: commerce was annihilated: agriculture was inefficiently carried on: the Jews were very rich, but did not circulate their money among others: the people were miserable: the crown was without resources: Spain was disturbed by insurrections against the person of king Henry: people's minds were in a state of excitement produced by their present misery, while they looked upon this monarch's downfall as the only sure way of remedying all the misfortunes which so

that the banks and exchange offices would not give reals for them except at a discount: there were many persons in Spain who made a living by exchanging, and many wholesale dealers who had in their houses silver money, besides reals, quarter reals, tarjas, and other gold coins, which they kept in bags, and doled out by weight and measure: if you don't believe it, go and ask for the tradesmen's books at Medina del Campo, Burgos, Toledo, and other places, and you will find that there were many more gold and silver coins in those days than the present." So said Valverde, just as the scarcity of Spanish money began to be felt, and the importation of foreign coins had commenced. Sarabía de la Calle, in his *Instruccion de Mercaderes* (Medina del Campo, 1544, id. 1547), writes thus: "Though the escudos del sol of France, the big ducats of Genoa, and the ducats of the Roman chamber pass in Spain, the half-pence (*parpallolas*) of France, the picholes of Genoa, and the quatrins of Rome are of no value whatever."

grievously afflicted them. These evils originated in the rash methods employed, against all reason and justice, by monarchs and people for the conversion of the numerous Jews who dwelt in these lands. They were forbidden to practise medicine and surgery, to keep their houses open for traffic with Christians, and, finally, to dispose of their goods and persons in the way that was most conducive to their own interests and to the increase of their substance. The Christians reaped the fruits of this barbarous policy during king Henry the Fourth's unhappy reign over Castile: for to this policy must be ascribed the abandonment of commerce by the Jews who were the only, or, at any rate, the principal persons engaged in it, and who kept it alive: and, as its destruction arose from the cause I have mentioned, the ruin of agriculture followed in its rear, and the kingdom, being destitute of the two principal nerves which keep the body of a state together, was ultimately reduced to the greatest weakness and distress.

SUMMARY OF BOOK THE THIRD.

COMMENCEMENT of the reign of the Catholic Sovereigns.—Character of Ferdinand the Fifth.—Eulogium on Queen Isabella.—First Inquisitors appointed for the punishment of converted Jews that Judaized.—Conspiracy of these persons at Seville.—Punishment inflicted upon many of them.—Pedro Fernandez de Alcaudete, treasurer of the cathedral of Córdova, burnt to death.—Establishment of the Inquisition.—Great assistance rendered by the Jews to the Catholic Sovereigns in their enterprise against Granada.—Decree for the expulsion of the unconverted Jews.—Presents offered by them to King Ferdinand for permission to remain in Spain.—The king, influenced by these, is anxious to revoke the decree.—Is prevented from doing so by the boldness of Torquemada.—The Jews quit Spain, and go to foreign kingdoms.—Some notices of their chequered fortunes in them.—Inquiry into the calamities which the Catholic Sovereigns brought upon Spain by expelling the Jews and persecuting the converts.—Bad policy of these monarchs censured.

BOOK THE THIRD.

AFTER the death of Henry the Fourth, who left the kingdoms of Castile and Leon in so prostrate a condition and reduced to such extreme distress, his sister Isabella maintained her seat on the throne, in spite of the pretensions of Juana la Beltraneja,[1] who was, or,

---

[1] Though acknowledged as his daughter by King Henry, she was supposed to be the child of Beltran de la Cueva, whence the name Beltraneja.— *Translator.*

at least, was said to be, the daughter of the deceased monarch, and who was married to the king of Portugal, who, by means of a powerful army, endeavoured to support in the field his claim to the sovereignty of these lands. Isabella, wife of prince Ferdinand of Aragon (the monarch in whose person the crowns of this latter realm and Castile were first united), was in a great measure enabled to overcome the king of Portugal's opposition to her consort's claims, and, accordingly, continued, with greater security than before, to sway the sceptre of the vast monarchy.[2]

King Ferdinand was, in the opinion of Antonio de Herrera,[3] *a man of excellent wisdom, and had he fulfilled his promises, there would have been nothing reprehensible in his conduct.* Others accuse him of being unfaithful in every transaction of life to the pledge he had given to his partisans, except when it suited his own convenience to keep it. They likewise charge him with insatiable ambition and unbounded avarice, and of allowing those vices to get the entire dominion over him.[4] Fray Prudencio de Sandoval, bishop of Pamplona, asserts that this king *had long since thrown his confessor overboard, as a troublesome merchant, telling the latter that he was more influenced in coming by*

[2] See Zurita's account of the war between Ferdinand the Fifth and Alonso king of Portugal. Anales de Aragon, latter half of book xix. and first half of book xx.—*Translator.*

[3] Comentarios de los hechos de los Españoles, Franceses, y Venecianos y otros capitanes famosos en Italia, Madrid, 1624.

[4] Anales de Aragon por Bartolomé Leonardo de Argensola, Zaragoza, 1630.

motives of personal interest than regard for his (the king's) *conscience.*[5] Finally, that well-known politician Niccoló Machiavelli, citizen and secretary of Florence, said, " That Ferdinand the Fifth might be looked upon as a new prince, inasmuch as he, from having been the mere king of a petty state, had, owing to his great reputation and glory, become the king of Christendom. No sooner did he ascend the throne than he turned his arms against the kingdom of Granada—an enterprise which was the foundation of his greatness; for the minds of the Castilian grandees, diverted by constant warfare from attending to political changes, did not observe that the king was daily increasing his authority at their expense, and supporting, with the fortunes of the people and the Church, those armies which were extending his power. Afterwards, with the view of attempting still greater undertakings, he artfully concealed his design under the mask of religion, and, by means of a cruel piety, drove the Moors out of his dominions, a stroke of policy truly deplorable and unexampled."[6] All the translators of Machiavelli's

[5] Historia del Emperador Cárlos V., primera parte, Valladolid, 1604. [Lib. i. cap. 50.—*Translator.*]

[6] Il Principe di Niccoló Machiavelli cittadino e secretario Fiorentino, Capítolo xxi. "Noi abbiamo nei nostri tempi Ferrando d'Aragona, presenti re di Spagna. Costui si può chiamare quasi principe nuovo, perchè d' un re debole è diventato per fama e per gloria il primo Rei dei Christiani: e si considerete le azioni sue, le troverete tutte grandissime e qualcuna straordinaria: Egli nel principio del suo regno assaltò la Granata, e quella impresa fu il fondamento dello stato suo. In prima ei la fece ozioso e senza sospetto di essere impedito; tenne occupati in quella gli animi de ' Baroni di

works are agreed that this famous politician alluded to Ferdinand the Fifth, when he said, " There now reigns a prince, whose name it is not expedient that I should declare, from whose mouth one hears nothing else but praises of peace and good faith, but had his actions corresponded to his words, he would, more than once ere this, have lost either his reputation or his dominions."[7]

If we adopt the opinion formed of Ferdinand the Fifth by his contemporary, who, next to Cornelius Tacitus, was the first of master politicians in the art of government; if we take into consideration the unworthy acts perpetrated by this king to the prejudice of the people of Spain, among which we must class the marriage which (after the death of his wife Isabella) he solemnized with Queen Germaine, in hopes of leaving a succession by her, now that the crowns of Castile and Arragon were united, we shall perceive that this monarch was not so great a personage as some individuals have asserted (in opposition to all reason and justice),

Castiglia,' i quali pensando a quella guerra, non pensavano ad innovare; e lui acquistava in questo mezzo riputazioni, ed imperio sopra di loro, che non se ne accorgevanno. Potè nutrire con danari della Chiesa e de popoli gli esserciti e fare un fondamento con quella guerra lunga alla milizia sua: la quale lo ha dipoi onorato. Oltre di questo per potere intrapendere maggiori imprese, servendosi sempre della religione, se volse a una pietosa crudeltà, cacciando e spogliando il suo regno de ' Marrani,' ne puo essere questo esempio più mirabile ne più raro."

[7] Capítolo xviii., "Alcuno principe dei presenti tempi, quale non è bene nominare, non predica mai altro che pace e fede, e dell' una e dell' altra è inimicissimo, e l' una e l' altra quando è l' avesse osservata, gli arebbe più volte tolto o la riputazioni o lo stato."

relying on the accounts of writers influenced by fear and the desire of flattering him.

It cannot, however, be doubted that many events of importance to the prosperity of Spain occurred in his reign; and yet the glory of them belongs not to him, but to the wisdom and virtues of his first wife, Queen Isabella; she was an illustrious matron, worthy to have lived in an age in which barbarous fanaticism—that secret foe to God, to the cultivation of the intellects, and to the happiness of mankind, did not influence the greater part of the human race.

Queen Isabella went down to Andalusia in July 1477, with Pedro Gonzalez de Mendoza, Grand Cardinal of Spain and Archbishop of Seville, while Ferdinand was using the greatest expedition in fortifying the castles and towns situated on the borders of Portugal. To this he was compelled by the continuance of the war with king Alonso, pretender to the crown of Castile, in right of his wife La Beltraneja.[8]

In the mean time, Isabella was busily engaged in establishing the order of the holy brotherhood, which was founded with the sole object of extirpating malefactors out of the uncultivated lands which harboured them.[9] Fray Alonso de Ojeda, prior of the convent of

[8] Zúñiga, *Anales de Sevilla*, p. 380, 381, see also note (²) p. 116.—*Translator*.

[9] Anales de Aragon, por Zurita, lib. xx. cap. 21, vol. iv. fol. 294. "Ferd. and Isab. organized the *Hermandad* ostensibly, as a mounted brotherhood, or *gendarmerie*, to protect the roads, but, in reality, as the germ of a standing army to be employed in beating down their too independent aristocracy." Ford's Handbook of Spain, vol. i. p. 313, Murray, 1845.—*Translator*.

dominican friars at Seville, observing the zeal of the Queen for the public good, represented to her the injury done to the Christian religion by the wicked lives of the Jewish converts;[10] and, accordingly, to remedy this evil, he urgently entreated her, in eloquent and forcible language, to grant the friars of his order permission to inquire into the crime of heresy—a privilege enjoyed by the friars of the same order in the kingdom of Aragon, of whom certain persons were nominated to the like commission, sometimes immediately by the pope, and sometimes by his vicegerents or provincials. Fray Alonso de Ojeda's importunities were backed by those of many persons of great virtue and in exalted situations; and Isabella was compelled to dictate a measure strong enough to weaken, if not destroy, the obstacles to the increase of the faith caused by Jews not really converted; she was, however, a woman of too generous a mind to be capable of deciding at once to give her consent to so flagrant an oppression of her subjects.[11] And, therefore, they were unable to extort more from her by their solicitations (although supported by the above arguments) than a recommendation to the priests, and particularly to the dominican friars, to show themselves energetic and faithful preachers, and to bring over [if possible] to the Christian religion those who, to their own misfortune, were wandering astray and living far from the light of truth which was necessary to the

[10] Llorente, *Historia Crítica de la Inquisicion*, cap. v. art. ii. sect. 3. —*Translator*.

[11] Llorente, cap. v. art. ii. sects. 3, 5, 6, 7, 8, 11, 18.—*Translator*.

salvation of their souls. Cardinal Pedro Gomez de Mendoza prepared a catechism for their instruction, and likewise framed some laws for the correction of all who refused conformity with the teaching of the gospel.[12]

But as it was afterwards discovered in the following year, 1478, that sundry Jews had met together on Holy Thursday night to Judaize, and that, after they had blasphemed Jesus Christ and His religion, and been apprehended for so doing, they had, on exhibiting proofs of repentance, been reconciled; new and urgent solicitations were made to the catholic king to establish in these realms the tribunal of the inquisition after the model of that established in Sicily.[13] This arose not so much from devotion as from the covetous desire of getting into his hands the great wealth,[14] of which the principal Jewish converts were then possessed; for, according to the ordinances of the tribunal founded in Sicily, one-third of the estates of heretics, on which an embargo had been laid prior to their confiscation, went into the pockets of the inquisitors.

By this means robberies were perpetrated with impunity; for as it was the interest of the judges that the

[12] Zúñiga, p. 386, column 1; Llorente, cap. v. art. II. sects. 14, 15, 17.—*Translator*.

[13] See Zúñiga, p. 386, col. 2; Llorente, cap. v. art. II. sec. 12.— *Translator*.

[14] That impudent fellow Zurita says that the funds raised by the confiscations, which went into the Royal treasury, were (after defraying the salaries of the inquisitors and ministers of the holy office, and providing food for poor criminals) *exclusively applied to religious purposes!* Anales de Aragon, lib. xx. cap. 49,vol. iv. fol. 324.—*Translator*.

accused should appear, in the eyes of the world, guilty of all heresies that ever existed, in order that they might make a prize of one-third of his estate, what rich man could expect mercy at the hands of those who looked upon his death or dishonour as the means of obtaining so pretty a picking, without incurring the slightest hazard in getting it?

King Ferdinand had, by his frequent military expeditions, exhausted his treasury and burdened his subjects with taxes, and, after selling a considerable portion of the church plate, called upon the regular clergy to pay him contributions to which they had not been accustomed, and which were, on that account, borne with greater reluctance; he also wearied the secular clergy with loans that he could never expect to repay out of his royal treasury, on which there were so many claims as yet unpaid; and as he now lost all hopes of replenishing it, and became perplexed at his inability to extricate himself from present troubles and to avoid future difficulties, while engaged in carrying on such long wars against the enemies to his crown, he looked to the Inquisition as the sole means of augmenting the royal revenue. This was the true reason why Ferdinand consented to what the dominican friars had, under the influence of their cupidity, so repeatedly and so urgently implored him to grant. He was one of the greatest politicians of his age, and one who travelled to his end without regarding the means employed in its attainment.

In the same year, 1478, while the Catholic Sovereigns

were at Seville, they received intelligence that the pope had issued his Bull and given his consent to the foundation of the so-much-desired tribunal of the Inquisition. But the Queen, who in all matters of business acted on the advice of the learned cardinal Mendoza,[15] opposed her husband's wishes,[16] rightly judging that if evils arose from the converts being allowed to live in the enjoyment of their liberty, and from their being exempted from molestation by persons who, under colour of inquiring into their morals, words, and even thoughts, might persecute them, far greater disasters must and would arise from the cupidity of judges desirous of finding them guilty, for the sake of enriching themselves with the estates of such as should have the dreadful misfortune to fall into their hands. And so, to pacify as well those who were exasperated at the excess of liberty allowed to the Jews, as the new Christians and those who contumaciously adhered to the Jewish law, she decreed, in the Cortes assembled at Toledo in 1480, that all observers of the Mosaic law should live apart from Christians, and wear the badges

[15] Like all other women, Queen Isabella had a will of her own. When cardinal Mendoza was on his death-bed, she and her husband went to visit and console him. Mendoza, however, availing himself of an occasion when Ferdinand had gone out of the room, charged Isabella in the most solemn manner, to cultivate a good understanding with the house of France, and also to marry her son John to Juana la Beltraneja; both of which proposals were anything but acceptable to her: and she, declaring that the cardinal had taken leave of his senses, abruptly rose up and took her departure. Zurita, *Historia del Rey Don Hernando,* lib. ii. cap. 4.—*Translator.*

[16] Llorente, cap. v. art. i. sect. 14; art. ii. sects. 7, 8, 9.—*Translator.*

appointed by the ancient laws and ordinances. This shows that the mandates of former sovereigns had become a dead letter. It was likewise enacted that the unbaptized Jews should retire to their quarters at nightfall, and suspend their commercial dealings till daylight. This is a clear proof that, in those times, the law which prohibited the Jews from making acquisitions, gains, bargains, and contracts with Christians, had fallen into abeyance. At last Queen Isabella, whose compassionate and benevolent heart had prevented her from consenting to the erection of the barbarous tribunal, was overcome by the solicitations of her avaricious husband and the dominican fraternity, who swallowed the bait of interest and scented the blood of those Jewish converts who had the greatest reputation for wealth, before they saw the hour approach in which, invested with the king's authority, they were to make prizes of the possessions belonging to so many unhappy beings, whose misfortune it was to be born in that calamitous age.[17]

In the year 1480, the Monarchs Ferdinand and Isabella appointed as Inquisitors Fray Miguel de Morillo and the presentee [18] Fray San Martin, and as Assessor priest Juan Ruiz de Medina, Doctor in Canon law.

[17] Llorente, cap. v. art. ii. sects. 17, 18, 19. It will be worth the reader's while, I think, to peruse the whole of the fifth chapter.— *Translator.*

[18] In the original, *presentado*, which Seoane defines thus, "a teacher of divinity who expects soon to be ranked as a master." See his dictionary. Perhaps, the expression answers to what, in Cambridge, we should call *an inceptor.*— *Translator.*

The persons elected were ordered to commence the exercise of their functions in the arch-diocese of Seville and in the diocese of Cadiz, where their zeal was required to bring those Jews back to the Christian faith, who were formerly converted and had now gone astray from the path of truth. These judges received letters from the Catholic Sovereigns which were to serve as their credentials to the civil authorities of the towns and cities, who were to provide them with lodgings. The letter addressed to the Council of Seville commenced thus :—

" Be it known unto you that We, observing that in our realms and seigniories there have been and still are some wicked Christians, apostates, heretics, and converts, who, after having received baptism and borne the name of Christians, have turned and do now turn back to the sect and superstition and perfidy of the Jews, &c. Willing and desiring to provide against this, and to check the evil and mischief from spreading farther, in case the aforesaid offences be not punished, &c., we have entreated our Right Reverend Father to provide a wholesome remedy for these things, and His Holiness hath consented to the prayer of our petition, and granted us a faculty which authorizes us to elect, and we have elected, two or three persons with defined powers, to act as Inquisitors, and to proceed, according to this apostolical authority, against the said infidels and wicked Christians, and all who countenance and receive them, and to prosecute and punish them as far as they are, by right of custom, entitled to prosecute and punish them. By virtue of the said faculty conceded to and accepted by us, and in the exercise of the same, we elect, nominate, and depute, as inquisitors into the said infidelity, apostacy, and heresy, the venerable and devout fathers, Fray Miguel de Morillo, Doctor of Divinity, and Fray Juan de San Martin, presented [19] Bachelor of Divinity, and Prior of the Monastery of St. Paul, of the preaching order, in the city of Seville.[20]

The Inquisitors did not go down to Seville to carry out these instructions till the year 1481,[21] owing to the various difficulties which they had to overcome: these were, in all probability, such as men usually experience, when any change is about to be introduced. An account of the entry of these judges into Seville, and of the plot devised by the Jews for the destruction of the former, is given in a manuscript of the day, written by an unknown author. As the notices contained in it are very curious, it will not be out of the way to copy some passages from it, which will stamp additional authority upon my history. "As soon as the Inquisitors and ministers of the holy Office entered Seville, the city was divided into factions which took different views of the case, some sided with the Inquisitors, some against them. *That which caused the greatest scandal and astonishment was the fact that this opinion affected*

---

[19] See note ([18]) page 124.—*Translator*.
[20] Zúñiga, pp. 388, and 389.—*Translator*.
[21] Zúñiga, p. 389.—*Translator*.

many men in power, and persons holding offices and dignities, inasmuch as they favoured its most obnoxious maintainers.

"The nobility and prebendaries declared in favour of the holy faith of Jesus Christ and His ministers: some persons went a league's distance out of the city to receive them, others proceeded as far as Carmona,[22] refreshed, entertained them, and paid them frequent visits.

"The Inquisitors proceeded to the Chapter-House of the Holy Church, where they presented and exhibited the Bulls and royal warrants, and then went out to the door of the Chapter-House, where they found the municipal body ready to receive them, and were conducted by them from the steps," [outside of the Cathedral],[23] "to the Guildhall, and were put into seats at the Guildhall and entertained by the Corporation. Then the prebendaries and aldermen (regidores) of the respective corporate bodies met together, and decreed that there should be a procession of the clergy and people on the following Sunday: and the procession took place with much solemnity, and the Inquisition was accepted by the people.

"Meanwhile a meeting took place between the following persons, viz. Suson, father of Susana, known by the name of the beautiful female; Benadeva, father of

[22] Carmona is six leagues from Seville.—*Translator.*
[23] There are flights of steps on three sides of this Cathedral, with a terrace of considerable width at the top of them. I think the ancient Chapter-house stood on this terrace.—*Translator.*

the Canon; Abalofia the odoriferous, who held the customs of the king and queen in pawn; Aleman, a person of low birth, and one of the numerous cadets of the same name ......, the Adalfes of Triana,[24] who still lived in the castle ......, Cristóbal Lopez Mondadura of San Salvador, and many other rich and influential persons, who attended the meeting, and lived in the towns of Utrera[25] and Carmona.

"What think ye, said these men, of those fellows who are coming against us? Are not we the persons of most consideration for our wealth in this city? Let us have a rising. You man here, bring so many of your men, and you man yonder, bring together as many as you can; and then they began to distribute among the ringleaders, arms, men, money, and whatever else appeared necessary. And if, said they, they come to arrest us, we will gain the people over to our side, and raise a tumult, and, by this means, put our aggressors to death and take vengeance upon our enemies. Then said a venerable old Jew, who was present, '*My sons, I think the people are ready, so be my life, but what! where are the hearts? Give me hearts.*'"

This conspiracy came to the knowledge of the Inquisitors, who immediately began to imprison all who were concerned in it, and even many who had nothing whatever to do with it. While they were getting up their cases, all nature seemed to shudder at the contemplation

[24] Triana is a suburb of Seville, on the opposite bank of the Guadalquivir.—*Translator.*

[25] Utrera lies between Seville and Jerez; it is four leagues distant from the former city.—*Translator.*

of the erection of a tribunal, so barbarous and so inimical to the human race. Andrés Bernaldez or Bernal, a writer of the day, and chaplain to one of the Inquisitors, speaks of the dreadful tempest which burst upon all the cities of Andalusia. " This fourteen hundred and eighty-first year, at the commencement of Christmas and afterwards, there fell so much rain and there rose such high floods that the Guadalquivir carried away and destroyed a part of *El Copero*, which contained eighty dwellings, and many other places on the bank, and the swollen waters rose near the rampart turret of Seville, by the ravine of Coria, to a greater height than they had ever been known to rise, and did not subside for three days, and it was feared that the city would be destroyed by the waters. At this time also a dreadful plague broke out, which ravaged these lands till the year 1488, with great obstinacy and severity: more than fifteen thousand persons died at Seville, and as many at Córdova; and at Jerez and Écija upwards of eight or nine thousand persons, and this was the case in all the other towns and villages."[21]

With such a festive entertainment did nature hail the institution of the Holy Office! On the one hand the Guadalquivir overflowed its banks, carrying in its course houses, trees, human beings, and cattle, while on the other, the plague spread desolation in the cities,

[26] History of the Catholic Sovereigns, Ferdinand and Isabella, M.S. cap. XLIV. [A considerable part of El Copero which had escaped destruction in the year 1481, was (according to the same writer, quoted by Zúñiga in his Anales de Sevilla,) swept away by the swollen waters of the Guadalquivir in 1485.—*Translator.*]

cutting the thread of many lives with the greatest rapidity. With these dreadful calamities before their eyes, these more than brutal judges of the Inquisition began to imprison and devise punishments for those who (having been baptized to save their lives and fortunes from the cupidity and hatred of the rabble, who had been instigated by certain wicked ecclesiastics or avaricious friars to destroy the Jews,) still observed the Mosaic law, though they did so with the greatest secrecy. "Those first Inquisitors," says Bernaldez, "had the burning-place [27] at Tablada prepared, together with those plaister figures of the four prophets, and in a very few days they found many ways of discovering those who were guilty of heresy, and commenced laying hands on the most culpable of both sexes, of whom several were found amongst the highest ranks, the veinticuatros,[28] the jurats, the bachelors of the universities, the lawyers, and men in greatest repute, whom they began sentencing to be burnt with fire. The first time they brought six men and women to be burnt, and saw due execution done upon them.[29] Fray

[27] "On the flat plain outside the walls" (of Seville), "called *El Prado de San Sebastian*, was the Quemadero or burning place of the Inquisition: here the last act of the tragedy of the *auto de fé* was performed by the civil power, on whom the odium was cast, while the populace, in the words of Cæsar, 'sceleris obliti de pænâ disserebant.' The spot of fire is marked by the foundations of a square platform on which the faggots were piled." Ford's Hand-book of Spain, vol. i. page 278. Murray, 1845.—*Translator.*

[28] *Veinticuatros* were certain magistrates of towns in Andalusia, so called because their number consisted of *twenty-four.*—*Translator.*

[29] In this very brasier of Seville, which, according to Bernaldez,

Alsonso Hojeda de San Pablo, a zealot for the faith in Jesus Christ, the most active person in Seville in bringing about this Inquisition, preached the sermon. A few days after this they burnt three of the principal and richest persons in the city: these were Diego de Suson who was reported to be worth ten millions: he was a great Rabbi, and appears to have died a Christian,[30] the second was Manuel Saulí, and the other Bartolomé Torralba. They also took Pedro Fernandez Benedeba, steward of the church for the dean and chapter (one of the most considerable of that body, who had arms in his house sufficient to arm a hundred men,) and Juan Fernandez Abalasia, who had been a magistrate for some time, and was a great lawyer, and many other persons of great wealth and consider-

was first employed in the year 1481 in the execution of six men and women for the crime of Judaizing, the Inquisition burnt its last victim, a woman condemned for Molinism, in 1782. *La Inquisicion sin máscara* by Natanael Jomtob (Don Antonio Puigblanch), Cadiz, 1811. Alonso de Fuentes in his *Cuarenta cantos de diversas y peregrinas historias* (Seville, 1545), says that the person who built the burning-place was himself the first to make trial of it and suffered the torture of its flames for Judaizing. This dreadful witness of human ferocity was destroyed in the year 1809, when Bonaparte's troops went down to Andalusia and its materials were employed in the erection of various fortifications at the gates of Seville. [The author has taken a few other passages from Puigblanch, whose work has been translated by Walton, portions of whose version I have not hesitated to adopt where I preferred it to my own.—*Translator.*]

[30] It is not true that Suson or Susan was converted to the faith at the last hour of his life. The anonymous writer of Seville, whose manuscript I have cited, says, that when the people were leading Suson to the flames, the rope was drawn too tight, and as he set up for a wit, he said to a bystander, "Lift up this Tunisian hood for me."

ation, whom they likewise burnt, and whose wealth could not shield them. On this all the converts took alarm, and fled in great terror from the city and archdiocese. And they placed them in Seville, and forbad them to depart from it on pain of death. And they set guards at the gates of the city, [and apprehended so many that they were at a loss where to put them].[31] Still many of them contrived to flee to the lands of their masters, and into Portugal and into the territory of the Moors........I have no desire, at present, to write any thing more about the mischief caused by this wicked heresy, and shall content myself with saying that as this fire is now kindled, so shall it continue to burn until it reach the end of the dry wood, which must blaze until the Judaizers be consumed, so that not one of them, nor even one of their children of twenty years old and upwards may remain alive, if infected with the same leprosy, even though less diseased with it than their parents." With such ardent and such brutal zeal did the clergyman Andrés Bernaldez write in praise of the Inquisition! And while the judges of this tribunal thus insolently and arrogantly strutted about Seville, the neighbouring city of Córdova had already been the scene of acts of the utmost severity.

One of the first persons reduced to ashes for the crime

---

[31] The words in brackets are not given in the author's text, but I have inserted them, as I find them in a note of his a few pages further on, and think they will make what follows clearer than it would otherwise be.—*Translator*.

of Judaizing[32] was Pedro Fernandez de Alcaudete, treasurer of that church. The discovery of his guilt is vulgarly reported to have been attended with a thousand marvellous particulars, such, for example, as the following: In the year 1483, when the procession took place on Holy Thursday,[33] at the time of placing the Most Holy[34] on the monument[35] of the Cathedral of Córdova, some persons observed that from one of the treasurer's shoes blood was issuing so profusely, that his foot was quite bathed in it. It seems that several people informed him of this strange occurrence, and that he was much troubled at the information, and, owing to the state of alarm he was in, could not utter a word. The Canons met him in the chapel of Acacio (ever since that time called the chapel *of blood*), and on pulling off his shoes, they found concealed in one of them the sacred form, which he should have consumed at the general communion, which had been that day

[32] Coleccion de los autos generales y particulares de fé celebrados por el tribunal de la ciudad de Córdoba, anotados y dados á luz por el Licenciado Gaspar Matute y Luquin (el docto filólogo Don Luis María Ramirez y las Casas-Deza) Córdoba, 1839.

[33] The festival commemorated by this name in the Spanish Church *is not Ascension day*, which *we* sometimes call *Holy Thursday*, but the Thursday in Passion week.—*Translator.*

[34] That is to say the consecrated wafer.—*Translator.*

[35] *Monuments* are wooden structures, placed in Spanish Cathedrals, on the Thursday in Passion week; that of Seville is the finest, it reaches to within a few feet of the roof, and is divided into several compartments (perhaps I might say stories), on each of which colossal figures are placed to represent scenes connected with our Saviour's Passion, &c. When lighted up at night, these monuments present a most brilliant and gorgeous appearance.—*Translator.*

administered. But this is altogether fabulous. The imprisonment of the treasurer resulted from the trial of a mistress living with him, upon whom punishment had been inflicted: on being accused of Judaizing, this woman at first denied, but afterwards acknowledged her guilt, and concluded by saying that Pedro Fernandez de Alcaudete, her paramour, in spite of his dignity of treasurer to the Cathedral, and of the Christian life he apparently led, was, like herself, an observer of the Mosaic law. When the Inquisitors went to take Alcaudete, he made an armed resistance, in which he was assisted by his servants, who killed the chief Alguazil of the Holy Office, who had made the best fight to clear a passage for himself; but in the end the servants were put to flight, and then the ministers laid hold of the treasurer, and after securing his person, took him to the prisons of the Inquisition, giving him occasional pushes as well as blows with the backs of their swords on his way thither; and into these prisons was he cast till Saturday the 28th of February, 1484.

On this day he was brought out to the public act, degraded from his orders, stripped of his ecclesiastical habits, and left with a cloth coat upon him: he was then handed over to the secular arm and condemned to be burnt alive. A yellow *aljuba*,[36] with long sleeves to it, was then put upon him, also a head-dress in the shape of a long cap (or mitre) terminating with a

[36] The dictionary of the Royal Spanish Academy informs us that the *aljuba* was a Moorish garment worn by Spanish Christians and Moors, but does not describe it; neither does Seoane.—*Translator.*

coloured tassel, and lastly a label, bearing in large letters, the inscription

THIS FELLOW HATH JUDAIZED.

In this fashion, riding on a donkey, was he conducted to the site appointed for the burning-place, where the sentence was carried into execution.

These and other instances of punishments inflicted by the Inquisition spread terror over the whole of Andalusia—so much so, that the people fled to foreign countries from well-founded fear of the brutal and inhuman acts that were perpetrated, without the slightest opposition, by the judges of the tribunal called *holy*. Hernan Perez del Pulgar, chronicler to the Catholic Sovereigns, in his account of the calamities which attended the establishment of the Inquisition in Spain, speaks thus: "at this period, in the cities and towns of Andalusia, and especially in Seville and Córdova, there were found to be four thousand houses and upwards, in which many persons of that race" (the Jewish) "dwelt; who, with their wives and children, withdrew themselves from the land. And although a large portion of that territory was depopulated by the removal of these people, and although it was notified to the Queen that trade was on the decline; *yet did she, lightly regarding the diminution of her revenues in comparison with the advantage gained by the purification of her territories, declare that, postponing all question of interest, she was determined to purge the country from that sin of heresy, believing that act of hers to be a service rendered to God and herself.*"[37]

[37] Parte 2ª, cap. LXXXVII., fol. 137.—*Translator.*

To what excess have our historians carried their flattery of royal personages! The learned Hernan Perez del Pulgar asserts that the Catholic Queen did not regard [the destruction of commerce and trade, nor that of her own revenues, provided she could root out the bad seed of those Christians in name but Jews in heart, that had been sown in her realms. It cannot be doubted that with the establishment of the Holy Tribunal the ruin of trade commenced, and though by its destruction the income of the crown began to diminish, this was trebled by the confiscated goods of so many wealthy persons. Suson alone was worth ten millions, probably of maravedis. In consequence of this, the hapless Jews fled from the Inquisitors (those robbers in towns), and abandoned the cities, to save their lives and properties in foreign kingdoms from the voracity of those wolves.[38] Other unfortunate converts went to Rome to complain of the evil proceedings of the ministers of the Holy Office. Pope Sixtus the Fourth, dispatched a brief, dated the 29th of January, 1481,[39] to Ferdinand and Isabella, Sovereigns of Spain, for the purpose of setting before their eyes the numerous complaints which had come to Rome respecting the first judges of the Inquisition at Seville,

---

[38] "On this, all the converts took alarm, and fled in great terror from the city and archdiocese. And they placed them in Seville, and forbad them to depart from it on pain of death. And they set guards at the gates of the city, and apprehended so many that they were at a loss where to put them." Andrés Bernaldez.

[39] Don Juan Antonio Llorente. Historia crítica de la Inquisicion, Piezas justificativas, No. 1.

for persecuting a multitude of persons who were thorough Catholics—for tormenting them with great cruelty—for declaring them heretics, with the view of condemning them to death, in order to get possession of their estates—and, in short, for passing sentence on them in so barbarous a manner as to force the people to flee away in terror to foreign lands, to which they looked for the safety of their lives. He concludes the brief by saying that the Inquisitors Morillo and San Martin deserved signal punishment and forfeiture of office, and that he was restrained, solely by respect for the authority of the Catholic Sovereigns, from taking the necessary measures for giving satisfaction to the multudes of persons aggrieved by the proceedings of such avaricious and unprincipled judges.

As a striking proof of the public opinion, that, in establishing the Inquisition, the Catholic Sovereigns had no other object than the replenishment of their exhausted coffers with the confiscations of the goods belonging to heretics, I shall copy a portion of the brief which the same Sixtus the Fourth issued on the 23rd of January, 1483, in reply to a letter from Queen Isabella, in which this lady asked to have the form and plan of conducting and directing the Inquisition settled for her at Rome, in order more effectually to increase the fruits to be reaped from the erection of this tribunal. The following words which we read in the afore-mentioned document are worthy of close attention:—

"Thou seemst to doubt whether We, on seeing the care thou employest in punishing with severity the perfidious persons who, in the guise of Christians, blaspheme Christ, crucify Him with their Jewish infidelity, and obstinately persevere in their apostasy, *shall think that thou doest it more from ambition and desire of worldly gain than from zeal for the faith and Catholic truth or fear of God;* but thou mayest rest satisfied that we have never entertained the slightest suspicion of this: *for, though certain individuals have whispered some things to cover the iniquities of the persons who have been punished, we have never been able to believe that any injustice hath been committed by thee or thy illustrious consort, our dearly beloved son.* We know your sincerity, piety, and devotion towards God. We do not believe every spirit; and *although we listen to the complaints of all, we do not, therefore, attach credit to them."* [40]

But there never was a time when the truth was not corrupted by historians, who are sometimes led away by

[40] Llorente.—Historia crítica de la Inquisicion.—Piezas justificativas, No. 3. "Quod autem dubitare videris nos forsan existimare, cum in perfidos illos qui Christianum nomen ementiti, Christum blasphemant et Judaicâ perfidiâ crucifigunt, quando ad unitatem redigi nequeant, tam severe animadvertere cures, ambitione potius et bonorum temporalium cupiditate quam zelo fidei et catholicæ veritatis vel Dei timore, certo scias ne ullam quidem apud nos ejus rei fuisse suspicionem. Quod si non defuerint qui ad protegendum eorum scelera multa susurrarint, nihil tamen sinistri de tuâ vel præfati charissimi filii nostri, consortis tui illustris, devotione persuadere nobis potuit. Nota est nobis sinceritas, et pietas vestra, atque in Deum religio. Non credimus omni spiritui. Si alienis querelis aures, non tamen mentem præstamus." [The whole of this curious bull is given by Llorente.—*Translator.*]

the grossest ignorance, and sometimes influenced by fear and given to flattery. What praises have they not lavished upon the catholic zeal of Ferdinand the Fifth, for exterminating the Jews who lived in his dominions under the cloak of Christians, as if in all this monarch's actions the increase of the faith were his ruling principle! What amount of merit have they not awarded to his unreasonable and unjust usurpation of the kingdom of Navarre (then in a state of schism), praising up to the skies the bold stroke of the Catholic king, and spreading the report that it was taken by him with the sole object of maintaining the unity of the faith in the Peninsula! Oh, poor mortals! How weak is your understanding and how easily deceived! A thing done out of mere covetousness and in opposition to Christian piety, is now proclaimed by your tongues to be an act of service rendered to God! An ambitious desire to augment the number and extent of seigniories attached to the crown is called by you zeal for the increase of religion!

Don Diego Hurtado de Mendoza, historian of the war of Granada, undertaken by Philip the Second against the rebellious Moriscos, and one of the ablest politicians, not only of those but of all ages, says, in a memorial presented to the Emperor Charles the Fifth:[41] "It is clear that when a person has a district within or near a seigniory, by which that province may be injured, the seigneur may with justice deprive that

---

[41] This work, in manuscript, and other papers likewise unpublished, are in the library of the author.

individual of the right of admission to it, and give him an equivalent for it in another quarter, in which he may dwell free from suspicion. *The best reason the Catholic Sovereigns could allege for their occupation of Navarre, was the injury which might be done in that quarter to the whole of Spain; and it was on this principle that the king of France acted,*[42] *when he took possession of Burgundy, which is the key to his kingdom... Among learned men this was, at that time, considered a better title than approbation or investiture on the ground of schism."* [43]

Thus did Ferdinand the Fifth throw a cloak of Christian piety over his ambition and avarice, deceiving by these means a large portion of the human race.[44] But how soever it may serve the interest and convenience of the wicked to conceal the truth from the eyes of all human beings, it succeeds, eventually, in shedding its light abroad and dispelling the clouds of falsehood, which may obtain a temporary triumph over

[42] "Upon the death of Charles the Bold, he" (Louis XI. of France) "seized with a strong hand Burgundy and Artois, which had belonged to that prince." Robertson's State of Europe, sect. 2nd.—*Translator.*

[43] Alluding to the Pope's permission to Ferdinand to conquer the kingdom of Navarre, which his holiness had declared to be in a state of schism. Zurita Historia del Rey Hernando, lib. ix., cap. 53. Abarca. Anales de Aragon, reign of Ferdinand, chap. 20.—*Translator.*

[44] I am strongly inclined to suspect that the author *deceives himself* in supposing that *Ferdinand deceived* any considerable portion of the community: it is far more probable that his wickedness was seen through by thousands, who durst not express their opinions respecting the conduct of this powerful prince.—*Translator.*

it and blind the human intellects, which always go hand in hand with ignorance and are ever fond of vulgar tales.

I am persuaded that, in discoursing thus about king Ferdinand the Fifth, I shall draw down upon myself the ill-will of many, who will be silly enough to accuse me of being a bad Spaniard, merely because I do not allow my pen to repeat the errors which, up to this time, have falsified the history of my country. But I ask those who would brand me with the imputation of being a bad Spaniard for speaking ill of bad Spaniards, is not the unhappy Jewish race, which, through its misfortunes, has been domiciled in these lands ever since the seventieth year of the Christian era, as Spanish as our own? Could difference of religious persuasion from that of the kings and a majority of the nation deprive the Jews of their country? A word in their behalf: if denied the title of Spaniards, have they not the title of men, and even a still stronger one than that of men, that of an unfortunate people? How then can I palm off covetousness and robberies as Christian acts? This would be equivalent to canonizing wickedness, and attributing to the doctrine of the gospel that which is diametrically opposed to it. Let writers influenced by fear and in the habit of flattering others praise up to the skies those exploits of kings and tyrants of the world that deserve to be buried in the dust and obliterated from the memory of man. Let them apply the name Great to him, who to the injury of more than a hundred thousand of his subjects, dictates measures which tend to the increase of his treasury, while he regards the sacrifice of human life as the mere overthrow of an obstacle to his acquisitions. Let them extol those who, to increase their seigniories, ruin commerce and agriculture, oppress tradesmen and farmers with taxes, and rob the earth of the hands which should be employed in its cultivation, in order that these same hands may grasp the lance instead of the plough and the spade, and be engaged in the destruction of their brethren. Let them, in short, proclaim that they are wonderfully Christian kings who, in opposition to the commands of Jesus Christ, oppress men who have not embraced the faith—who think that the understandings of men can be led by violence into the belief of what is repugnant to them, and attempt to convince their opponents, not by reason, which distinguishes us from brutes and savage animals, but by force, which levels us to the grade of the brute creation. This style of preaching the Gospel is unworthy of men who call themselves Christians, for it is forbidden by Jesus Christ. Be it left to Mahomet and those who preach falsehoods to convey their religion to men's understandings at the point of the sword. Truth needs no force to obtain credit for itself, and they who take violent means to exalt it, are its enemies rather than defenders; because injuries done under the pretext of enforcing truth, carry with them hatred, contempt, and reproach. For how can the oppressed love those who are the cause of their oppression? How can persons think it possible to travel by the high road of wickedness to that of goodness? How can they attach any credit to the truth when it is presented to their eyes with every appearance of falsehood? It is true that Ferdinand the Catholic rescued the kingdom of Granada from the dominion of the Moors: that the Canary Isles, discovered in the reign of Henry the Third, were conquered in his time: that he furthered the expedition undertaken by Christopher Columbus for the discovery of the New World, which was foretold by Seneca in one of the choruses of his Medea:[45] that he incorporated the city of Cadiz and the marquisate of Villena with his crown: that he confiscated the county of Pallas: that he regained Rousillon and Cerdagne for the county of Barcelona, which had been mortgaged to Louis the Eleventh, king of France, by John the Second of Arragon: that he conquered Mazalquivir,[46] Oran, and Bujia: that he protected the kingdom of Naples from French aggression.[47] But all our historians have committed an

[45] The learned Ferdinand Columbus, in a manuscript prepared by him, in which he compiled all that he found written in the ancient Greek and Roman authors respecting America, puts down in the margin of Seneca's verses: *This prophecy was fulfilled by my father.* This manuscript is in the library of Seville cathedral. [My friend, Mr. Clark, in his *Gazpacho*, page 221, says, " Columbus himself, in a memorial which I have seen in his own hand, appealed to this ' prophecy,' as he called it."—*Translator.*]

[46] Sometimes called Alcázar-quiver.—*Translator.*

[47] See Monarquía de España por Pedro Salazar de Mendoza, lib. III. tit. VII. caps. 3, 5, 6, 8, 9, 10, 11, 18, and lib. III. tit. VIII. cap. 2. Zurita, Anales de Aragon, lib. xx., *passim*, but particularly chapters 25, 47, 54, 56, 57, 58, 87, 88, 89, 90, 91, 92. Historia del Rey Hernando, lib. I. caps. 7, 10, 13, 14, 19, 20, 38; lib. v. caps. 34, 51, 52, 53, 54; lib. VI. cap. 15; lib. IX. caps. 1, 14, 15. Abarca, Anales de Aragon, reign of Ferdinand, caps. 1, 2, 3, 4, 6, 13, 15, 19, 21, 23.—*Translator.*

error, and, in my opinion, *a great* error, in their narratives of the lives of kings: they measure the good actions of monarchs and the benefits which their good government confers upon their subjects by their successful battles, by the cities they have won, by the glory they have acquired in their military enterprises. Triumphs these are, indeed, and worthy of praise, but unworthy of occupying, as they do, not only the principal place in their histories, but the whole of the reader's attention with the accounts of marches and countermarches of armies, the sites of sieges and positions of military encampments, the assaults made upon cities, the enemies' attacks in open field or amid rugged sierras and mountains, the number of killed and wounded, and other things which, from such constant repetition as well as from their own tiresome nature, are apt to weary the mind.

Some persons[48] will say that Ferdinand the Fifth's prudence was not limited to the mere care of augmenting his states and territories, but was extended to their prosperity and improvement. How vain are their assertions, and how easily may their incorrectness be exposed! Of this I shall give clear proofs in the course of my history: for the present, I must attend to matters connected with the Inquisition and the persecutions raised against the converted Jews.

[48] I suspect that the author particularly alludes to Zurita and Abarca. It is very surprising that a man of such learning and generally good judgment as Mr. Prescott should eulogize the former historian in the manner he does.—*Translator.*

In the year 1483, Fray Tomás de Torquemada, an inferior judge of the Holy Office, was elevated to the rank of Inquisitor-General in the kingdoms of Castile and Arragon.[48] In order to double the confiscations and increase thereby the profits of Ferdinand the Fifth, he ordered a large number of this king's subjects to be burnt.[49] The children and families of these persons were reduced to the greatest poverty; but what did the depopulation and misery of his subjects signify to this monarch, provided the extent of territory subject to him was increased by his conquests? what cared he if, owing to the wars which he was obliged to sustain for the preservation of his conquests, he saddled unhappy Spain with the weight of heavy taxes, which, though they made her powerful abroad by the force of arms, reduced her to extreme misery at home, as was more clearly seen afterwards in the latter years of Philip the Second's reign, and throughout the reigns of his successors Philip the Third, Philip the Fourth, and that blockhead Charles the Second[50]?

[49] Zurita, Anales de Aragon, lib. xx. cap. 49; Zuñiga, Anales de Sevilla, years 1483 and 1524.—*Translator.*

[50] " Spain, the head of such an extensive monarchy, was the only country impoverished by its contributions towards the preservation of such vast possessions: this was more particularly the case in the loyal realms of Castile: the distress was occasioned by the new taxes, which Philip imposed with the consent of the states: this was the commencement of the depopulation and troubles which, in course of time, came upon Castile; and this kingdom, once so opulent, began to decline in consequence of the rapidity with which burdens it was unable to bear were laid upon it..... ; and the minds of the subjects were filled with no slight astonishment, when they thought of the many millions that had come from the Indies during

Torquemada, in order to persecute the Jews with redoubled severity, created four inferior tribunals;[51] one at Seville, another at Córdova, a third at Jaen, and the fourth at a town of La Mancha, then called Villa (but now Cuidad) Real. The last-mentioned tribunal was afterwards transferred to Toledo,[52] in which city the Inquisitors began to preach to the converts and urge upon those who persisted in Judaizing the necessity of denouncing themselves to the Holy Office; for by such a proceeding they would escape with slight punishment, whereas this would not be the case if informations were laid against them by others. No Jews appear to have presented themselves to the tribunal to ask for mercy and abjure the errors into which they had relapsed: on the contrary, they are reported to have formed a conspiracy, the design of which was to occupy the avenues of the four streets through which the procession was in the habit of passing on Corpus day,[53] to take pos-

his" [Philip the Second's] "reign, and they commented on the strange historical fact that in the year 1595, in the space of eight months, thirty-five millions of gold and silver, which would have sufficed to enrich every prince in Europe, had passed the bar of San Lúcar, and in 1596 there was not a single real in Castile, and they asked *what had become of the wealthy rivers or seas of gold, and into what channel had they flowed?*" Gil Gonzalez Dávila: Vida y hechos del rey Don Felipe III. [lib. I. cap. 16. The San Lúcar here mentioned is San Lúcar de Barrameda, at the mouth of the Guadalquivir.—*Translator.*]

[51] Zúñiga, Anales de Sevilla, año 1484.—*Translator.*
[52] In 1485, Páramo, lib. II. tit. II. cap. 7.—*Translator.*
[53] The first Thursday in June is, if my memory fail me not, the day on which the procession of the consecrated wafer (or Corpus Christi, as Romanists term it) usually takes place in Spain.—*Translator.*

session of the city gates and the cathedral tower, to put all the Christians to death, and make a declaration against the continuance of the royal authority, which had given countenance and aid to the barbarity that had been displayed in oppressing and plundering the towns. But this conspiracy was discovered on Corpus eve by the corregidor,[54] who apprehended some converts, and, by torturing them, succeeded in obtaining accurate information of the whole plot formed by the unhappy Jews to punish the robbers of their estates, the destroyers of their houses, the defamers of their race, the persecutors of their persons and their consciences. When this came to the knowledge of the corregidor, he ordered one of the culprits to be hanged at the time of the procession, as a warning to the rest; and on the following day, Bachelor Latorre (one of the ringleaders in the conspiracy) and four other converted Jews underwent the same punishment. And as the number of the offenders was so considerable as to render it impossible to punish them all, for they could not condemn the majority of its inhabitants without depopulating and otherwise injuring the city, the covetous inquisitors determined, though with much reluctance, on reducing the punishments to pecuniary fines, instead of total confiscation of property. They, eventually, drew from these sources large sums of money, which the king received with much pleasure and satisfaction, as they sufficed to keep his armies in pay for a considerable time.

[54] A corregidor is "a magistrate appointed by the king to govern a district." *Seoane's Dictionary.—Translator.*

At this season the authorities of the Holy Office called upon the Rabbis of the synagogue at Toledo to swear in their presence, according to the Mosaic form, that they would acquaint the tribunal with the names of all converted Jews who had obstinately persisted in Judaizing, and also threatened them with heavy penalties, death not excepted, in case of a breach of their oath. In addition to this, they ordered the Jews to put up in their synagogues certain large placards OF EXCOMMUNICATION, *according to the usual form adopted by observers of the Mosaic law*, fulminated against all Jews who, when acquainted with the names of persons formerly converted to the Christian religion and now gone astray from it, should not give information of the same to the holy and pious tribunal. So fond were the Inquisitors of excommunicating, that *they wanted the Jews themselves to excommunicate each other!* [55]

This caused an increase in the number of the accused, the imprisoned, the reduced to ashes, and, in a word, the robbed. Andrés Bernaldez, who was both a witness to all these atrocities and a friend to the judges of the Inquisition, relates that " since the year '88 [1488], the Inquisitors of Seville had burnt more than seven hundred persons, reconciled more than five thousand, and punished some who had already been in gaol four or five years and upwards with perpetual imprisonment: while others they dragged out of their prisons to clothe them with red sambenitos,[56] with crosses on them before

---

[55] See Llorente, cap. VII. art. 2, last paragraph.—*Translator*.
[56] There were also *yellow* sambenitos. The sambenito is a large

III.]	THE JEWS IN SPAIN.	149

and behind; and in this way they had to walk about for some time; after which these were taken off them, that the land might not be additionally disgraced by the sight of such exhibitions." Hernan Perez del Pulgar, in his Crónica de los Reyes Católicos, declares that "two thousand of these (Judaizers) were burnt on different occasions in some of the cities and towns, and others condemned to perpetual imprisonment."[57]

The cupidity of the Inquisitors and king Ferdinand, not satisfied with the amount, considerable as it was, of the confiscated properties of the heretics, invented a new plan to increase it: they determined to institute legal proceedings against some converted Jews who had been very rich, and who, fortunately for themselves, were no longer alive. As a matter of course, these were found guilty, and by this means the funds of the royal treasury were augmented, and the Inquisitors became more and more eager to make similar prizes. The aforesaid Hernan Perez del Pulgar writes that "a *large number* of these" (deceased Judaizers) "was found, whose goods and hereditaments were taken and applied to the king's and queen's exchequer."[58]

scapulary, worn by persons condemned of heresy or strongly suspected of it, and on other special occasions: the word is a corruption of *saco bendito*, which Mr. Prescott seems to doubt: I find, however, that Páramo, in his Latin history of the Inquisition, *always* renders it by the words *saccus benedictus.—Translator*.

[57] Parte 2ª, cap. 77.—*Translator*.

[58] Parte segunda, cap. 77; Páramo (lib. II. tit. ii. cap. 3) says, "Similiter etiam in eos qui non multo ante decesserant, Inquisitio facta est: quorum autem crimina probabantur, eorum ossa si inventa essent, concremata sunt. Hi fuerunt numero non pauci, quorum tum filii declarabantur publicis honoribus ac muneribus indigni; tum vero bona omnia Regum erario confiscabantur."—*Translator*.

The avarice of Ferdinand the Fifth would not even allow him to respect the dead. He ordered their bodies to be disinterred and converted into ashes by the devouring flames, and, at the same time, he despoiled the children and heirs of the deceased of the estates which they had honestly and legally inherited, and thus reduced them to extreme poverty. This was the act of that king so much eulogized in our histories by his flatterers, who either were foolishly deceived or durst not speak the truth. It was on the confiscations that all his zeal for the increase of the Christian religion in his lands and seigniories depended: it was on the confiscations that his desire to maintain the unity of religion in his dominions—an action about which his panegyrists have cackled so much—depended. It is true that he applied the proceeds of them to the conquest of other lands; but, in doing this, he impoverished his own: it is likewise true that it was he who opened the door to his successors to carry the fame of Spanish valour into foreign kingdoms, at the expense of commerce and agriculture in Spain: but as the Spaniards made proof of their valour by injuring foreign states, the only fruits they reaped of it were the envy and admiration of the vanquished and oppressed, while Spain herself became odious to every province in the world, which felt the burden of her arms and the tyrannical rule of her kings.

In the year 1485 many Judaizers, disgusted at the measures adopted against them by Pedro de Arbues (then an Inquisitor and now a saint!), determined to put him to death; he was slain while on his knees in the metropolitan church of St. Saviour's at Zaragoza, at the hour of matins, while the other canons were praying in the choir. Pedro de Arbues was accustomed to go armed with a coat of mail under his dress, and an iron casque to protect his head; the casque was concealed by a cap placed over it: whence it appears that the saint was prepared for a like mischance, though his being accoutred in so warlike a manner was not of the slightest avail to him. The old Christians rose up against the converted Jews, of whom several were apprehended; acts of faith (*autos de fé*) were holden, which terminated in the burning alive of many persons concerned in the death of the saintly Inquisitor, and the funds of the royal treasury received an additional increase from the confiscated wealth of the delinquents. Hernan Perez del Pulgar, speaking of these men, says, " *all their goods* were applied to the king's and queen's exchequer, *and these* were very considerable."[59]

[59] I have not been able to find these exact words in Pulgar, and hardly know whether the author refers to the concluding sentence of the last paragraph but one, or not. It does not appear to me that the historian of the Catholic Sovereigns there alludes to the murderers of Pedro Arbues, whose death he does not even mention. A minute account of this tragical occurrence, and of its fearful consequences to those concerned in it, may be seen in Zurita's *Anales de Aragon*, lib. xx. cap. 65. Llorente tells a story current in Spain (founded, he says, upon a forged document), that the saint appeared, after his death, to one Blas Galvez, and charged him to tell Alonso de Aragon, Archbishop of Zaragoza, to inform Ferdinand and Isabella that seats in heaven among the martyrs were reserved for them, *for having established the Inquisition*. The saint also commissioned Galvez to inform the Inquisitors that glorious seats among the martyrs in

Any one would imagine that, with all the confiscations above mentioned, the two Catholic spouses must have been very powerful; but it is well for him to know that, in entertaining such a notion, he wanders very far[60] from the truth.

King Ferdinand and Queen Isabella, in spite of the excellent traffic which they carried on through the medium of their Inquisitor, were reduced to the lowest ebb of poverty, which was thus occasioned: when they found the kingdom in a state of extreme destitution, instead of applying a remedy to it, they occupied themselves with making conquests, on which they spent the little stock of their own, in addition to large sums which were not their own, but were exacted from those converted Jews who had been punished by that tribunal, which was composed of wolves and other ferocious and blood-thirsty wild beasts, that prowled about the world in the disguise of human beings.

In order to show the amount of the sums expended by the Catholic Sovereigns on the war of Granada, I

heaven were also prepared for them, *out of respect for their firmness in upholding the Inquisition, and that they might be assured they had done well in committing so many persons to the flames, inasmuch as all whom they had punished with death*, save one, *were condemned to hell!* "What a pity," says Llorente, "that the saint *did not declare the name of this person!*" He proceeds to give a host of reasons to *prove* that the document on which the story was founded is a forgery: one of them will suffice. The saint speaks of Ferdinand and Isabella as *Their Majesties*, a title which the Emperor Charles the Fifth was the first Spanish monarch who ever assumed. See Llorente's *Historia Critica de la Inquisicion*, cap. VI. art. 4.—*Translator.*

[60] Literally, *a hundred millions of leagues*. A moderate distance!—*Translator.*

shall cite Hernan Perez del Pulgar's account of the way in which things were conducted at the blockade of Baza,[61] and the plan adopted by the Queen for supplying the whole Christian camp: for though I am not fond of inserting many quotations from ancient authors in my histories,[62] it will not, for all that, be out of the way to introduce some in this place, as they will give additional authority to my work, and silence those who do not believe many truths, which, if they rested on my bare assertion, would thereby run the risque of being discredited. Now these are the words of Pulgar (as they appear in his afore-cited chronicle) respecting the blockade of Baza: "Since, owing to the difficulties and losses incurred by the transport of supplies, no tradesman, induced by the hope of deriving a profit therefrom, would bestir himself to bring any for sale, the Queen ordered fourteen thousand beasts to be hired, in order that the army might be provisioned. Moreover, she ordered all the wheat and barley that could be procured in all the cities, towns, and villages of Andalusia, and in the lands belonging to the Masterships of Santiago and Calatrava, and in the territories lying between the Priorate of San Juan and Ciudad Real, to be bought up, and charged certain persons to receive it, and others to convey it to the mills, requesting the millers to grind it......the barley and flour

[61] Baza is a town in the province of Granada, and about sixteen leagues north-east of the city so called.—*Translator*.

[62] Here I must beg leave to differ from the author, though I see no reason why he should make an apology for quoting any *good* writer, ancient or modern.—*Translator*.

were received by officers appointed by the Queen, and by them conveyed to a place called the granary. The receivers were bidden to sell it to the soldiers at a fixed price, which neither rose nor fell. Taking into account the cost of the wheat and barley, and the price at which these commodities were sold, and other expenses incurred, the loss on this commercial transaction *was ascertained to be forty millions of maravedis and upwards, in the space of six months.* But, *in addition to the other expenses incurred,* the Queen was obliged to make this outlay for the provision of the camp, in order to remove all grounds of complaint about the insufficiency of the supplies. Moreover, as the blockade of this city was a protracted one, and as time had consumed a large portion of the money of which the Queen was possessed at its commencement (and which was derived from the indulgence and subsidy and from her own revenues), she determined to raise a loan in all her dominions in support of this war. And with this object she dispatched letters to all the cities and towns, calling upon them each to lend her a certain sum according to the assessment respectively made upon each person. In addition to this, she wrote to the prelates, ladies and gentlemen, tradesmen and private individuals, to lend her money according to their ability. And as they all knew that the Queen was sure to repay the money she borrowed, every one lent her as much as he was able. Some ladies and gentlemen and other persons, aware of the strait she was in, even though they had not been called upon, seeing how she spent her money, voluntarily came forward and lent her large sums of gold and silver. And as these loans, which might amount to a hundred millions, were not sufficient to defray the continual expenses that occurred in the course of the war, she resolved to mortgage a portion of her revenues for a certain amount of maravedis, which were to remain as a permanent charge on those revenues, payable to all persons who chose to become purchasers of them, and *she was to pay ten thousand maravedis for every thousand she received.* And to the numerous persons in her realms who had become purchasers of these maravedis, she ordered documents to be given, by which they were put in possession of revenues accruing from certain cities, towns, and villages in her realms, which they were to have and to hold, every year, until the money which the Queen owed them was paid off. *By this mortgage of her revenues a large sum of maravedis was raised; but as this money was spent and yet did not suffice to defray the heavy expenses incurred by the constant pay*[63] *and other things connected with the war, the Queen sent all her gold and silver jewels, trinkets, pearls, and precious stones, to the cities of* Valencia *and* Barcelona, *to be pawned, and they were pawned for a large sum of money."*[64]

Whenever the war of Granada was carried on with renewed spirit, the expenses of the Catholic Sovereigns

---

[63] Of the troops, I suppose.—*Translator.*

[64] Pulgar. Crónica de los Reyes Católicos. Parte III. cap. 3.—*Translator.*

increased, while there was a corresponding decrease in the number of sources whence the money flowed in: hence it was that, urged to it by necessity, they determined on applying to those unconverted Jews who were reputed to be the most wealthy to supply them with heavy loans, payable on the surrender of Granada. This appears from the accounts of many historians.[65]

As soon as the Sovereigns gained possession of this city, which they did on the 2nd[66] of January, 1492, they found themselves under the necessity of paying their debts to their Jewish creditors, as they had promised to do; but, owing to the exhausted state of their treasury, they were unable to fulfil their word; for the sums of money which they had expended in a war of such long duration and with such varied and strange fortunes, were enormous, and during the war their revenues decreased daily: and while they were in this dilemma, Ferdinand the Fifth, as the best plan he could think of to get rid of the debt, issued a decree, on the 31st of March, 1492, that all the Jews who dwelt in the vicinity of the Aljamas of his kingdom,

---

[65] I have not seen any *direct authority* for this statement. Pulgar, in his *Crónica de los Reyes Católicos*, parte 2ª, caps. 14 and 64, states that Ferdinand and Isabella borrowed large sums of money from the *Christians* and *Jewish converts*, and that the Pope granted them a subsidy from the *revenues of the clergy:* under these circumstances, we very naturally infer that the unconverted Jews had also to contribute a portion of their funds.—*Translator.*

[66] Zurita, Anales de Aragon, lib. xx. cap. 92. Mariaña, Historia General de España, lib. xxv. cap. 18. Pedro Salazar de Mendoza, Monarquía de España, part. III. tit. iii., cap. 6. Abarca, Anales de Aragon, reign of Ferdinand the Fifth, chap. 3.—*Translator.*

should turn Christians within the space of four months, or be banished from it.[67]

"Be it known unto you," said the Catholic Sovereigns, "and we will have you to know (for we have been informed that there have been and are certain wicked Christians in our realms), that in the Cortes holden by us at Toledo in the year 1480, we ordered all the Jews in all the cities, towns, and villages within our realms to live apart from other people, and we gave them Jewries and separate places, where they might live on in their error, and be stung with remorse for it, while in their state of separation: moreover, we ordered that an Inquisition should be made in all our realms and seigniories, which, as ye know, was made twelve years ago, and still continues to be made; whereby, as is notorious, many culprits have been detected, according to the statements made to us by the Inquisitors and many other persons, religious, ecclesiastical, and secular: and forasmuch as the greatness of the mischief which hath befallen and still befalleth the Christians through the association, conversation, and intercourse which they have kept up and do still keep up with the Jews, who pride themselves on their success in subverting people from our holy Catholic faith, is palpable........
In order that the Jews and Jewesses aforesaid may,

[67] Zurita, Historia del Rey Don Hernando el Católico, lib. i. cap. 6. Abarca, Anales de Aragon, Ferdinand the Fifth's reign, chap. 4, Páramo, lib. ii. tit. ii., cap. 6. This writer limits the time allowed the Jews to remain in Spain to *three* months. *Trimestri tempore præstituto* are his words.—*Translator*.

from the aforesaid day till the end of July, make better disposition of themselves, their goods and properties, we, by the present decree, receive and take them under our royal protection, favor, and countenance, and grant security to them and their goods from the present time till the last day of July aforesaid, in order that they may go about in safety, and sell, barter, and alienate all their property, moveable or immoveable, and freely dispose of it according to their pleasure. During the said time, let no hurt, injury, or offence be offered to them, either in their persons or property, contrary to justice: all offenders against this our royal letter will have to answer at their peril for any such breach of law. We also permit and authorize all Jews and Jewesses to carry all their goods and property out of all our said realms and seigniories by sea or by land, provided they consist not of gold or silver, or coined money, or other things prohibited by the laws of our realms" [to be exported], " or prohibited articles of merchandize."[68]

I shall prove that Ferdinand the Fifth, in issuing his decree for the expulsion of the Jews, was influenced solely by interest: he was not provided with money sufficient to pay so many and such considerable creditors as they were, and, by obliging the Jews to be converted to the faith, he knew that the Inquisition would institute proceedings against the most wealthy of them, and thereby cause all their riches to pass into the royal

[68] See Zurita and Abarca, same chapters as cited in last note. —*Translator.*

coffers. I am now going to relate a fact which will corroborate my opinion, inasmuch as it will clearly show that, in all his undertakings, Ferdinand the Catholic looked merely to the triumph of his own ambition in the conquest of lands and dominions, and to the success of his cupidity in seeking for money to carry out his designs. The Jews, who were well acquainted with the character of the king, made him an offer of thirty thousand ducats, on condition that he and his consort should revoke the edict which had been issued for their expulsion. As the smell of the money had now disposed Ferdinand to be prevailed upon by the solicitations of the Hebrews, and as their design was known to the Inquisitor Torquemada; this scoundrel, availing himself of the privilege of entering into the king's chamber, to which (as being the king's confessor) he was entitled, brought in an image of Christ crucified, which he had concealed in his dress, and showing it to the king and queen exclaimed, *Judas once sold the Son of God for thirty pieces of silver. Your Highnesses are thinking of selling Him for thirty thousand. Come, my Lord and Lady, here you have Him, sell Him.*[69] Such is the account of this occurrence given by Posevino in his *Apparatus Sacer* and Luís de Páramo in his work *De sanctâ Inquisitione,* authors as fanatical as they are ancient: this furnishes us with a very clear proof of the self-deception of those writers who corrupt the

[69] Páramo, lib. II. tit. ii., cap. 6. The passage is quoted from *Posevino* by Prescott in his history of Ferdinand and Isabella, vol. II. p. 125, ed. 1846.—*Translator.*

truth, and believe the above-related occurrence to have been a fiction invented by foreigners, for the purpose of casting a slur upon the fair fame of the Catholic Sovereigns, or rather of Ferdinand the Fifth. Torquemada himself, proud of having defeated the king's favourable intentions towards the poor unfortunate Hebrews, issued a furious edict, (denouncing most terrible anathemas against all who should disobey it,) that no Christian, after the time specified in the royal schedule, should give food or any thing else to unconverted Jews.[70]

It is said that the Spanish Jews then wrote to their brethren of Constantinople to ask advice and counsel of the latter as to what they had best do in the present emergency, and that the Jews of Constantinople answered them with the brevity that the case required, and with such dispatch as the remote distance of one country from another would admit.

I have seen several specimens of the documents, every one of which appears to have been written by a different author. In order that the reader may convince himself of this I shall here transcribe a couple of the epistles sent, with the answers to them.[71]

LETTERS FROM THE JEWS OF SPAIN TO THEIR BRETHREN IN CONSTANTINOPLE.

"Honoured Jews, salvation and grace : Be it known unto you that the king of Spain, by public

[70] Páramo, lib. II, tit. ii., cap. 6, sect. 6. Zurita, Historia del Rey Don Hernando, lib. I. cap. 6.—*Translator.*

[71] The reader cannot expect that in a translation this difference of style should be so apparent as in the original.—*Translator.*

proclamation, ordereth us to turn Christians and is anxious to deprive us of our estates, taketh away our lives, destroyeth our synagogues, and so vexeth us in other ways that we are in a state of doubt and uncertainty how to act. We beg and entreat you by the law of Moses, to have the kindness to assemble together and acquaint us, as soon as possible, with the result of your deliberations. Chamorro, chief of the Jews in Spain."

LETTER ON THE SAME SUBJECT IN A DIFFERENT STYLE.

" As brethren and persons of the same persuasion as ourselves, who are equally interested in our misfortunes, we inform you of what is going on here, with the object of hearing your opinion and being guided by it in our proceedings: the king of Spain hath lately begun to use much violence and severity towards us, particularly in the profanation of our synagogues, in putting our children to death, and in taking possession of our estates: the worst of all is that he commandeth us to turn Christians within four months, or depart from his realms. Be particular in sending us your opinion on every one of these points, as we shall be guided by it. The trouble which overwhelmeth us preventeth us from coming to a decision. The mighty God Adonay be with you and us."

ANSWER FROM THE JEWS OF CONSTANTINOPLE.

" Beloved brethren in Moses, we have received your letter, in which ye mention the troubles and afflictions that ye endure, of which as great a portion hath fallen to our lot as to yours. This is the opinion of the great satraps and rabbis. As for what ye say about the king of Spain's ordering you to turn Christians, ye should do so, as ye have no other course to follow. As for what ye say about his commanding you to be deprived of your estates, make your sons tradesmen, and thus deprive the Christians of theirs: and as for what ye say about their taking away your lives, make your sons physicians and apothecaries, and deprive them of theirs: and as for what ye say about their taking away your synagogues from you, make your sons clergymen, and let them profane and destroy the Christian religion and temple. As for what ye say about the vexations with which they harass you, contrive to get your sons government-appointments, whereby they may subjugate your oppressors, and ye may be avenged of them. Do not act contrary to these directions of ours; for ye will find by experience that, though now in a low condition, ye will soon come to be regarded as men of some consideration. Usuff, chief of the Jews of Constantinople."

THE SAME ANSWER IN A DIFFERENT STYLE.

" We have received your letter, and felt as much concern and pain as it is possible for us to feel at your troubles and want of tranquillity: and as for our opinion that ye ask, after conferring with the most learned rabbis and cleverest men of this synagogue, we think that the best and last remedy for all these evils is to baptize your bodies, but to continue mentally stedfast in your conformity with the requirements of our law, and by so doing ye will be enabled to take vengeance on them for all the injuries they have done you: for if they have profaned your synagogues, make your sons clergymen, and then ye will profane their churches; if they have slain your fathers, make your sons physicians, and ye shall slay their fathers; if they have taken estates from you who are tradesmen, contrive to make their estates soon fall into your hands; by so doing ye will be avenged on them for what they have done, and intend to do, to you. The mighty God Adonay be with you."

But these documents are altogether apocryphal. The real author of them was Cardinal Siliceo, Archbishop of Toledo, who gave out, when he published them, that they were taken from the archives of his church. In making this announcement he had two objects in view: the first of which was to circulate the report that many Jews had turned clergymen for the sake of living in greater security from the Inquisition; the second was to obtain from the court of Rome the statute of purity,[12] which was to affect those who held prebends or benefices in that diocese. Then it was that the apocryphal letters mentioned in the first book of this history were dispersed throughout Spain in answer to the forged ones of Cardinal Siliceo: in fact this was a paper warfare. The Cardinal declared that all persons of Jewish

[12] That is, purity of blood. See note to page 2.—*Translator.*

descent ought to be expelled from the prebends, benefices, and dignities of the Church of God; for the majority of those Jews who remained in Spain after the expulsion of their race from that country, acting upon the advice of the Constantinopolitan rabbis, undertook those charges which best suited their interests.[73] Those Jews who were really converted asserted their right to be admitted to such dignities, inasmuch as their ancestors had opposed the death of Christ—a notion founded on that letter attributed to the synagogue of Toledo. The fact of Cardinal Siliceo being the person who strove hardest for the statute of purity in this metropolitan city, and the fact that the aforesaid letter was attributed to the Jews of the Toledan synagogue who did not consent to the death of the Saviour of the world (for that was no less than the head and principal synagogue of all the Spains in those days, just as the cathedral of that city is the head of all the churches in these), make me suspect that these documents on both sides were, one and all of them, forged for the purpose of upsetting the arguments of their opponents.

As the Jews had no choice left them but either to turn Christians, quit Spain, or die, they began to sell off all their goods; and as the time allowed them to do so was so short (for Ferdinand the Fifth had even taken this into his calculation), they were obliged to part with

[73] Abarca says that the Jews, on whom penance was imposed by the Inquisition of Castile, were *not Spaniards* but *Portuguese*, either by birth or extraction. Can national prejudice be carried further than this? See Reign of Ferdinand V., chap. 4.—*Translator.*

THE JEWS IN SPAIN.

their properties for very inadequate prices, and sell them for what the Christians chose to give for them; and, according to Bernaldez, *they would barter a house for a donkey, and a vineyard for a small piece of cloth or linen.*[74]

In July 1492, three thousand persons and upwards quitted Spain by Benavente for Braganza in Portugal: by Zamora, for Miranda in Portugal, thirty thousand: by Ciudad Rodrigo for El Villar in Portugal, thirty-five thousand: by Alcántara for Marban in Portugal, fifteen thousand: by Badajoz for Yelves in Portugal, ten thousand: so that by Castile alone, ninety thousand Jews left Spain for Portugal. By Rioja for Navarre went two thousand persons and upwards: by Biscay for the port of Laredo, three hundred families, which embarked for places beyond the seas: from Andalusia and the territory of the Mastership of Santiago by way of Cadiz, eight thousand Hebrews and upwards. Such, in short, was the case all over Spain. Bernaldez, on the authority of a rabbi whom he had converted to Christianity, asserts that the number of Jews expelled from Spain exceeded a hundred and sixty thousand. Zurita[75] augments the number to four hundred thousand, and Juan de Mariana[76] relates that it amounted to eight

[74] This passage is quoted in the history of Ferdinand and Isabella by Prescott, who laments that Bernaldez's works are not in print, as, being an eyewitness of the war of Granada, he would probably correct many errors now current respecting it. See Páramo, lib. II. tit. ii. cap. 6, sect. 11.—*Translator.*

[75] Historia del Rey Don Hernando el Católico, lib. I. cap. 6.—*Translator.*

[76] Lib. xxvi. cap. 1.—*Translator.*

hundred thousand. Lastly, Pedro de Abarca[77] says that there were a hundred and *sixty* (*sesenta*) thousand families.

Gonzalo de Illescas, speaking in his *Historia Pontifical* of the expulsion of the Jews by the Catholic Sovereigns, says : " By this holy and rigorous law more than twenty-four thousand families and establishments of Jews were compelled to quit Castile. They sold all their possessions, and those who went by sea had to pay the king two ducats a head. Many of them went into Portugal, whence they have, since then, been expelled. Others betook themselves to France, Italy, Flanders, and Germany. I was acquainted with one at Rome who had once resided at Toledo. A very considerable number of them went to Constantinople, Thessalonica, Cairo, and Barbary. They carried our language along with them, and have preserved it to this day, and delight in speaking it; and it is certain that, in Thessalonica, Constantinople, Alexandria, Cairo, and other commercial cities as well as in Venice, they employ no other language than the Spanish in buying and selling and transacting business. When I was at Venice, I was acquainted with a great many Jews of Thessalonica, who, though mere lads, spoke Castilian as well as, if not better than, I did. Very great, indeed, are the profits which the Grand Turk derives from the tributes paid

[77] Anales de la Corona de Aragon [cap. 4 del Rey Fernando el Católico. In my edition it is *seventy* (*setenta*). I should observe that all the writers cited in this paragraph, except perhaps Bernaldez, *qualify* their statements by such expressions as these: *it is reported, it is supposed,* &c.—*Translator.*]

him by these people; and it is said that Bajazet, who was living when they betook themselves to his dominions, was in the habit of exclaiming (when persons puffed off to him the wisdom and discretion of the Catholic Sovereigns), *I do not understand the wisdom of the Spanish Sovereigns; since, when they had such excellent slaves as these Jews, they banished them from their territories.*"[78]

When these unhappy people departed from their homes, the Christians, seeing that many of them were suffering from the fatigues of travel, that some of the sick and convalescent were either journeying on foot or mounted on miserable steeds, were moved with compassion towards them, and are said to have exhorted them to receive baptism and to put an end to their present and future calamities. But these entreaties were of no avail, since the Jews, disgusted at the rigorous orders of the Catholic Sovereigns, obstinately determined to adhere to their law even to death; being persuaded that God would work miracles on their behalf, similar to those he had formerly wrought in Egypt, and that the land in which they were about to take up their abode, was the land of promise. This was the opinion of all except a few, who, though not convinced of the Messiah's advent, turned Christians, partly from fear of the inconveniences attendant upon travel, and partly from their strong affection for their native country.[79]

[78] Seg^a parte, lib. vi. cap. 20, sect. 2.—*Translator.*
[79] See Ferreras, Synopsis Histórica de España, año 1492, sect. 17. —*Translator.*

Notwithstanding the injunctions which the Catholic Sovereigns had issued to prevent the Jews from carrying away with them either gold or silver, they took with them large quantities of both these metals, laughing in their sleeve at the vigilance of their cruel persecutors, and bringing the gold and silver away, concealed in the trappings of their beasts or in the inner garments of the women.[80] Intelligence of this trick was conveyed to the Catholic king, who, thereupon, found a new pretext for feeding his insatiable avarice. Accordingly, on the 2nd of September, 1492, he issued a warrant, signed by himself and his consort, for holding a commission of inquiry in the archdiocese of Toledo, respecting those Jews who, in defiance of his injunctions, had taken out of these realms gold, silver, money, or prohibited articles, and also for discovering what goods they had sold to the Christians, and for the immediate sequestration of all such goods. Thus did the Christians have to pay out of their pockets for the offences committed by the Jews who were now out of the kingdom! This proceeding of Ferdinand the Fifth would be considered an extraordinary one, were we unacquainted with his motive for it; but it shows us that this monarch cared nothing about the exigencies of his treasury, for when they began to trouble him, he instantly hit upon an expedient for replenishing it, and dictated some measure for the confiscation of the estates of his wealthiest and most powerful subjects.

[80] Bernaldez, quoted by Llorente, cap. VIII. art. i. sect. 8. Ferreras, año 1492, sect. 19.—*Translator.*

But the calamities of the unhappy Hebrews did not terminate with their expulsion, by the order of the Catholic Sovereigns. Out of five-and-twenty vessels that sailed from Cadiz and Port St. Mary, bound for Oran and filled with Jews, seventeen, under the command of Pedro Cabron, were shattered on the high seas by a dreadful storm, and, in order to repair the damage, he was obliged to anchor in the waters of Cartagena. A hundred and fifty persons landed at that port, and after applying for and receiving baptism, set out for old Castile. The vessels went on to Málaga, and under colour of going to ask for provisions to continue their voyage, four hundred more families disembarked, and embraced Christianity, whilst the remainder of them set sail for Fez. The Jews who went to Portugal obtained permission from John the Second to live in that kingdom for six[81] months: this permission was granted them on condition of their paying him a crusado each. There they waited to see what kind of reception and entertainment had been given to their brethren who went to Fez, for it was commonly reported that they had been plundered at sea by pirates and in Africa by the Arabs of the country. At the expiration of the six[81] months, seven hundred families and upwards still remained in Portugal, each of which had to pay the king the tribute of a hundred crusados, besides an additional hundred jointly, and a capitation tax of eight crusados for each individual. On this the remaining Jewish families determined to go to the African port of Arcilla and thence

[81] Ferreras and Abarca say *eight*.—*Translator*.

to Fez, in March 1493; but as some of them went in Moorish ships, the Moors, eager to possess themselves of the goods and chattels of the Jews, murdered a large number of them on the high seas, although contenting themselves with merely plundering the majority. On receiving this intelligence the Jews resolved not to enter the Moorish territories, owing to their well-grounded suspicion that in them they would be likely to suffer new disasters: accordingly, they formed a kind of encampment in the neighbourhood of Arcilla, where they continued for some months without coming to any decision. But seeing at last that in every direction to which they turned their eyes, misfortunes stared them in the face, they notified to Count Borba, the Portuguese commandant of the prison-fortress of Arcilla, their desire to embrace Christianity and to return to Spain, and requested him to provide them with means to put their plans into execution.[82]

This Portuguese gentleman, touched with a feeling of compassion for the calamities of the Hebrews, took opportune measures for satisfying the wishes of that unhappy race; and, assisted by him, many families

[82] See Páramo, lib. II. tit. ii. cap. 6, sect. 11. Llorente, cap. VIII. art. i. sect. 9. Ferreras, año 1492, sects. 20, 21, and año 1493, sect. 16. Zurita, Historia de Hernando el Católico, lib. I. cap. 6. The following passage from the Historia Geral de Portugal, by Lemos (quoted by Dunham, in his history of Spain and Portugal), will show that the exiles had to undergo even greater hardships than those mentioned in the text: "Naõ he dizivel a persiguiçaõ que fizeraõ os Mouros á esta escoria das gentes. Elles os affrontaraõ, os roubaraõ, os escarneceraõ, e á vista dos frais e dos maridos dormiaõ com as mulheres e as filhas."—*Translator.*

kept continually pouring into Andalusia till the year 1496,[83] some of which had already embraced Christianity, whilst others intended to follow their example. The remainder of them went to Fez, where they met with insults of every description, and were plundered by the barbarous rabble, which in all respects (save religious creed) resembled the brutal judges of the Holy Office. Another party of Jews, who were expelled from Spain, arrived in nine caravels at Naples, and as these persons had on their voyage contracted various kinds of diseases, occasioned by the numbers huddled together in such small vessels, they carried such a terrible plague with them to the Neapolitan kingdom that, in the capital of that state alone, upwards of twenty thousand persons fell victims to its ravages."[84]

The Jews compared their expulsion from the realms of Spain to the calamities which their forefathers endured, when Zion was destroyed and her inhabitants dispersed all over the world, in the times of Titus and Vespasian. Equal to those, if not greater, were the misfortunes which befel the Jews when they quitted these realms, on which they looked with the same love as Palestine;[85] for ever since the destruction of Jeru-

[83] See Ferreras, año 1492, sect. 21, and año 1493, sect. 16.—*Translator*.

[84] See Abarca, Anales de Aragon, reign of Ferdinand the Fifth, chap. 4. Zurita, Historia del Rey Hernando el Católico, lib. I. cap. 6. —*Translator*.

[85] See Zurita, work and chapter referred to in last note.—*Translator*.

salem they have regarded Spain as their new country, and hence originated that affection for Spanish things which they cherish to this day, holding it, as they do, to be the highest honor to them that they are descendants of those who were expelled from Spain by the Catholic Sovereigns, and speaking the Castilian language in all its purity, and keeping in perpetual memory the Inquisition, which they porutray as a most cruel and voracious fury. Such is their abhorrence of this tribunal, that they have even endeavoured to find in the prophecies of the Old Testament passages directed against its ministers.

[*The author here gives an account of some Jewish poets, with extracts from whose works he fills three pages, which, not to fatigue the reader, I omit.*]

Those Jews who lived in concealment in Spain, when writing to their brethren in foreign kingdoms accounts of the persecutions and other punishments to which the Holy Office rendered them obnoxious, were obliged to be extremely guarded in the expressions they used: this tribunal they mortally hated because of its present acts of oppression, and also on account of its having been the engine which wrought most powerfully in procuring the banishment of their race from Spain. And yet there are some who imagine that when the Catholic Sovereigns dictated that measure, they were not influenced by cupidity, but holy zeal for Catholic unity in Spain![86]

[86] See Abarca, Anales de Aragon, reign of Ferdinand the Fifth, chap. 4.—*Translator.*

Mistaken, indeed, are they who hold such notions as these! Ferdinand the Fifth never thought about the religious unity of the Spanish monarchy. Although his hatred was often on the very verge of bursting upon the court of Rome, it remained locked up in the prison of his own breast for some years. But at last it came to an open exhibition on the occasion of an apostolical legate having carried into the kingdom of Naples several excommunications, all of them prejudicial to the prerogatives of his crown. He then wrote to Count Ribagorza, his viceroy, lieutenant, and captain-general, that famous letter, which has seen the public light, at different times. Among the intemperate expressions which we find in it, directed against Pope Julius the Second, author of the offence above mentioned, the following occur: "We have been exceedingly troubled, annoyed, and aggrieved at all of this, and are very much astonished and displeased at your conduct, when we consider how important and how prejudicial to our interests, prerogatives, and royal dignity that act was, which hath been done by the apostolical legate; particularly as it hath been done in express violation of our rights, and is such an act as hath not been done before within our memory to any king or viceroy of our realms. *Why did you not comply with our wishes and strangle the legate who presented the brief to you?* It is quite clear that the Pope will not limit his proceedings to that kingdom, if he discover that in Spain and France he is allowed to act thus, but will do the same thing in other kingdoms, for the sake of extending his jurisdiction. But good viceroys proceed in a summary way with such fellows, and by the infliction of a single punishment, prevent others from making similar attempts."[87]

In another passage of the same document he gives

[87] This letter, dated Burgos, the 22nd of May, 1508, was not known in Spain, until that famous writer, poet, and politician, Don Francisco Gomez de Quevedo y Villegas, a great friend of the Duke of Osuna, at that time Viceroy of Naples, found it, while examining some papers in the archives of that kingdom. An Italian gentleman asked him for a transcript of it, with which Quevedo furnished him; accompanying, however, some of its boldest clauses against the Pope with notes, observations, and exculpatory remarks, all of which were published in the last century, in the first volume of the *Semanario Erudito*. At a convenient season, Quevedo forwarded another copy to Spain, which was addressed to Don Baltasar de Zúñiga y Acevedo, grand knight-courtier to Philip the Third, and afterwards a favourite of his son Philip the Fourth, together with the following letter, which is in my library, in a volume of divers manuscripts: "A gentleman of Italy asked me for that letter—a circumstance I took care to state in the reply I sent him, with that letter enclosed in it: and in order that by this freedom I might not be too openly exposed and put in the power of men who cloak their malice under the garb of religion, I accompanied the letter with these notes, apprehending and fearing that such strong expressions and arguments as those employed by that great king might prove dangerous when viewed by other eyes than those of your Excellency, and that none but persons of your experience can duly appreciate that which would scandalize a mind of inferior mould. I wished to send it you for the sake of amusing one of your leisure hours, and have no doubt that the communication of this writing to a person of so well-regulated a mind as yours, will tend to the service of His Majesty in the matter of jurisdiction. God grant your Excellency long life and health.—Torre de Juan Abad, April 24th, 1621. Don Francisco Quevedo." [Ferdinand's letter is too long to insert in this place: from the tenor of it, I think he suspected that his viceroy had been tampered with, especially as he orders him *to strangle the legate, if he can catch him.*—*Translator.*]

utterance to these highly significant words, which show his intention to become a schismatic. "We have written on this occasion to Jerónimo de Vich, our ambassador to the court of Rome, what you will see in the copies of our letter to him, which we transmit with this; *and we are positively determined, should his Holiness refuse to revoke the brief, as well as the acts performed by its authority, to deprive him of the obedience now paid him by the realms of Castile and Arragon,* and to take such other steps and make such other provisions as a case of such gravity and emergency requires."

Whence it appears that the idea of religious unity never entered into the head of Ferdinand the Fifth: for had he entertained any such notion, how could he have come to such a resolution as to renounce his allegiance to the Pope, and introduce schism into his realms? Be it observed that if, in this matter, Ferdinand did not actually satisfy his wishes, he was not restrained from doing so by want of inclination, but fear of those very arms which he himself was employing against the king of Navarre, to deprive that monarch (by virtue of the Papal authority) of his realms and seigniories, which were then in a state of schism.[88]

---

[88] "The Catholic king had no intention of ever restoring that state, which he considered as part and parcel of his dominions, nor did he entertain the slightest scruple of conscience about the matter, and this he repeatedly asserted. The grounds on which he justified his decision were three: the first of these was the Papal sentence, which deprived the reigning Sovereigns" (Jean d' Albret and his wife Catherine) "of that kingdom: the second was the bestowal of her right to that kingdom upon the Sovereigns of Castile by the Princess

On the other hand, the Catholic Sovereigns, in ordering the banishment of the Jews, acted in direct opposition to the rules of justice and the honor of the Gospel, and instead of rendering a real service to the Spanish nation, did it an infinity of mischief, the effects of which we feel even to this day.

By their religious intolerance they opened the gates of persecution against those who were acquainted with the Hebrew and oriental languages, for they looked upon such persons as if they were Jews; and by this proceeding they put an end to the study of those languages in Spain, to the serious detriment of the mental culture and learning of their subjects.

The first restorer of Spanish literature, after the revival of the arts and sciences in Europe, was also the first learned man who suffered from the power of the Inquisition. In the comments which Don Antonio

---

Blanche (first wife of Prince Henry, who afterwards reigned in Castile by the title of Henry the Fourth), when her father king John of Arragon delivered her into the power of Gaston de Foix and her sister Leonor, both of them her declared enemies, whose sole aim was to put her to death, in order to secure to themselves the succession to Navarre, and it was right that he should avenge the death of Blanche by taking their kingdom away from the grandchildren of those who perpetrated that foul deed. The third reason was the claim to that crown which Queen Germaine set up after the death of her brother Gaston de Foix; for though, in virtue of this title, the king, her husband, could not unite that realm to Castile, we may suppose that he did so with her consent, for we find that three years afterwards Ferdinand renounced his own right in the Cortes at Zaragoza, and transferred it to Prince Charles, afterwards king of Castile and Arragon." Mariana, Hist. Gen. de Esp. lib. xxx. cap. 24.
—*Translator.*

Lebrija[89] put in the dedication of his Latin Grammar (in the year 1495), addressed by him to the Catholic Queen Isabella, he declared that as he had just finished writing his ideas on the antiquities of Spain, he was now resolved on devoting the remainder of his life to the study of sacred literature.

At what period Lebrija first entered upon this useful task, it is impossible to ascertain; nevertheless, from conjectures more or less probable, we infer that it was about 1497 or 1498 at the latest. He not only read the Holy Scriptures, but scrutinized every passage and even every word, comparing the Latin Vulgate (which was in print in his time,) as well as several manuscript copies of that version, with the original Hebrew and Greek, besides consulting some of the Fathers of the Church and ancient Biblical commentators; and whenever the discovery of a clerical error or inaccuracy in the Latin translation resulted from his labors, he suggested the true reading of the passage. Moreover, when he came to a word of recondite signification, he was wont to search the dictionaries and Scripture-interpreters, in order to ascertain what exposition they had given to it; and when he perceived that they had not caught its true import, he took care to make this manifest by forcible reasons and sufficient authority.

When the news of this useful undertaking of his was divulged, the fanatics were in a state of excitement, and many Doctors, who prided themselves on their learning,

[89] See Bibliotheca Hispana, under word ANTONIUS. Llorente, cap. x. art. iii., sect. 8.—*Translator.*

were greatly exasperated: these fellows imagined that the Vulgate did not admit of improvement; that it had ever been preserved in its primitive integrity by a species of miracle; and therefore were scandalized and horror-stricken, when they heard of a man having the presumption to suppose that any passages in the standard Latin text could be found to require emendation.

At this their conceit was so deeply wounded, that they could not patiently endure the thought *that a mere master of Latinity* (as they called Lebrija), *a title of no value or authority*, should dare to lay his hands upon the sacred books: *for*, said they, *even granting the necessity, which there is not, of correcting any passage of the Vulgate, this would be a matter within the peculiar province of the Masters of Divinity; not that all Masters of this divine science would be so qualified, but only those who should receive the sanction and authority of a Supreme Pontiff or a General Council.*

This horde of presumptuous theologians, frantic as though an attempt had been made to pull down the fortress of the Catholic faith and raze it to its foundations, began to storm with rage and declaim against the laborious Antonio de Lebrija, calling him *rash and sacrilegious.* So much did they talk against this learned man, that the news of what he had done came to the ears of Don Fray Diego de Deza, then Bishop of Palencia, one of the greatest monsters of cruelty,[90] who,

---

[90] Llorente, Hist. crit. de la Inq. cap. ix. art. i. sects. 1, 2.—*Translator.*

to Spain's dishonour and the disgrace of human nature, ever held the office of Inquisitor General: he was a man, in short, who so mortally hated both the Hebrew and Greek texts of the Holy Scriptures, that he determined not to allow a trace [91] of them to remain in the Peninsula; and so, with the same brutality as those who, when denouncing a person as a Judaizer, used to say, "*Give me the Jew and I will return him to thee burnt*," he incessantly persecuted the Hebrew and Greek Bibles, prying into the most hidden corners in search of them, with lighted torches always in his hands, ready to reduce the copies of them to ashes.[92]

Exasperated at the laudable toil of Lebrija, Deza presented himself before the Catholic Sovereigns and requested them to give him an order to proceed against that illustrious man, for he well knew the Queen's partiality to literary studies, and did not dare to make an attack upon him without first obtaining the royal permission to do so.

Deza then forcibly carried off all the manuscripts of

[91] Nam bonus ille præsul (Deza) in tota quæstione sua nihil magis laborabat quam ut duarum linguarum ex quibus religio nostra pendet neque *ullum vestigium relinqueretur*. Lebrija en su Apología al lector. [Walton says that this work, though not printed, circulates in a manuscript form. The passage from Lebrija, given in this note is quoted by Nicolás Antonio in the Bibliot. Hisp.—*Translator*.]

[92] Si Hebraicorum voluminum lectione nobis interdicitur, si Hebræos codices eliminant, dissipant, lacerant, adurunt, si Græcos libros minime putant necessarios, in quibus prima illa nascentis ecclesiæ jacta sunt fundamenta, in chaos illud antiquum antequam literæ essent inventæ confundemur, atque duobus sacræ Scripturæ voluminibus orbati in sempiterna noctis caligine versemur necesse est. Lebrija en la Apología. [See also Llorente, cap. x. art. iii., sect. 8.—*Translator*].

Lebrija that contained notes on the Holy Scriptures, and committed them to the flames; thereby defrauding posterity of the fruit which it might have reaped of his Biblical labors.[93]

Distressed at this act of the Inquisitor, and apprehensive of falling into disgrace with the Catholic Sovereigns, Lebrija addressed to Don Fray Francisco Ximenez de Cisneros, Archbishop of Toledo, a brief and eloquent defence against the accusations of his enemies; in which, not being able to contain himself, he burst forth into exclamations of grief and indignation to the following effect: "What! then it does not suffice for me to enslave my own understanding in compliance with the faith, respecting the dogmas it proposes to me, but I am moreover bound to confess myself ignorant with regard to certain truths, which I know, not on grounds either dubious or supported only by probable reasons, but resulting from irrefragable arguments and palpable demonstrations! What slavery is this, which, under the title of piety, does not permit me to manifest my way of thinking in matters by no means injurious to the faith? What! did I say manifest? nay, that does not even allow me to write down my opinion for my own use and within the secrecy of the closet—not even to mutter it within my teeth, or make it the subject of my meditations."[94]

[93] Lee Llorente, cap. x. art. iii., sect. 8.—*Translator.*

[94] An mihi non sit satis in iis quæ mihi religio credenda proponit captivare intellectum in obsequium Christi, nisi etiam in iis quæ mihi sunt explorata, comperta, nota, manifesta, ipsaque luce clariora, ipsa veritate veriora, compellar nescire quod scio, non allucinans,

The false theories respecting the correctness and purity of the Vulgate outlived the death of Lebrija's persecutors, and to the misfortune and injury of theological studies and of some Masters of Divinity, one set of divines after another handed down to posterity the maxims which they had successfully inherited, as a kind of heir-loom, from their predecessors: hence it was that after the Council of Trent had decided in favor of the authenticity of the Vulgate, these opinions had many advocates.

The Tridentine fathers, it is true, allowed the use and authority of the Hebrew and Greek texts: but in consideration of the respect with which the Vulgate had been received from the first ages of the Church, and of its containing nothing contrary to religious doctrine and good morals, it was their will and intent only to decree that, thenceforward, Expositors of the Holy Scriptures, in their commentaries, glosses, and scholia; Masters in their disputations; and Preachers in their lectures or sermons, should use that version to the exclusion of all other *Latin* ones. It is likewise true that some Doctors who attended the council at the time the decree was drawn up, particularly the Jesuit

---

non opinans, non conjectans, sed adamantinis rationibus, irrefragabilibus argumentis, apodicticis demonstrationibus colligens? Quam mala hæc servitus est, aut quæ tam iniqua, velut ex arce dominatio, quæ te non sinat, pietate salva, libere quæ sentias dicere? Quid dicere? Immo nec intra parietes latitans scribere, aut scrobibus immurmurans infodire, aut saltem tecum (*mecum*?) volutans cogitare. Lebrija en la Apología. [Lebrija is better known, out of Spain, by the name of Ælius Nebrissensis.—*Translator.*]

Alonso Salmeron,[95] and the Franciscan Andrés de Vega,[96] lost no time in publishing in print that the design of the Fathers in council was the same as we have above stated it to have been. But of what good was all this? Testimonies of such weight and publicity were either unknown or disregarded.

The illiterate theologians, blinded by the word *authentic*, which had been employed by the Council, gave the decree a wrong interpretation, and stoutly maintained that the Vulgate was to be regarded with the same veneration as if it had dropped down from heaven, or as if the Holy Spirit had guided the translator's hand: by this means they finally carried their point and got their way of thinking to be generally, or all but generally, received.

Now the evil did not stop here: in the code of rules used by the officers of the Inquisition, the respect due to the Vulgate was set down, almost as a point of

---

[95] See Bibliotheca Hispana, under word ALPHONSUS.—*Translator*.

[96] Andrés de Vega, in the fifteenth book, ninth chapter, of his work entituled, *Tridentini decreti de justificatione expositio et defensio*, addresses these words to Calvin: "Et ne dubites de his, verissime possum tibi allegare pro his amplissimum et observantissimum dominum sanctæ crucis Cardinalem, de pietate et de literis et studiosis omnibus optime meritum, qui illi sessioni et aliis omnibus præfuit, ac pridie quidem quam illud decretum firmaretur, et postea, non opinor semel, mihi testatus est nihil amplius voluisse patres firmare. Itaque nec tu, nec quisquam alius, propter hanc approbationem vulgatæ editionis, impeditur, quominus, ubi hæsitaverit, ad fontes recurrat et in medium proferat quicquid habere potuerit quo juventur et locupletentur Latini, et vulgatam editionem ab erroribus repurgent, et quæ sensui Spiritûs Sancti et ipsis fontibus sunt magis consentanea assequantur."—[Page 755 in 4to edition of 1621.—*Translator*.]

doctrine, in the terms above explained: the consequence of which was that some learned and pious men were treated by its tribunals as offenders against the faith, for having shown their preference for the original texts of the Sacred Books and for having paid deference to them.

To this class belongs *Alfonso de Zamora*, first professor of Hebrew in the University of Alcalá, and one of those who laboured most in preparing the edition of the Complutensian Bible: this person, after the death of his protector Cisneros, was robbed of the fruits of his labor and pains by the machinations of two perverse men, who were shielded by the authority of a brutal Inquisitor.[97]

Of the same class was the Augustine friar *Luis de Leon*, professor in the University of Salamanca, who passed nearly five years in the Inquisition of Valladolid, bitterly lamenting the narrow limits and obscurity of the dungeon in which he lay, and complaining of his persecutors in these well-known lines:

> "Here envious hate and slanderous tongues
> Have made me pass my life:
> Happy the scholar who retires
> Far from worldly strife:
> The man who communing with God,
> Content with humble fare,
> Lives all alone, and envies not,
> Him envy's tongue will spare."

Thus did he bewail the mortal hatred and excessive

[97] See Biblioteca de los Rabinos Españoles; and Bibliotheca Hispana, under word ALPHONSUS.—*Translator.*

tyranny of his calumniators, the unfair advantages they took in attacking him, the forgetfulness of some friends, the vain and useless sympathy of others, the dilatoriness of the proceedings against him, and their doubtful result.[98]

Such a one was the famous master *Fray Alonso Gudiel,* likewise an Augustine friar and a great preacher, who perished within the prison walls of the tribunal of the Holy Office: his corpse was thence removed and delivered to the monks of his order, to be by them interred, though by no means sure of remaining in that continual peace and quiet usually conceded to the dead, for his cause was still proceeded with, and in the interim his bones ran the risque of being disturbed.[99]

Another of these was *Martin Martinez Cantalapiedra,* professor of Hebrew in the schools of Salamanca, who fell into the clutches of the Inquisition of Valladolid, from the dark dungeons of which he eventually came forth to the light of liberty, though with his forehead stained with the same black dye as that with which some passages of his printed works had been ordered to be smeared.[100]

Of the same class was *Gaspar de Grajar,* abbot of Santiago de Peñalba in the cathedral church of Astorga,

---

[98] Bibliotheca Hispana, under word LUDOVICUS, and Llorente, cap. xxv. sect. 58.—*Translator.*

[99] Nicolás Antonio gives a brief notice of Alonso Gudiel in the Bibliotheca Hispana, under word ALPHONSUS, but makes no mention of his imprisonment or the persecutions he suffered.—*Translator.*

[100] See Bibliotheca Hispana, under word MARTINUS, and Llorente, cap. xxv. sect. 22.—*Translator.*

who was tried in the fire of the same crucible, and ended his days in prison, deprived of the comfort he would have derived from hearing that declaration of the soundness and orthodoxy of his tenets which was made after his death.[101]

Such another, lastly, was *Benedicto Arias Montano*, a professed monk of the order of Santiago in the royal convent of San Marcos de Leon: he was a great theologian (a fact clearly proved by the number of valuable works of his that are in print), and one of the most famous doctors present at the Council of Trent. It is well known that he was the principal commissioner employed in editing that Bible, which was called *Royal*, because undertaken by the king; *Philippine*, because executed at the expense of Philip the Second; *Antwerpian*, because printed at Antwerp; *Plantinian*, because printed at the press of Plantinus; *Polyglott*, because it is in many languages; *Montanian*, because this famous doctor (as we observed) undertook the editorial part of the work, in which labor he was assisted by the Universities of Paris, Louvaine, and Alcalá de Henares.[102]

Leon de Castro, professor of Hebrew at the University of Salamanca, a jealous man who could not endure the thought of Philip having committed the editorship of the Bible to a doctor of Alcalá, began to declaim against and find fault with it; he even went so far as

[101] Nicolás Antonio mentions this writer in his Bibliotheca Hispana, under word GASPAR, but says nothing about the persecutions he endured nor of his imprisonment.—*Translator*.

[102] Bibliotheca Hispana, under word BENEDICTUS; Montanus's preface to this Bible, and Llorente, cap. XXIX. art. ii. sect. 1.—*Translator*.

to assert that in the most important parts of the work, Árias Montano had followed the erroneous readings usually given to them by the Jews, to the great injury of the Christian religion. On this the Inquisitors made a fuss: those of Toledo determined, with the assent and consent of Cardinal Gaspar Quiroga, that these readings should be examined and qualified: this was done, and the respect due to the multitude of learned men and exalted personages who took part in the publication of this Bible, was trampled under foot by the Inquisitors, who paid no regard to the consultations previously holden by the aforementioned persons, nor to the care they employed in order to execute their undertaking in the best manner possible.[103]

[103] Pedro de Fuentidueña, in a letter, still in manuscript, addressed to Cardinal Stanislaus Osius, respecting the persecution raised against the pious Benedicto Árias Montano (an intimate friend of his), in consequence of the printing of the Polyglott Bible at Antwerp by Plantinus, says: " Ex hac enim schola Salamantina prodierunt, et in ea versantur, qui has modo tragœdias excitarunt........ Adripiunt enim causam........ex concilii decreto, quo decernitur ut hæc ipsa vulgata......in publicis lectionibus, disputationibus, prædicationibus, et expositionibus, pro authentica habeatur, et ut nemo eam rejicere quovis prætextu audeat vel præsumat. Hæc sunt legis verba, quæ quidem ita illi accipiunt, ut non modo qui de ejus aliquid auctoritate detraxerit, sed qui vel punctis et apicibus vulgatæ editionis fidem non adhibuerit, hæreseos crimen incurrisse clament: deinde non licere jam confugere ad Hebræos et Græcos codices, immo vero illos per hanc Latinam vulgatam editionem esse corrigendos. Hæc ego non scriberem nisi interfuissem publicis disputationibus theologicis, quibus id agitari et pertinaciter defendi ac animadverti...... .Hi vero mordicùs tenent solam vulgatam editionem incorruptam esse; Hebræos vero codices et Græcos corruptos atque depravatos jam olim fuisse. Vulgatam editionem volunt unicum esse canonem Divinorum omnium scriptorum: aliis hæc non probantur. Res ut plena offen-

The theologians of the University of Alcalá had, with the assistance of Árias Montano, pointed out the mode to prepare this edition of the Bible; they were commissioned to do so by the Supreme Council of the Inquisition, to which Philip the Second, the munificent patron of the undertaking, had entrusted the business. For the execution of this task, the king himself supplied Árias Montano with instructions that were in conformity with the determinations of the Complutensian divines.[104] Many eminent doctors of the University of Louvaine and other places assisted Árias Montano's learning with their useful observations and valuable manuscripts. Everything was examined with the most scrupulous minuteness when the Bible was issuing from the press; and, as a seal and safeguard to such important and such pious labors, Pope Gregory the Thirteenth himself expedited a brief of approbation, which was printed at the commencement of the work.[105]

To this no regard was paid, for the whole attention of the Inquisitors was directed to the clamours of Leon de Castro, an insolent madcap, in whom the person of Ruffinus, St. Jerome's adversary, was revived. For, after the example of Ruffinus, he said the Hebrew text had been corrupted by the Rabbins, and consequently

sionis et quæ serpat quotidie longius non sine periculo multorum." [See Bibliotheca Hispana; Biblioteca de los Rabinos Españoles, chapter on R. Abraham Husque; and Llorente, cap. xxix. art. ii. sects. 2 and 5.—*Translator*.]

[104] *Complutum* was the ancient name of Alcalá.—*Translator*.

[105] Llorente, cap. xxix. art. ii. sect. 1. Biblioteca de los Rabinos Españoles, in voce *Abraham Husque* (p. 524, col. 2), and Árias Montano's preface to his Bible.—*Translator*.

that all who, with Jerome, set up the authority of the original Hebrew, were actually Judaizers and sworn enemies of the Church. To such a pitch of perverseness was this opinion carried by unsound divines, that father José Sigüenza, in his excellent life of St. Jerome, fifth book, second discourse, said, *On discovering that persons know two letters of the Hebrew language, they suspect them of Judaism: ignorant must they be, indeed, who entertain such notions as these!* [106]

It was no slight triumph to Árias Montano that the new Polyglott should have been allowed to circulate without notes or comments: and considering the custom and practice of the Inquisition, it might be regarded as a wonderfully strange thing that this tribunal should not have instituted proceedings against the illustrious doctor who edited the work, for the purpose of arresting and imprisoning him, did we not know that large sums had been expended on the Polyglott; that its magnificence and beauty were the admiration of all Europe; and that as it bore the name of the monarch who had ordered it to be published, Philip the Second was obliged, for the sake of his own interest as well as his credit, not to allow of the work being impugned, inasmuch as the like consent on his part must redound to his own shame. He, therefore, took care that the Bible should be submitted to the censorship of father Mariana,[107] who pronounced in favor of Montano, not-

[106] Sigüenza was sentenced to a year's imprisonment by the Inquisition of Toledo. Llorente, cap. xxv. sect. 98.—*Translator.*

[107] Mariana was a long time immured in the prisons of the Inquisition. Llorente, cap. xxv. sect. 64. Bibliotheca Hispana, under word JOHANNES.—*Translator.*

withstanding the pertinacity of his companions the Jesuits, who, owing to the disgust they felt at the freedom with which he spoke as well as wrote against them, wished Mariana to give an adverse decision: proof of this may be seen in the extremely rare documents which I publish as an Appendix to this history, for the purpose of undeceiving such fanatics as disbelieve in the subtle wiles and wickedness of the Jesuits.

Such of the Spanish theologians who had been arrested as did not belong to the noble class, on seeing the miserable state of oppression and ignominy to which their superiors were reduced, believed themselves to be threatened with the same lash, and all of them became dispirited thereat. Owing to the state of alarm they were in, some condemned themselves to the observance of a perpetual silence respecting the Vulgate and the original versions of Scripture, or endeavoured to explain them in a qualified sense—the offspring of fear rather than ingenuousness;[108] whilst others, abandoning the side of truth, went over to the multitude, this being the only means by which they could promise themselves security from molestation. From that time

[108] Father Basilio Ponce, an Augustine friar, in the introduction to his fourth *expository question*, writes thus: "De Sacræ Scripturæ ratione et ejus in varias linguas translationibus multa scribi possunt et scitu digna, et cognitu pernecessaria. De quibus qui recte scribere poterant, aut scribere noluerunt, aut parcius id fecerunt, argumentum invidiosum veriti. Qui vero aut judicio aut necessaria ad judicandum eruditione carebant, scribere ausi sunt. Itaque quædam perperam, plura inconsiderate, pleraque inerudite scripserunt."

the Holy Books were given up to unskilful hands, and in the following ages the theologians of the Peninsular schools became entangled in the meshes of futile and complicated questions,[109] and the oriental languages were banished from their halls. These are the precious fruits which Spain has reaped from her unworthy treatment of such distinguished persons! These are the fruits of which the Catholic Sovereigns sowed the seeds, when they destroyed the Hebrew Bibles and persecuted the learned, solely because they preferred the original versions of the Scriptures to the Vulgate edition of them!

But if by the religious intolerance of the Catholic Sovereigns and their unjust proceedings against the Jews, injury was done to the literature of Spain, no less injury was done to her commerce, and subsequently to the whole of her realms, by the expulsion of that race, and the arrival of Genoese and other foreigners, who established houses of trade and commerce there: these houses were, generally, dependent upon the principal ones in the mercantile cities of Italy and other towns, and their establishment was productive of serious evil.

The whole commerce of Spain fell into the hands of foreigners, and while they grew rich, this country

---

[109] I have seen theological works printed in one or two folio volumes, in which the attempt is made to ascertain from texts of St. Augustine, St. John Chrysostom, and other holy fathers of the Church, whether chocolate is an eatable or a beverage! And without going further, who has not read the *Ente dilucidado*, in which there is a long discussion as to whether hobgoblins possess the sense of touch or not?

became weaker and weaker and declined in a wonderful manner. The Spaniards ceased to be mercers and manufacturers; consequently the immense sums of gold and silver imported from America did not contribute to the restoration of Spain, but only helped to enrich foreign kingdoms.

Much outcry has been raised against the Spanish economists of the sixteenth and seventeenth centuries for petitioning for the abolition of free trade. But they were travelling on the road which led to truth and justice. What more efficacious remedy than the one proposed by them could have been devised for the eradication of the evils endured by a nation, in which not one of the natives either kept a mercer's shop or became a merchant?

In the seventeenth century, no sooner had Philip the Third issued his decree to prevent his subjects from dealing with those of his enemy, the king of England, (reviving that decree which Philip the Second had published at the commencement of the war between him and his rival Elizabeth,) than some learned men, anxious for the prosperity of Spain, began to think of a remedy for the evils from which she was suffering, owing to her want of money as well as population in many of her finest cities.[110] And after divers arguments, they came to the conclusion, that the introduction of foreign agricultural produce and articles of foreign manufacture into these kingdoms had operated more

[110] See Gil Gonzalez Dávila's Vida y hechos de Felipe III., *passim*. —*Translator*.

powerfully than any other cause in producing the greater part of those evils.

Don Matéo de Lison y Biedma, seigneur of Algarinejo, veinticuatro of Granada, and representative in Parliament for that city in the year 1621, among his other speeches and notes committed to the press, published a treatise on the introduction of foreign merchandise into Spain, of which the following is an extract: "The introduction of foreign merchandise into these realms has been attended with much evil to them, for the foreigners carry off the gold and silver coin paid for these articles, grow rich and powerful, while they cause a diminution in your Majesty's revenues, drain the coffers of your subjects, whom they deprive of the means of gaining a subsistence by art and industry, and, in the interim, themselves keep advancing. Now since God has made your Majesty so mighty a lord, and since you have in your lands and seigniories mines, treasures, and all things necessary for the support of human life, as well fruits of the earth as riches acquired by art and science, and have no need to depend upon any foreign kingdom, may it please your Majesty *to order this evil to be remedied by prohibiting, in the most inoffensive manner possible, the admission into these realms of merchandise wrought and manufactured abroad.* Then will the same thing happen as in one ship cut off from communication with another; if the people on board speculate and gamble, the money and the treasures contained in the ship may, indeed, change hands, but must remain in possession of the same community."[111]

Before Lison de Biedma had petitioned Philip the Fourth in the Cortes to prohibit the importation of foreign merchandise, Dr. Sancho Moncada, in his *Restauracion Politica de los Pueblos de España*, attempted to prove that the only remedy for the present state of things was the enforcement of the following regulations, viz.: that none but Spaniards should carry on trade and business in Spain; that raw materials, to be afterwards manufactured abroad, should not be exported from these realms; and that articles of foreign manufacture should not be imported.

Licentiate Pedro Fernandez Navarrete, in his *Discursos Politicos*, likewise expresses himself in similar terms.

Jerónimo de Ceballos, in his *Arte real para el buen gobierno de los reyes y príncipes*, speaks thus: "Wealth and plenty cannot exist, so long as the subjects are in want of employment and none can be found them: this want might be remedied by prohibiting absolutely the importation of foreign cloths and manufactured silks, or by at least insisting that all which shall be imported in future be of standard weight and quality; due respect being had in the working of them to the ordinances of Spain, for it is not fair that the natives of these realms should be fettered with laws and ordinances and be liable to informations and punishments

---

[111] This simile, notwithstanding its singularity, must, I think, be admitted to be a good one.—*Translator*.

for transgressing them, while foreigners are exempted from such restrictions, and actually introduce mere imitations, for which they carry off our money; *a thing which would be endurable, were they to take merchandise of Spanish manufacture in return.*"

Such was the language used by Ceballos, with respect to the trade carried on in Spain by foreigners exclusively. Fray Jerónimo Bolívar, Francisco Martinez de la Mata, Cristóbal Perez de Herrer, Luís de Castilla, Damian de Olivares, Miguel Caja de Leruela and others have expressed themselves on this subject in the same or similar terms.

But though the grounds on which these economists based their arguments appeared strong to persons reduced to poverty, and, consequently, both anxious for a change in their circumstances and eager to discover the means of effecting it, their arguments were not, at the time, considered to be based on reason and truth, but on that undue love of country to which they had been conducted by the crooked path of error.

Let this appear from the opposition some of them made to the restrictions on free trade—restrictions which lasted only during war time, and even then only affected that nation against which the Spanish arms were employed. Let the same thing also appear from the treaties of peace in which it was stipulated that there should be free trade between the subjects of both kingdoms.[112]

---

[112] In the year 1604 a treaty of peace and another of commerce were ratified between Philip the Third of Spain and James the First

The majority of the economists looked to the abolition of foreign trade as the best means of improving the condition of Spain. In that age foreigners were the only, or at any rate the principal, persons who carried on the commerce of this country, and these men put the most exorbitant prices on the merchandise which they introduced from abroad; for, unacquainted as the Spaniards were with the value of the goods just turned out of the factories, they paid whatever price was asked for them.[113]

So completely was Spain given up to the cupidity of foreigners, that in their commercial dealings they made their own will stand for law. The few manufactures then existing in this country were burdened with most grievous taxes: whence we naturally infer that it was owing to these taxes that the cloths manufactured in these realms could not compete in lowness of price with those introduced from foreign countries. Hence it was that purchasers looked for such merchandise as combined excellence of material with cheapness: hence, in a word, the Spanish factories neither yielded a profit to the owners of them, nor helped to

---

of Great Britain. Gil Gonzalez Dávila, Vida y hechos de Felipe III., lib. II. cap. 16. Rapin's History of England, Book XVII.—*Translator*.

[113] "The names of many of the streets—C^e Francos, Genoa, Alemanes, Placentines, &c., are the surest evidence that traffic was chiefly managed by foreigners, and this even in Seville—the heart of the vaunted silk and other manufactures of Spain." Ford's Handbook of Spain, vol. I. p. 242, 2nd column, Murray, 1845. I recollect at Cadiz a Calle de Flamencos *Borrachos* (*Drunken* Flemings' Street). —*Translator*.

improve their incomes: on the contrary, these were vainly and unprofitably squandered away.

Such were the fruits that Spain reaped from the expulsion of the Jews[114] and the arrival and settlement of foreign merchants in the Peninsula. Of what use to us were the riches of the New World, which were no sooner acquired than employed as a bridge of passage into foreign kingdoms? A century after the Genoese houses of commerce were established in Spain, there were neither eyes enough to weep for the calamities introduced by bad government and the recklessness of our kings, nor hands to repair the ruined state of the Peninsula. Of what avail to Spain was the external grandeur of being mistress of so large a portion of the globe, when to support that grandeur she herself became wretchedly poor and miserable, and all her children humbled and disheartened? How many disasters did not the Catholic king's wars in Italy bring upon these unhappy kingdoms? But what could be expected of a monarch who had no regard for the welfare of his subjects, and only looked to the increase of his own power and greatness? The

[114] *The statute of purity*, which was originally enacted for the purpose of eradicating Judaism and Mahometanism, became afterwards the instrument of persecution of Christians owing to false informations, &c., and many of *these were expelled from Spain* also. So sensible had the Spanish nation become of the evils occasioned by this statute that, in the year 1618, Don Gabriel Cimbron presented a petition in the Cortes to Philip the Third, praying for a modification of it. Gil Gonzalez Dávila, Vida y hechos de Felipe III., lib. II. caps. 85, 86. In his history of this reign he shows the deplorable state of weakness o which Spain was then reduced.—*Translator*.

Spaniards, flushed with the victories they had gained during the whole of the sixteenth century, neither heeded the calamities which begun to harass these kingdoms, nor considered who was the sole author of them. In the seventeenth, these had increased to such an alarming extent, that all who were anxious that the Spanish peninsula should not be for ever merged in the lowest abyss of misery, saw the necessity of providing a remedy for them. But now it was all in vain. Literature and commerce were prostrate, nor could Spain make head by force of arms against all the calamities which had commenced showering down upon her,—in fact she had not hands in which to put them, much less vigorous ones to wield them. Thus all those lands and seigniories, in the vain attempt to preserve which so much blood had been spilled, so many lives sacrificed, and such large sums of money expended, (sums sufficient to enrich a nation and make it powerful,) were miserably lost![115]

Another evil which Ferdinand's policy bought upon Spain was the war with the Moriscos, who, no longer able to endure the oppression and misery to which they had been reduced, were continually rebelling. This

[115] Don Francisco Quevedo thus expresses himself in one of his sonnets:

"If in a league all did combine
To take from thee, O Spain,
The lands which now thou callest thine,
They'd with more ease regain
Those very lands (which are their own),
Than thou by boldest fight
Would'st hold what only thine is shown
By conquest's hateful right."

king, in order to get possession of Granada, granted the Moors the conditions they demanded prior to its surrender. The principal of these were:

"That their Highnesses and successors for ever should allow Abí Abdelihí, his alcaides, cadis, mestis, alguazils, captains, good men, and all his people, both great and small, to live according to their law, and should neither suffer them to be deprived of their mosques, towers, or almuedans, nor allow the income and rents derived therefrom to be touched, nor interfere with their present manners and customs.

"That no Moor or Mooress should be compelled to embrace Christianity against his or her will: that no maid, married woman, or widow, who from motives of love might wish to turn Christian, should be allowed to do so, until she had been examined.

"*That no person should be allowed to ill-treat by deed or word the Christian men or women who, before these capitulations, had become Moors; and that if any Moor should have a renegade wife, she should not be compelled to turn Christian against her will, but should be interrogated in presence of Christians and Moors; and the same thing should be understood to apply to the children, both male and female, born of a Christian woman and a Moor.*"

In conclusion, the words with which the king and queen bound themselves to observe the capitulations to the letter are these:

"We promise and swear to you on our royal faith and word, that each of you may go out to cultivate your estates, and pass wherever you choose in these our kingdoms, to seek a livelihood wherever it can be found; and we will command that you be left in the same enjoyment of your laws and customs and of your mosques, that ye now are."[116]

But instead of ratifying these promises, Ferdinand the Catholic broke his royal word, which, as a Christian prince and a gentleman, he was bound to observe. It was one of the first objects of the clergy to try and bring home the truth of the Catholic faith to the Moors through the medium of preaching.[117] But as their preaching was not attended with the rapid success that was looked for, Cardinal Cisneros resorted to the arbitrary measure of inquiring who were renegade Moors or children of renegades, for the purpose of employing compulsory means to make them embrace Christianity. And here it must be observed that this step was taken in direct violation of that article in the capitulations which said, *" That no person should be allowed to illtreat by deed or word the Christian men or women who, before these capitulations, had become Moors; and that if any Moor should have a renegade wife, she should not be compelled to turn Christian against her will, but should be interrogated in presence of Christians and Moors; and the same thing should be understood to apply to the children, both male and female, born of a Christian woman and a Moor."*

[116] Luís Mármol de Carvajal. *Historia de la Rebelion del reyno de Granada*, lib. 1°, cap. xix. [fols. 22, 23, 24.—*Translator.*]
[117] Ferreras, Synopsis Histórica, año 1499, sects. 9, 10.—*Translator.*

Thus did Ferdinand know how to fulfil his word: thus did he show his respect for the Gospel! What might not the Moors say about his observance of treaties and the credit of his oaths? The conquerors of Spain allowed the Christians who chose to remain and dwell among them (whence they were called Mozárabes) to live in the exercise of their religion and to have their temples. But the Christians, not considering that the breach of their sworn promises could be attended with no other result than the discredit of evangelical doctrine, accepted in the articles of peace the condition which allowed the Mahometans to continue in the free enjoyment of their religion without oppression or molestation, and then deprived them of their temples, and forcibly compelled them to embrace Christianity. If Mahomet be reproachfully, though falsely,[118] charged with preaching his doctrines with the Koran in one hand and the sword in the other, what might not be said of the Christians by men whom they subjected to punishments, and on whom they forced another creed?[119] The Catholic Sovereigns, by their mode of

[118] Though I think it may be questioned whether Mahomet *literally* preached his doctrines with the Koran in one hand and the sword in the other, there can be no doubt that he was a cruel persecutor.—*Translator.*

[119] Casiodoro de Reina, translator of the Bible into the Castilian tongue (Ferrara, 1555), says, "In order that the newly-converted Moors might be well instructed in the Christian religion, Friar Jerome, first Bishop of Granada, was of opinion that the Holy Scriptures should be translated into Arabic. This pious intent was opposed by Fray Ximenez de Cisneros, who gave reasons, not taken from the word of God nor from the words or deeds' of the holy Doctors, but from mere human judgment, and consequently repugnant to that word:

procedure against the Jews and Moors, acted neither more nor less than in direct opposition to the dictates of reason and justice; thereby kindling hatred to the Christian faith in the greater part of the world, and opening the door to the destruction of the study of oriental literature, to the injury of all science[120] (as appeared in course of time in the seventeenth century), and depriving us of Spanish merchants, in order to supply us with Genoese, whose cupidity only served to swallow up all the gold of our country, as well as that which came to us from the Indies: and, finally, owing to their excessive oppressions, they bequeathed a civil war to Spain, and, by their expulsion of the Jews and Moors who refused to embrace Christianity, depopulated the kingdom.

thus was the translation, which would have conferred so much benefit upon those poor ignorant Moriscos, put a stop to."

[120] The greater part of those men of eminence in Canon Law, Theology, and the liberal sciences, whom Spain produced in the sixteenth century, pursued their principal studies at foreign Universities: among these persons may be numbered Melchor Cano, Don Pedro Guerrero, Don Martin Perez de Ayala, Andrés Laguna, &c.

SUMMARY OF BOOK THE FOURTH.

CHEQUERED fortunes of the Jews in Portugal.—They begin to be oppressed there.—The new Christians of Portugal pardoned for their crimes of heresy and apostasy.—Jewish writers.—The Holy Office unable to eradicate Judaism from Spain.—Persons of note burnt to death for Judaizing.—Notice of some autos-de-fé against the Jews (or Judaizers) up to the year 1800.—Abolition of the tribunal.—Cessation of Judaism in Spain.

BOOK THE FOURTH.

THE Jews, after their admission into Portugal, were no less unfortunate than the other exiles from Spain. In the year 1493, when king John the Second conferred the seigniory of St. Thomas's isle upon Don Álvaro de Caminha, he obliged the latter to people it, and, for this purpose, ordered that all the Jews should have their sons and daughters of tender age taken away from them, and that after the baptism of the latter, these should be handed over (as was done) to Don Álvaro for the purpose of peopling the said isle of St. Thomas.[1]

Orders were also issued by king Emanuel, in 1496, that all the Hebrews who dwelt in Portugal should quit that kingdom, save children under fourteen years

---

[1] Osorius. *De rebus gestis Emanuelis regis Portugalliæ*, lib. prim. Monteiro. *Historia da Santa Inquisiçaõ*, parte 1ª, liv. seg°, cap. 2. —*Translator.*

of age, who were to be left behind. The more wealthy Jews represented to the king that they would embrace Christianity without further opposition, provided he would do them the favour not to institute any inquiries against them for the space of twenty years; and so, on the 30th of March 1497, king Emanuel accorded to them the privilege which they so earnestly solicited. On this many were baptized, and those who did not choose to become acquainted with the truths of the Christian faith, went to Africa and elsewhere.[2]

But this determination on the part of the Jews did not put an end to their misfortunes. In the month of April 1506, the people of Lisbon rose up against them, at the instigation of two Dominican friars, who exhibited an image of Christ crucified which emitted a very vivid light. A converted Jew observed that this miracle was nothing else than the reflection of the sun's rays upon a curtain, and as the news of this discovery began to spread all over the city, the friars, alarmed at the prospect of losing the alms and other offerings brought into their convent by the devotion of the people, in consequence of the virtue of that portentous image, stirred them up against the Hebrews. Numbers of this race were slain by the barbarous and superstitious rabble; but as king Emanuel was much displeased at this tumult, he had several

[2] Ferreras, Synopsis Histórica de España, año 1496, sect. 18. Osorius, lib. prim. Monteiro, parte 1ª liv seg°, cap. 43. This author accuses another writer of having *calumniously* stated that Emanuel and his son John granted the Jews *the privilege of exemption from examination as to matters of faith.—Translator.*

of the authors and ringleaders apprehended, and ordered severe examples to be made of them. The two Dominican scoundrels who were the promoters of the sedition, were strangled; and in order to punish the knavery of those men who, to make a gainful traffic in divine things, dared to deceive superstitious persons in so shameless a manner, the Dominican convent at Lisbon was suppressed. The same king, in 1507, renewed the privilege given to the baptized Jews, and it was afterwards confirmed by John the Third. And when the attempt to establish the Holy Office in Portugal was made, Pope Clement the Seventh was informed of all these exemptions.[3]

It is said that a letter was then written by some Jews who were settled in Rome and other cities of Italy to their brethren in the Lusitanian kingdom, recommending the latter to flee therefrom, and go with their families to the abovementioned land: this letter is given by several authors, among others Torrejoncillo, in his *Centinela contra Judios*.

[3] Ferreras, año 1506, sects 33, 34. Osorius, lib. prim. Monteiro, parte 1ª, liv. segº, caps. 43, 44. This writer says that the convent was suppressed for a few months only, namely from the 28th of May till the 24th of October, when it was restored by Pope Julius the Second. According to him, the tumult mentioned in the text was attended with most fearful consequences to the Jewish converts, of whom 1930 (women included) were slain at Lisbon and in its neighbourhood, and afterwards burnt in the Rocio (a large square) and in the Strand. His account of this tumult is thus given: "Andava o povo taó amotinado, que com furia diabolica, (segundo dizem algumas memorias) mataraõ no espaço de tres dias, em Lisboa e seu termo 1930 pessoas, assim de homens como de mulheres dos novamente convertidos. Os que matavaó em Lisboa, os queimavaó logo no Rocio e na Ribeira."

"Your Honors[4] must surely be aware that the holy Father and Cardinals gave permission in the Ecclesiastical Court for an inquiry to be made in Portugal respecting the privileges granted by the kings of that realm, and determined that, if agreeable to the state, order might be given to the Bishops to take upon themselves the guardianship of the civil law; than which nothing can be more reasonable or expedient: that prisoners should not receive pardon from the state, but that referees should decide their causes before the Bishops, in whose presence they might allege the illegality of the arrest of prisoners who had not relapsed, and might set forth the inconvenience resulting from the existence of so large a number of persons supported by begging, to whom the Bishops were objects of suspicion; first, because from being Bishops, those men come to be Inquisitors, and secondly, because as ministers of the king, they are obliged to have an eye to his honor, and so condemn the prisoners, whose number favors the escape of some and makes the state hesitate to pardon others. The ambassadors of the King and the Emperor have, in concert with the holy Father and Cardinals, adopted a method which will serve as a key to our previous statements: they made a short cut and ordered that, for the future, general expediency should be disregarded; whence to one

---

[4] In the original, *Vuessas Mercedes:* in the English versions of Don Quixote this expression is generally rendered Your *Worships,* but the translation of them that I have given is that which I believe to be the nearest approach to their real meaning.—*Translator.*

who looks beyond mere temporal things, it appears like inspiration to see that pardon is accorded to condemned persons, whether under arrest or at large, whether absent or present; that they are let go freely, unconditionally, and unpunished, and allowed to depart in peace whithersoever they will: that from the day of their release and the verification of their pardon till the expiration of six months, no inquiry into their offences may be instituted: that all persons in Portugal who wish to quit the realm may freely do so, without being arrested openly or secretly, and pass through bordering lands and countries with the safe conducts which will be given them; and when the six months are expired, as rigorous an inquisition into their lives is conceded as that which is now in force in Castile."

"Your Honors may know and believe that Dr. Pedro Hurtado and his companion rendered much service to this cause, for which they deserve to be rewarded of God and of those who are His. The holy Father, like an upright man, seeing what were the wishes of the king's and emperor's ambassadors, granted a bull for Portugal as he had done for Castile, which, in compliance with the promises he had made to the Cardinals, and on account of his desire to get rid of the obligation he was under to them, and to have the business off his hands, was a severe one; whereby it seemed to be entirely of God that these six months were granted by the king of Portugal to the Jews, in order to enable them to quit that realm freely, for which purpose they have a safe conduct provided them.

We are well aware that men have reason to regret being separated from their native country, their wives, and their children. But they, and even those that have children, must expose themselves to every thing in exchange for their redemption from captivity, for there are many self-evident reasons why not a single individual of our nation should remain in Portugal, and refuse to come hither. The first of these reasons is, that God remembers us and sets us at liberty, as He did those who were in Egypt. The second (which ought to be remembered) is, that however innocent soever they be, they are liable to be put to death at Lisbon. The third is, that the king and ambassadors have determined to establish as rigorous an inquisition over them as that which is in force in Castile. The fourth is, their great rejoicings at the time of the execution of the acts of faith, insomuch so that when they burn persons they have banquets, show themselves at the windows, and erect platforms as they would do on occasions of great festivals and bull-fights. The fifth is, that all persons of the envied race are so much disliked by the people; of which a practical proof was exhibited in the unfavourable reports made of them in the Cortes. The sixth is, that when they arrest a man, they deprive him of his estate, as is the custom in Castile, and allow him but two maravedis a day for his support. The seventh is, that, notwithstanding men's innocence of the crimes imputed to them; in order to escape punishment, they confess their guilt and sue for mercy: whereby they forfeit the possession of their children and estates, and go begging from door to door for the love of God,[5] and if the persons of whom they beg be householders they demand of them their estates, for they find their own to be legally forfeited, as happened in Castile not long since, when judgment was given against one *Labaredas*. Let your Honors consider these and other things, of which it is needless to remind you: and since God is pleased, of His mercy, to remember this people, it becomes you not to show yourselves ungrateful for it, but to escape from so many discomforts, and to be thankful for such goodness as this which He showeth you in providing you with a port to escape from the power of your enemies: those who are allowed the privilege of quitting that kingdom and come with their wives, will do well to escape from their present oppression, and have reason to regret not having done so before. Now since you have the opportunity, have the sense to avail yourselves of it and come; for this country is rich, fertile, and extensive—a country in which you may live and enjoy yourselves. It is expedient that the poor should come in company with the rich and assist them in the management of their estates; for when the people went forth out of Egypt, both rich and poor escaped from the land. Blessed may he be considered that lendeth a helping hand and thereby diminisheth the severe fatigue of his relatives! Let not the poor suppose that, owing to their poverty, they shall be in want of any thing, for all who

---

[5] A trade very extensively carried on in the present day by the *Christians* of Spain.—*Translator*.

have hitherto come here, have soon after their arrival been richly supplied with all the necessaries of life, and filled with joy at having escaped, through God's hand, from their subjection and captivity.

"Now, ye gentlemen of the envied race, who dwell yonder, we should be glad to know what entailed estates ye have, which can make it worth your while to abide so many hazards. We tell you that though ye lead the life of St. Augustine, this will be of no avail to you, except with God; for should ye be accused before the people, ye will assuredly be punished, your properties will be sold, your children will be degraded, and in order to punish you, the evidence of two witnesses will never be wanting; nay, to obtain their freedom, your slaves will state things to have happened that never did happen. Since this is so evident, ye ought to rouse yourselves from your lethargy, to be watchful and to follow my counsel; for if ye do not, ye will deserve severe punishments, without being able to allege either reason or ignorance when called to account, which God forbid; for God preserveth man in three ages, and even the last of these is good, and all of them are good. Wherefore, gentlemen, ye should all of you in general and each of you in particular take this into consideration, and should exert yourselves to comfort one another in your journey to this land of Italy; for now is the time that the men are known who will liberate themselves from their present troubles (for ye are aware that ye have a sharp sword suspended over your heads by a single thread), and not when each man's offences are brought forward (which God neither order nor permit!). Many of the envied race have immoveable property in Portugal, which it will be painful to them to abandon and forfeit; others who must necessarily have goods scattered about in different places will not be able to collect them together; all these must do the best they can to emancipate themselves from such terrible misfortunes; for they who had immoveable property in Castile were punished as well as those who had much property lent out; and as things present must be judged of by things past, let all whom it may concern look to their own affairs and beware of trusting to bulls of protection, for in such times as these, those bulls will avail them nothing, for I well recollect a man being hanged at Lisbon with the privileges suspended from his neck; I remember also that as Count Benavente was killing a man who had the king's own royal security or privilege, he said to Ferdinand: 'I would sooner have taken from him some good cuirasses.' Wherefore let all beware of God's wrath, when they begin to do execution (which God forbid!), and no blame ought to be imputed to them for procuring the establishment of an inquisition in their country like to that in Castile; for the king's heart is in the hands of God, who is served in all that he doeth.

"Let the persons who come bring with them all things needful for their support, and they had better bring all that they do not immediately require in bills of exchange on Lyons, Venice and other towns in Italy. Let the bills be drawn on two persons in whom ye can place the greatest confidence, and let it be expressed in them that each of the two persons is bound for the whole amount of the bills drawn upon him, and that the payment of so many golden crusados or escudos is to be made in gold; for should it be merely stated that the payment of so many crusados is to be made, this expression will imply payment in coins worth only 336 maravedis apiece; whereas the crusados and escudos go for 320, and the golden crusado is worth 368 maravedis. I say that some well-disposed men should come over land to France, Lyons, and Gerona, for the security of the bills they may bring; and let those who bring merchandise come to Flanders, France, and Genoa; and should they go in that direction, the Arragonese[6] ships are fine vessels and have good crews. Persons who go by La Pulla expose themselves to danger, and the safest way is through France, Antwerp, Genoa, and Civita-Vecchia, near Rome; further information can be obtained there. Blessed be He that ordereth the times and maketh the firmament above; and cursed be every one of my nation who shall not listen to my counsel and act upon it; and if he refuse to leave that kingdom for a place of safety, upon him and all who are disobedient, as well as upon their wives and children, and upon all the people of this nation, may the following curses fall, and fall so heavily that when they die they cannot be buried in a double tomb. Cursed be the hour of your birth. May every hour

---

[6] No part of the present *province* of Arragon extends to the sea, but the ancient *kingdom* of that name included Valencia.—*Translator.*

of your lives be sad and defiled with the red blood of the calf which your fathers worshipped. May ye experience dreadful grief of your own creation and unmixed sorrow; may the scab be upon you, upon all your race, and upon your children. May every thing in the world run counter to your prosperity. God smite you with the plague wherewith He slew those who left the swine's flesh in Egypt. Such calamity enter into your gates, that ye and your families may rise in the morning crippled like the sister of Moses. May ye be stoned like those who were discovered gathering wood on the sabbath-day. May fire break out in your houses and burn you, as it broke out in the tent of Korah and burnt him and his company. May ye and all your descendants be ashamed and go down to hell together, like Dathan and Abiron. The curse of mount Gilboa be upon you and all your posterity. May ye be burnt like those who would have stoned Moses and Aaron. May ye fall into the hands of justice, as did the Israelites. May serpents breed in your houses to bite you as they bit those whom God punished for murmuring against Him. May every house ye inhabit be accursed and excommunicate, and may stones fall upon you as ye enter them, as the walls of Jericho fell. May ye be robbed in the court of the Palace or in the house of India. Such misfortune befal you and your wives in the end of your dark days as befel the wife of the Levite in the city of Gibeon. May the hand of the Lord be uplifted against you to smite you in the extremities of your bodies, and may ye rot like the men of the cities of Gazor. Accursed and excommunicate be all your race and all your children, and may your bodies be cast to the dogs, like that of the prophet in Selva. May evil come upon you, and may your heart be broken for some treasonable crime in which ye shall be detected, and may ye be hanged like Ahitophel, David's brother-in-law. May your toes be cut off, as were those of the men of the tribe of Judah. Cursed be ye, and may ye be slain by wild animals and savage beasts, as the captive youths whom Elisha cursed were slain by bears. May ye be sold in the lands of the Moors, as the Jews were sold in Egypt by Ptolemy. May ye be carried piecemeal out of your houses, as king Antiochus was by the priests of the temple. May ye be constrained to eat swine's flesh. May ye and your children be hanged by the neck, as the Jews were in the city of David, by command of Anteus. May ye be ignominiously hanged by the Queen's command, as Haman was by command of Esther, in accordance with the dream that he dreamed. May all I have said come upon you, if ye refuse to depart from that kingdom: accursed be ye all, as I say, while my house and those who live in it continue in freedom and peace, and in security from all mishaps, while we enjoy our good acquisitions in these extensive lands, which are lands of promise here, and which ye refuse to enjoy, and do not deserve to see."

The new Christians of Portugal did not much appreciate the counsel given them in this letter, for they continued to live in that kingdom: which shows that they were not so much persecuted there as was imagined: only they could not patiently endure that in cases of inquisition, the property of criminals should be confiscated; and in order to repair the mischief resulting therefrom, in the year 1577 they made a composition with king Sebastian, paying him two hundred and twenty-five thousand ducats, in consideration of which, they obtained security from him that for ten years they should not be molested in their possessions.[7] This point being settled, many of the Jews still living in seclusion in Spain, who had miraculously escaped from the clutches of the Inquisition, went into Portugal, where they increased to a great extent. Others, unwilling to forsake their country, remained in Spain. Of both these Jewish clans, the number who cultivated the study of literature was great.

In the solemn *auto de fé* celebrated at Seville on the 14th[8] of April, 1660, eighty persons (men and women included) were punished for judaizing. Many effigies, representing criminals in exile in foreign lands (which, fortunately, the barbarous scourge of the Inquisition did not reach), were reduced to ashes. One of these exiles was Captain Enrique Enriquez de Paz, better known by the name of Antonio Henriquez

---

[7] Gil Gonzalez Dávila, *Vida y hechos del rey Felipe III.* lib. II., cap. 16.—*Translator.*

[8] Llorente says *the thirteenth;* cap. xlviii., año 1660: in the 26th chapter, speaking of this *auto de fé,* he only mentions two or three persons who were punished.—*Translator.*

Gomez, a resident at Seville, knight of the order of San Miguel, and son of another Portugese judaizer, named Diego Henriquez Villanueva.

It is reported of this man that, once when he was at Amsterdam, he chanced to meet a Spanish friend of his lately arrived in that country, and on the latter saying to him, *Oh! señor Enriquez, I saw your effigy burnt at Seville!* he immediately burst out laughing and answered, *I do not care a fig for that.*[9]

Antonio Enriquez Gomez wrote some works in prose and verse,[10] of which the best known is *El siglo Pitagórico y vida de Don Gregorio de Guadaña:* this book is written with extreme grace and elegance, though in very flowery language. He also composed several comedies of mediocre merit, among which may be reckoned, *La prudente Abigail, A lo que obliga el honor, Amor con vista y cordura, Contra el amor no hay engaños,* &c.

[*The author proceeds to give an account of several Jewish poets, with specimens of whose poetry he fills ten or twelve pages, which I shall not inflict upon the reader.—Translator.*]

[9] The expression in the original is *allá me las den todas:* literally translated, it will not make sense, but I have given its meaning according to the Dictionary of the Royal Spanish Academy.—*Translator.*

[10] *La culpa del primer peregrino,* Roham, 1644, Madrid, 1735, a poetical work. *Luís dado de Dios á Luís y Anna, y Samuel dado de Dios á Elcana y Anna,* Paris, 1645, in prose. *Política angélica,** Roham, 1647, in prose. *La torre de Babilonia,** Roham, 1649, Madrid, 1670, in prose. *Academias morales de las Musas,** Madrid, 1660, Barcelona, 1704, a poetical work. [* These three works are not mentioned in Don José Rodriguez de Castro's Bibl. de los Rab. Esp.—*Translator.*]

Great is the number of Spanish Jews who wrote works on jurisprudence, philosophy, morality, mathematics, and medicine, besides translations of the Old Testament, and Commentaries upon it.

Among the eminent physicians of the Jewish persuasion there was a noted one in the sixteenth century, named Juan Rodrigo, a native of Castelo Branco, who from fear of the Inquisition fled to a free country, where he published several works; some of them under the name of Amato Lusitano, others under that of Juan Rodriguez de Castel Blanco. The aim of his writings was to give instructions for the preservation or restoration of human health.[11]

Just at this time lived Cristóval Acosta,[12] a native of Africa, whose parents were Jews expelled from Spain: this man, after many years' pilgrimage in Asia, came to the Peninsula, professed Christianity, and settled in the city of Burgos, where he published a work entituled, *Tratado de las drogas y medicinas de las Indias orientales con sus plantas dibujadas al vivo por Cristóval Acosta, médico y cirujano que las vió ocularmente. Un tomo en 4to.* 1578. (Treatise on the drugs and medicines of the East Indies, with the plants that produce them, drawn to the life, by Cristóval Acosta, physician and

---

[11] "Amati Lusitani primum exegemata, cum nomine Roderici de Castillo Albo, in duos priores libros Dioscoridis, Antuerpiæ prodierunt anno 1536." Albert Haller, *Bibliotheca Botanica*, lib. I., cap. 36. José Rodriguez de Castro, in his Bib. de los Rab. Esp. says he died at Thessalonica.—*Translator*.

[12] This famous physician and surgeon is not mentioned by Don José Rodriguez de Castro, in his Biblioteca de los Rabines Españoles.

surgeon, who saw them with his own eyes. One volume 4to. 1578).

The first person who wrote the medicinal history of the East Indies was the Portuguese doctor, García de Orta: this work he committed to the press at Goa, and gave it the following title: *Coloquios dos simples, drogas, é cousas medicinais da India.* (Colloquies on the simples, drugs, and medicinal things of India).[13]

Though this work possesses considerable merit, not merely from being the first of its kind, but also because it proceeds from the pen of so learned a man as García de Orta, it is disfigured by many serious errors. Let us hear what Gaspar Acosta says of these *Colloquies*, in the preface to his treatise on the drugs and medicines of the East Indies.

"As this work of his treats of divers medicines, plants, and other things pertaining to human health, so does it introduce much useless and irrelevant matter; for in this treatise he was obliged to adopt the form of dialogues, in which the speakers are wont to amuse themselves and wander from the main subject, and at

[13] Aníbal Briganti translated these *Coloquios* into Italian, and had them printed at Venice in 1582. Carolus Clusius put them into Latin for the use of the Germans, and Antoine Collin into French for the benefit of his countrymen. Other foreign writers have made long and excellent commentaries on this work. Albert Haller, speaking of the author of it in the first volume of his *Bibliotheca Botanica* [lib.v., cap. 314], says, *Garcias ab Orta primus glaciem fregit ipsamque naturam vidit.* [Clusius's work bears this title: *Aromatum et simplicium medicamentorum apud Indos nascentium historia, primum quidem Lusitanica lingua διαλογικῶς conscripta à D. Garçia ab Horto.* —*Translator.*]

every step we meet with numerous errors: the good fame and credit of the author will not allow us to attribute these to him, but to the carelessness of the printers at Goa, where he wrote and where printers are not so expert as in these parts: still these errors do not fail to annoy and disgust the reader. This work had another serious defect, viz. the omission of the paintings and drawings of the plants; this was owing to Dr. Orta having been occupied with graver matters which were of more importance to him. Thinking that this book might be of great use to our nation, were the good things contained in it pointed out and demonstrated by illustrations and figures for the better understanding of them; persuaded too that this could only be done by an experienced eyewitness of the plants; and zealous for the good of my country, and moved thereto by the love which I owe to my neighbours; I determined on executing this task, and on making exact drawings of each plant, taken from its original root, as well as of many other things which I have seen."[14]

So then if García de Orta be deserving of great credit for having been the first to make known in his vulgar tongue the medicinal history of the vast territory of the East Indies, Gaspar de Acosta deserves no less credit for having added thereto and corrected it, as well as for having represented in small drawings

---

[14] Carolus Clusius's book is illustrated with beautiful engravings, which Nicolás Antonio says were not copied from Acosta's work. " Clusius stirpium iconismos à Costa editos, *ut ineptos, prorsusque dissimiles, rejecit,*" Bibliotheca Hispana.—*Translator.*

the greater part of the plants, of which, in the course of his treatise, he demonstrated those virtues, excellent qualities, and properties, which render them beneficial to human health.

Licentiate Juan de Costa, Professor in the University of Salamanca, was in the habit of saying, that after a careful comparison of both books, he came to know *that Orta only drew the outlines, and that Acosta filled in the vivid colours, for what the former had begun the latter completed.*"

The same licentiate, a friend of the author, likewise observes that this work " was not, like any other, prepared in the quiet of his native country, but during a sad and bitter captivity, which Acosta had to endure in Africa, Asia, and China. One may well conceive the pains it cost him while there, to make trials and experiments upon all the plants and drugs about which he has written."[15]

He not only made his own observations, and consulted all the Greek, Latin, and Arabic authors who have treated on the subject, but in his wanderings through the Indies communicated upon it with the best and most distinguished Arab, Persian, Turkish, Brahminical, Chinese, and Malay physicians, not to

---

[15] Nicolás Antonio speaks thus of Acosta: "Christophorus Da Costa.... Africana et Asiatica longi temporis peregrinatione, multisque experimentis, etiam inter barbaras illius orbis gentes in captivitate, et ærumnis manens, medicam artem et botanicam, quibus sese addixerat, egregiè promovit scribens (mutuatus tamen magnam partem à Garcia de Orta, quod nec ipse dissimulat)." Bib[a]. Hisp., under word CHRISTOPHORUS,—*Translator.*

mention those of other countries who lived in that age.[16]

Thus was he enabled to write his work with so much effect, and to call it *a true representation and likeness of many medicinal plants unknown and unseen by any ancient writers who have handled this subject.*

When Acosta committed this treatise to the press, he was engaged in the composition of a longer and more elaborate one, which was to give a full description of the principal herbs, plants, fruits, birds, and animals, terrestrial as well as aquatic, that are found in the East Indies, of which, up to that time, drawings had not been taken, and of which, till then, very little had been written by physicians and philosophers. But, to the extreme regret of the literati, either Acosta was overtaken by death ere he completed his task, or if he did accomplish it, his work has not yet come to light.[17]

Cristóval Acosta's book was afterwards translated into Italian[18] with this title: *Notice of the Drugs of India*, and published at Venice in 1585. It was likewise translated into French by Antoine Collin.

[16] "Horti Malabarici 800 Tabulæ supra mille stirpium figuras continent, et Coromandeliæ medicis multo majorem in re herbaria diligentiam inesse demonstrant, quam vel in Græcis fuerit, vel demum ante Clusium et Gesnerum in Europæis." Albert Haller's *Bibliotheca Botanica*, lib. I. cap. 1.—*Translator.*

[17] See Nicolás Antonio's Bib. Hisp., under word CHRISTOPHORUS. —*Translator.*

[18] By Francisco Zeletti: its Italian title is *Trattato Di Christophoro Acosta, Africano, Medico et Chirurgo.* I have not seen Antoine Collin's work.—*Translator.*

THE JEWS IN SPAIN.

The Spanish Jews not only practised medicine with so much benefit to the human race, but devoted themselves to the study of history as well. One of these was Pedro Teixeira,[19] who published a book with this title: *Pedro Teixeira: De el origen, descendencia y sucesion de los reyes de Persia y Harmuz, y de un viage hecho por el mismo autor dende la India hasta Italia por tierra.* Amberes 1610. (Pedro Teixera's account of the origin, descent, and succession of the kings of Persia and Harmuz, and of an overland journey from Italy to India, taken by the same author. Antwerp, 1610).[20]

The best historical account of Persia that has been written will be found in this work: it is based on Persian manuscripts, and particularly the Chronicler Tarik[21] Mirkond's narrative. Teixeira was, perhaps, the only author who introduced foreign names into

[19] The author is mistaken: in the Preface to his History (p. iii.) Teixeira says that he wrote the first book of it in Portuguese, which was his mother-tongue (*mi lengua materna Portugueza*), but was recommended by his friends to publish it in Spanish, and that, following the advice given him, *he translated it into that language*, in which he also wrote the second book of his history.—*Translator*.

[20] When Don José Rodriguez de Castro formed his *Biblioteca de los Rabinos Españoles*, he had not Teixera's work before him, for he gives no further account of him than this: "*Pedro Teireira:* he is thus cited by Barrios, in the 58th page of his *Relacion de los pöetas Españoles*—*Pedro Teireira translated the history of the kings of Persia from Persian into Spanish:* he wrote an account of his journey from India to Italy, and died at Verona." [In Spanish handwriting, the letters *r* and *x* are very much alike.—*Translator*.]

[21] This word should have been omitted: Teixeira says in his Preface (p. iv.) that *Tarik* means *a chronicle*, and that Tarik Mirkond signifies Mirkond's Chronicle.—*Translator*.

the Castilian language just as they were written and pronounced [in their own]; a thing which other Spanish historians have not done. His reasons for doing so are the following: "Proper names, whether of men or places or of anything else, may strike you as being harsh and difficult to be pronounced: I might easily have accommodated them to our vernacular tongue, but preferred putting them in their own characters because of the confusion which is usually produced by altering them; for if writers or translators of histories had always adopted the plan of describing persons and countries as described in their own language, and had not altered their orthography, we should have much less difficulty than we now experience in understanding who those persons were, and what those countries are."[22]

But bidding adieu to my notices of eminent Jewish writers, it is time to enter upon the examination of a question which has not yet been treated of by any of those who have employed their pens to narrate the acts of the Holy Office. The Inquisition was established[23] for the purpose of eradicating Judaism; but Judaism maintained its ground till the Inquisition was abolished. This assertion, which has not yet been made by any author, may require to be confirmed by strong proof: this I am about to produce for the purpose of undeceiving many who still believe they see in this barbarous tribunal the bulwark of the Catholic faith, whereas in reality it has been a mere fortress

---

[22] Fourth page of his Preface.—*Translator*.
[23] Nominally.—*Translator*.

(alcázar) of fanaticism—an upholder of error, instead of a strong arm to repress it. After the Inquisition had been established at Seville forty years, the number of persons burnt in that Archbishopric alone exceeded four thousand, and in Andalusia alone the number of persons reconciled[24] and expatriated was above a hundred thousand.[25] At this time more than five thousand houses were shut up: their occupants (either destroyed by fire, or compelled by forfeiture of property to depart, or else driven by fear into foreign lands,) were exterminated by the fury of the Holy Office. To these destructive acts perpetrated by the tribunal at Seville, let those be added which were done by the other tribunals of Spain. In the year 1501, at a single act (auto) sixty-seven women were reduced to ashes at Toledo for judaizing.

It is not my intention to give a detailed narrative of the autos-de-fé directed against the Jews by the Pharisaical Inquisition in the sixteenth, seventeenth, and eighteenth centuries, for besides the difficulty of such an undertaking, I should weary the reader; I shall therefore content myself with relating those autos at which certain persons of note went forth to meet their fate, or certain individuals, in defiance of the tribunal's wrath, persisted unto death in adhering to their law.

[24] Reconciliation: ."Absolution from censures incurred by a heretic who confesses and repents." Llorente's Glossary of terms peculiar to the Holy Office.—*Translator.*

[25] Bernaldez, cap. 44. Páramo, De Sanct. Inquis. lib. II. [tit. ii., cap. 3.—*Translator.*]

In the report of the auto-de-fé celebrated at Mexico in the year 1549, we read the following statement respecting the execution of several judaizing criminals: "Thirteen victims in person were relaxed[26] and cast into the burning-place; all of whom, through mercy, were strangled before they were burnt, except Tomás Trebiño de Sobremonte, in consequence of his insolent rebellion and the diabolical fury with which (even though he began to feel in his beard, before he was placed on the scaffold, the fire that awaited him,) he burst forth into execrable blasphemies,[27] and drew the blazing faggots towards him with his feet. In the same fire they also consumed the bones of seventy persons together with their effigies, besides those corresponding to ten fugitives."[27]

Licentiate Juan Paez de Valenzuela, author of the account of the general auto-de-fé celebrated in the city of Córdova in the year 1625, speaks in the following terms of Manuel Lopez, one of the relaxed: "Though all possible means and all particular pains were taken to bring him to the knowledge of the truth, they were ineffectual. On asking him whether he had resolved at last to renounce his obstinacy, he answered that he was travelling on the road of truth, that all other roads

[26] In the Holy Office lingo, persons condemned by the Inquisitors and then handed over to the secular arm in order to be burnt, were *relaxed.—Translator.*]

[27] If a man died while his trial was pending in the court of the Inquisition, and after his death he were condemned by that tribunal, his body was exhumed and burnt, as well as his effigy: when a fugitive was condemned, he was merely burnt in effigy.—*Translator.*

were wrong, and that he sought the salvation of his soul, which was secured to him by that law of his. After he had been admitted to frequent audiences before the Council, which was composed of numerous lawyers and learned qualifiers[28] of this Holy Office, who endeavoured to remove his errors and bring him to acknowledge the truth, he all along persevered in his stubborn obstinacy, and asserted that the law which he obeyed was the law of truth which ought to be observed. Continuing in his obstinacy and obduracy, he was sentenced to relaxation and handed over to the arm of the Royal Justice to be burnt alive. It was about nine o'clock at night, when the Royal Justice had got ready the executioner, alguazils, ministers, criers, and beasts, on which they mounted the relaxed and led them out of the city to a spot appointed for the burning-place, called *El Marrubial;* this is a level plain, on which was erected a marble gallows, near which were five boards, with a ring attached to one of them, and a great heap of faggots ready. On their arrival at the place, they applied the garrote[29] to the three women and the aforesaid Antonio Lopez; and as soon as the strangling of these persons was accomplished, they piled up the faggots, to which they set fire and cast into the flames one by one the

[28] "Theologians appointed by the tribunal of the Inquisition to examine books and propositions." Dictionary of the Royal Spanish Academy.—*Translator.*

[29] "An iron instrument applied to the throats of criminals, by which they are strangled." Dictionary of the Royal Spanish Academy.—*Translator.*

effigies of the relaxed, in the names of the persons whom those effigies represented. When this was done, they placed the said pertinacious Manuel Lopez on the board with the ring attached to it, and commenced burning it whilst he was alive. Before they lighted the part on which he was standing, all the Dominican, Franciscan, Carmelite, Trinitarian, and Jesuitical monks who had accompanied him and the others, took singular pains and showed much affection in their endeavours to convert him; and as this was impossible—for the tears and entreaties of his parents who had just been burnt, and who had more than once this day attempted, with apparent sincerity, to effect his conversion, were of no avail—they kindled the fire more fiercely, though without eliciting from him the slightest token of contrition. Such was the subjection to which the devil had reduced his soul and body, and such his obstinacy, inflexibility, and obduracy! though, in consequence of this, the fire in its wrath got such a powerful hold on his body as to leave him and the others who were burnt with him reduced to a cinder; and such was the concourse of people that had come out to witness this doleful spectacle, that, although the site was a spacious plain, neither coaches, horses, nor human beings could move! It is well worthy of notice, for the confusion of these and all other Jews,[30] that a Franciscan monk having, before Manuel Lopez's head was put inside the ring, proposed to him some strong reasons why he should acknowledge

[30] A sensible man would read *Inquisitors* instead of *Jews.—Translator*.

our Lord Jesus Christ and renounce his errors, he answered him[31]—

* * * * * *"

These were the fruits which the Inquisitors reaped of the barbarous punishments inflicted on the persons of judaizers, and of their attempts to convert them to the Christian faith, at the moment when they were going to be reduced to ashes for not embracing it. Hence it appears that the judges of the Holy Office surpassed in cruelty the heathen in the times of Nero; for the latter never required of the Christians whom he put to death that they should turn pagans at their dying hour.

Don José de Pellicer, in his *notices* (avisos) of August the 2nd, 1644, says, " An act was kept by the Inquisition at Valladolid, and among those who suffered punishment was one Don Francisco de Vera, son of Don Lope de Vera, a knight of St. Clement and a man very respectably connected; his accuser was his own brother: he had been six years in prison. They burnt him alive for denying the Messiah's advent and other articles of the faith, though in point of birth and lineage he wanted nothing to make him an old Christian. He interpreted the Bible in his own way; it was impossible for him to be converted, and he finally died, impenitent and obstinate, in the law of Moses."

In the notices of August the 9th, in the same year, we likewise read these words: " They tell many tales about that unfortunate wretch who was burnt alive

---

[31] The words omitted are grossly blasphemous.—*Translator.*

for judaizing at the auto of Valladolid, and declare that he was nicknamed *Judas the Believer*."

There were many criminals who courageously defied the wrath of their judges, for whom they showed supreme contempt and even derided them, and went so far as to scoff at all the ceremonies performed at the autos-de-fé. In the report of the act celebrated at Mexico in the year 1569, we read these words: "Francisco Lopez de Aponte, a most contumacious and malicious atheist, while on the platform resembled a devil emitting sparks from his eyes, and beforehand gave signs of his eternal condemnation. When they carried him from the half-moon or steps to the centre of the theatre to hear his sentence, he walked with a haughty air, and instead of standing up on the raised platform, as he ought to have done whilst his sentence was reading, he soon sat down. When he returned to the half-moon, mocking the confessors who assisted the other condemned persons (for this horrid fellow refused to accept their services and remained alone by himself), he said, *What think ye, fathers? have not I played my part well?*"

Not only did the Jews ridicule these mitre-and-cassock-executioners, but also made signs to each other to keep firm in their adherence to their law, and endure with courage the death and martyrdom which awaited them. In the narrative before cited, the following statement is made: "Diego Diaz, whilst on the stage, absolutely declared himself to be a Jew, and both he and the two culprits Aponte and Botello kept on making signs, as if animating each other to die in their own lame faith: on being reproved by one of the friars who attended upon him, he (Diego Diaz) replied, *'Well, father, is it not right we should exhort each other to die for God?'* However, on being answered that, as a Jew, he did not die for God, but rather in disgrace with and under offence to Him, he became totally hardened, refusing any longer to hold the holy cross in his hand."

In this manner did they act now that all other means of communication were denied them; for as the cruelty of the Inquisitors surpassed that of Diocletian, Nero, and those other Emperors who were the scourge of Christianity, they did not allow the criminals to get a sight of each other till the hour of punishment had arrived, nor did they at any time suffer them to speak to each other. The tyrants of Rome did not hinder the martyrs from communicating with each other, either in prison or on their way to the scaffold, or at the time of their execution; but they were heathen emperors, while these were judges of the Holy Office of the Inquisition and divines! Husbands were not even informed of the arrest of their wives till the hour of the auto-de-fé had come, and even then, all they could do was to glance a parting farewell at each other, for they were forbidden to do so in words by those monsters of cruelty, unworthy to bear the title of men, much more of priests—those monsters fiercer than cannibals, who, not obeying the letter of the Gospel which they did not understand, but shielded with theological texts which they interpreted as they chose, had stifled in their hearts every feeling of humanity, and were more worthy of belonging to the rank of beasts than of men; and I am not disposed to class them with all beasts, for the lion is a noble animal, whilst in them appeared only the desire to satiate themselves with human blood and the brutal ferocity of tigers and hyenas!

In the afore-cited narrative of the auto-de-fé celebrated at Mexico in the year 1659, we read the following words: " Francisco Botello behaved so shamefully on the stage, that when one of the confessors who attempted to convert him from Judaism, begged him to consider whether he were in heart a Jew, for his wife was also there and had been put to penance, he lifted up his eyes to behold her with as much joy and gladness as if it had been the happiest day of his life, and made great exertions to speak to her; but this object he was unable to attain, for they removed him two steps lower down."

How many judaizers did not then endure with the greatest fortitude the horrible deaths appointed them by the Inquisitors! At the third of those four autos-de-fé celebrated at Majorca in 1691, in which thirty-four criminals, after being strangled, were committed to the flames, three persons were burnt alive for being impenitent Jews: their names were Rafael Valls, Rafael Terongi, and Catalina Terongi. "On seeing the flames near them," says the author of the report, "they began to show the greatest fury, struggling to free themselves from the ring to which they were bound, which Terongi at length effected, although he could no longer hold himself upright, and fell sidelong into the fire. Catalina, as soon as the flames began to encircle her, screamed out repeatedly for them to withdraw her from thence, although uniformly persisting in her refusal to invoke the name of Jesus: on the flames touching Valls, he covered himself, resisted, and struggled as long as he was able. Being fat, he took fire in such a manner that, before the flames had entwined around him, his flesh burnt like a firebrand, and bursting in the middle, his entrails fell out."[32]

Not only did the unhappy Jews undergo that most fearful death appointed them by those cannibals who styled themselves priests of God,[33] but oftentimes did they cast themselves into the flames, in order that they might the sooner enter upon a happier state of existence. José del Olmo, seeing that some criminals cast themselves into the fire, and knowing how detrimental to the Inquisition, or at least to Christianity, the cruelty of the judges of the Holy Office had been, sets down these words in his narrative of the general auto-de-fé celebrated at Madrid on the 30th of June, 1691: " It may be objected by some incautious man that such and such persons threw themselves into the flames—just

---

[32] Francisco Garau. La fé triunfante en cuatro autos celebrados en Mallorca, el año de 1691.

[33] Mr. Ford styles the first Inquisitor Torquemada, not inappropriately, *the first priest of Moloch.—Translator.*

as if true courage and the senseless brutality exhibited in a culpable waste of life, to be followed by eternal damnation, were identical." As Olmo knew that those who died so heroically were regarded as martyrs, he anticipates the arguments of the Jews with this logic: "It is not their death but the cause for which they die that makes men martyrs, and error is frequently known to imitate the achievements of truth."

Notwithstanding all that has been written by the fanatical Olmo to please the gentlemen of the Inquisition, whenever I reflect upon the constancy of the Spanish Jews in not abandoning their law, in spite of the wrath of the Holy Office, and the courage with which they died when discovered and brought to punishment, I call to mind the words written by Lucifer, Bishop of Cagliari, in the fourth century of the Church, to the Emperor Constantius, in the name of all the other persecuted Christians.

"Welcome the raging billows and violent whirlwinds to buffet us at thy bidding. We shall continue always more and more unmoveable; and far from foundering in the storm, the greater the dangers that surround us, the more freely shall we breathe; for the Christian does not easily yield to wickedness, and degrade himself by that weakness which follows its commission; on the contrary, in proportion to the attempts made by tyrants to debase him, does he manifest the greatness of his soul. Persecution is on the increase; the glory of Jesus Christ's soldiers increases equally; and far from being driven from the palæstra by the application of tortures, those very tortures make us fly to the encounter with additional agility. That this is true thyself wilt confess, when thou seest us appear in defence of the faith in all parts of the empire with like intrepidity, neither deceived by thy detestable blandishments, nor terrified by thy threats, nor overcome by the cruelty of thy tortures—seeing that we are strengthened by the Lord who hath promised to be with us till the end of the world.

"Now seeing that we are covered with the shield of Jesus Christ, clad with the mail of His holiness, and guided by His Spirit; moreover, keeping ourselves inflexible in our resistance to any suggestion which may be offered with the view of inducing us to forget our dignity, we shall adhere to the course we have hitherto pursued. We are sensible to pain, it is true, when our bodies are tortured; but we also show by our example that no violence can compel the wise man, in violation of his honor, to recede from his opinion and fixed determination; and that it is highly advantageous to one to suffer for God, who is the truth itself. As for other matters, I care not whether thou orderest me to die by the driving of a nail into my head, impalest me alive, crucifiest me, roastest me by a slow fire, castest me down from a rock, or drownest me in the depths of the sea. Nor do I care whether my carcase becomes food for the birds and wild dogs, nor whether in thy sight and for thy cruel pleasure the wild beasts tear it in pieces and devour it, leaving nothing but the bare bones; for in the end I shall find safety and appear unhurt in the presence of God."[34]

Expressions similar to these were uttered by the unhappy Hebrews when they were persecuted by those wicked Christians. And let not those silly persons who still defend that odious tribunal, by the rule of contraries styled Holy, presume to say that cruelty cannot fairly be imputed to its judges, because that after they had condemned a heretic, they declared him no longer subject to their jurisdiction, inasmuch as by his crime he had rendered himself amenable to the civil power, and that when they handed him over to it, they did not ask to have his life taken away. This proceeding of the judges of the Inquisition reveals the thorough hypocrisy of their character; for when they delivered up the criminal to the secular arm, they acted like the Jewish priests who, though the real authors of our Saviour's death, answered Pontius Pilate, when he urged them to judge Him according to their law, *that it was not lawful for them to put any man to death!* Hence we gather that, in wickedness and perversity, Inquisitors and Pharisees were very much alike.[35]

---

[34] This and the preceding paragraph are a mere analysis of a few passages from Lucifer's letter, which fills thirty-six pages of larger paper than this and in smaller type. The letter contains arguments against Arianism and religious persecutions; it is written with the boldness (would I could also add the meekness!) of a martyr. See 29th volume of the *Collectio Ecclesiæ Patrum*, Paris, 1842.—*Translator*.

[35] I was travelling four years ago from Santiago de Compostella to La Coruña, and as I sat with the diligence driver, heard him call out in a drawling tone to an unruly mule, "ma-ch-o-o-o,

Let all who imagine that persecutions are the only means of bringing back to the bosom of the Church those who have departed from her, take warning from the events that occurred in Spain in connexion with the tribunal of the Holy Office. In the fifteenth, sixteenth, and seventeenth centuries they did nothing else but arrest and punish judaizers, as appears from the numerous accounts of autos-de-fé printed in those times. Yet, in spite of all such severities, there were judaizers in Spain in the eighteenth century. On the 28th of October, 1703, Diego Lopez Duro, a native of Osuna, was burnt alive in the city of Seville at the age of twenty-six. In the same city also Fray José Diaz Pimienta was reduced to ashes in 1720; and at other autos, celebrated in that city in the same century, the bones of Don Diego de Avila (a native of Málaga, and resident and administrator-general of the royal revenues of Carmona), Don Diego de Espinosa (a native of Alhama, and resident of Cadiz, and principal excise-officer in that city), Francisco Diaz

---

ma-ch-o-o-o, eres tan féo como la Inquisici-on" (*He-mule, he-mule, thou art as ugly as the Inquisition!*) As he was a man of a humorous disposition, I observed to him that the mule should be called "Inquisitor General;" to which he demurred, saying "that although the obstinacy of the animal was quite equal to that of an Inquisitor, he feared the mule was a heretic, and consequently that the comparison would not hold good:" on which I informed him that an Inquisitor-general had once been summoned to appear before the tribunal of the Holy Office and answer the charges brought against him. His scruples were at once removed, and *he promised me that the next mule he bought should bear the name of Torquemada.*— Translator.

de Espinosa (also a native of Alhama and resident and administrator of revenues at Cadiz), were burnt, as well as the bones or the persons of many unhappy prisoners punished for judaizing.

So large was the number of the judaizers in the last century! The multitudes of them who dwelt in Córdova and its vicinity were also punished by the Inquisition with extreme cruelty. At Valladolid the same attempts to eradicate Judaism were made, but without effect. Nearly three centuries had now elapsed since the establishment of the barbarous and iniquitous tribunal, and during that period it had constantly and with persevering obstinacy laboured to destroy the large bodies of Jews residing in these realms under the garb of true Christians.

In the seventeenth century, notwithstanding so many punishments, certain infamous placards were affixed to the principal houses in some of the cities and towns with these words on them, *Long live the law of Moses and death to that of Christ, for all laws but the former are false.* There was but one man who attempted to put a stop to these evils, and at the same time to restore the want of population which Spain had brought upon herself by her two expulsions of the Jews and Moors. This man was the Count Duke of Olivares.

To gain his ends, he ordered several Jews, who were descendants of those that had been banished from Spain, to come from Thessalonica and other cities to deliberate with him and help to devise a plan for their own and their countrymen's return to these kingdoms and re-establishment in the same. With this object in view he tried to cut down the power of the Holy Office. The coming of these Jews and their stay at the court[36] were much spoken against and opposed by the Council of the Inquisition as well as by the Council of State. But the Count-Duke, relying on his own powerful influence with the king, laughed at all their opposition.

The Inquisitors now seeing that they were on the point of losing their power, as well as the property of so many unfortunate judaizers, which either was already or eventually would be confiscated, determined on representing to Philip the Fourth the great injury which was now resulting to the integrity of the faith from the residence of those Jews at the Court. For this purpose Cardinal Santa Balbina, Inquisitor-general, appeared in the king's chamber and spoke to him with that bold zeal which the interests of himself and the rascals whom he had at his beck imperiously demanded. Philip the Fourth then remembered that he was son of Philip the Third, and grandson of Philip the Second, and allowing himself to be led by the arguments of the Inquisitor, he pledged his word that he would order the Count-Duke of Olivares to compel those Jews to retire, not merely from the Court, but also to depart from all his realms and seigniories. Thus were the good intentions of the favourite to repair the evils from which Spain was suffering for want of population, commerce, and wealth, frustrated; and so rapidly did these evils increase

[36] It is very common in Spain to call Madrid the Court.—*Translator.*

that they now began to threaten the downfal of this unfortunate and ever ill-governed monarchy.

But what fruits did the King and Inquisitors reap of the constant persecutions raised against the judaizers? None that were of any service to them, if we except the confiscations. These men only brought odium upon the doctrines of the Gospel, which did not authorize them to perpetrate such atrocious and inhuman acts. If this be not the case, let the defenders of the Inquisition show us how many Christians there were in foreign kingdoms where Jews dwelt, and in which the tribunal of the Holy Office did not exist, that abjured their religion and conformed to the Mosaic law. In Spain, on the contrary, the more autos-de-fé, the more deaths and the more losses of caste[37] promoted by the Inquisitors, the more were the persons that judaized; and these individuals did not consist exclusively of persons belonging to the families of the punished, but of those also who were descended through all their branches from old Christians. Let Don Lope de Vera, who was burnt at Valladolid in 1644, and Fray José Diaz Pimienta, who suffered at Seville in 1703, be adduced as instances of what I have just said. The judaizers, instead of deterring others by the example of their deaths, made new proselytes; for multitudes who witnessed the stedfastness and courage with which those unfortunate men underwent the dreadful punishment of the bonfire, were convinced that God had

---

[37] *Infamias de linajes.—Translator.*

animated their hearts in that bitter and critical moment, and that, inasmuch as they obtained such a blessing as this from heaven, there could be no doubt whatever that they died in defence of the truth. Whereupon they canonized those men as martyrs, and themselves abjured the Christian religion, and went over to the ranks of Judaism. And this is the reason why there were so many judaizers living in Spain in the fifteenth, sixteenth, seventeenth, and eighteenth centuries, in defiance of the wrath of the Inquisition: which is a very clear proof that persecutions were the means of inciting many to follow the Mosaic rite; for in foreign kingdoms no Christian ever thought of becoming a Jew, while in our own there were many who did so, and these, not persons in the lower ranks of life, but gentlemen and people highly distinguished in every department of literature. Even at the commencement of the present century, or rather in the year 1799, a man named Lorenzo Beltran was punished by the Inquisition of Seville for being a judaizing heretic.

There were judaizers living in Spain till the time that the tribunal of the Holy Office was abolished in the war of independence, and though afterwards revived, it ceased to be a religious tribunal, but was converted into a political one; in the prisons of which, persons who could not be charged with the commission of any crime, but whom the government considered it unsafe to allow to be at large, were confined for an indefinite period.

Let the innumerable narratives of autos-de-fé existing in print and in manuscript from the fifteenth to the commencement of the present century be read, and by them it will be known how large was the number of judaizers then living in Spain. And then let it be seen what is the number of Christians who now forsake the Evangelical doctrine and embrace the Mosaic law:—this will show that the Inquisition, instead of destroying Judaism, was, through its barbarous and inhuman punishments, the means of rendering the Christian faith odious, and of inducing many persons of note, who were attracted by the example of the martyrs burnt in its flames, to go over to the ranks of Judaism.

RECAPITULATION.

A LARGE number of the Jews who escaped from Jerusalem, when that city was destroyed by Titus, settled in Spain, where they lived unmolested. The ancient Spaniards, in the Council of Elliberis, began to issue decrees to their prejudice, but the invasion of Spain by the Goths hindered the enactment of decrees still more injurious to the Israelites. While the Goths continued in the Arian faith, the Jews lived free from oppression; but as soon as the former were converted to Christianity, the unhappy Hebrews were cruelly persecuted by them. Every king and every council devised some new law against them more severe than any of those already existing. The fruit which the Goths reaped of their barbarous acts was the invasion of Spain by the Arabs and the overthrow of their empire. The Jews then assisted the conquerors with their arms, garrisoned the principal cities, and regained their liberty.

As the Hebrews were not persecuted by the Arabs, the Christians suffered the former to live in peace in their territories. In those times flourished many learned Jews, particularly at Córdova. The Christians, as soon as they began to conquer cities, began also to oppress the Hebrews, and in proportion to the number of the cities they acquired, did they increase their oppressions of that race: and since many of the Christians owed large sums of money to the Jews, they excited the fanaticism of the people against them, thereby causing frequent tumults and murders. In dread of these calamities, many of them became Christians, especially after the famous dispute of the Spanish Rabbins with Jerónimo de Santa Fé, in the presence of the Antipope Pedro de Luna.

Ferdinand the Fifth, styled the Catholic, being engaged in wars, of which his revenues would not cover the expenses, decided on establishing the tribunal of the faith for the purpose of filling his treasury with the proceeds of the confiscations.

He called upon several of the Jews to supply him with money to carry on the Granada war, and promised to pay them as soon as he should conquer that city. Instead of paying his debts, he ordered the Jews who refused to embrace Christianity to depart from Spain within the space of four months.

In spite of its flames and of the robberies it committed, the tribunal of the faith was unable to eradicate Judaism from Spain. Since the abolition of that tribunal, no Spaniard has abjured the Christian faith to embrace the Mosaic law.

APPENDIX.

ADVERTISEMENT.

The following Instruction, written to Philip the Second by the illustrious Dr. Benito Árias Montano (the Spanish Jerome), a professed Monk of the order of Santiago in the Royal Convent of San Marcos de Leon, and one of the most distinguished of the Doctors who were present at the Council of Trent, is in manuscript, in the library of the Author of this History.

INSTRUCTION FOR PRINCES RESPECTING THE MANNER IN WHICH THE FATHERS OF THE COMPANY CONDUCT THEMSELVES.

THAT the order of the fathers of the Company in Christ's vineyard was planted by the work of the Holy Spirit, as a tree which was to produce both an antidote to the poison of heresy, and flowers of religious and Christian works, of such exquisite sweetness that their very fragrance might constrain sinners to abhor the bad odour of their sins and walk in the good path of repentance, is clearly shown by the manner in which this plant was put into the ground by its first cultivator, St. Ignatius, of glorious memory; and truly may I say it was watered with the charity of those first fathers who gave it life; that it was cultivated according to its first planter's directions, and produced two branches, one of love towards God, the other of love towards our neighbour: and so, the fruits reaped in the good education of the young, in the conversion of souls and the increase of the Catholic faith, were abundant; but the devil, who labours as hard to destroy and undo the works and designs of God as others strive to carry them out, took such advantage of the very greatness and increase of this order as, in a short time, to pervert the ends for which it was instituted; for with as much subtilty as artifice, instead of those two first branches of charity (now nearly withered), he grafted in two others, one of self-conceit, the other of expediency, from which such injury is done to the Christian community as cannot, perhaps, be surpassed;—all which I purpose showing in the progress of this discourse, wherein I protest before God that I am not influenced by interest or passion, but simply by my zeal for the public good (to promote which I was sent into the world), and by my desire that when Christian princes become acquainted with their arts and devices, they may make such provision against them as they shall judge it to be most expedient for them to make.

Now it must be known that when first this order of the fathers of the Company was instituted, efforts were made in many places to enlarge it, principally with the view to the education of children, a thing wanted in every city in the kingdom; and thus in a few years this order, owing to the favour of several princes, spread wider and further than any other order in many. It was this aggrandisement, which ordinarily creates in our minds a change of habits, that aroused in the successors of St. Ignatius such love to the Company, that, thinking their own to be more useful to the Church and more serviceable in the reformation of manners than all religious orders in the world, they determined among themselves to extend it with such art and industry, and to found upon it the true defence of Christianity and the real welfare of the Church, or (to use their own term) the sole patrimony of Christ.

It now needed the acuteness of an Aristotle and the eloquence of a Cicero to explain the marvellous way, which from its novelty seems incredible to many, whereby these fathers extended their order; but I shall content myself with merely noting down some things, leaving a wide field open to other geniuses to form the opinion which may to them appear the most probable; I shall therefore propound some points which may supply the reader with a foundation on which to build his theories.

I must premise that these fathers did not suppose that their order could acquire that pitch of preeminence to which they aspire, by mere teaching, preaching, and administering of the sacraments, or other like religious exercises; for though they were at first (as I have already stated) received with open arms and caressed by many, they observed in course of time that (either from dissatisfaction with them, or from other causes, whatever they might be,) the affection and devotion of many had cooled; wherefore, doubting whether their order, still almost in its infancy, had made its last effort and acquired its full preeminence, they devised other means for aggrandizing it.

The first plan they adopted was to bring all other religious orders into bad odour with princes, and afterwards with as many others as they could, by showing up their imperfections, and then with good and dexterous management they procured their own grandeur through the oppression and fall of other persons: by this means they have made themselves masters of many abbeys as well as the large revenues attached to them, of which, through their representations, they have deprived those religious communities to which they originally belonged.

Their second plan was to meddle with matters of state, interesting and gaining over the majority of the Christian princes to their party by the most artificial and subtle method that ever was known; of which, as it is difficult to dive into, so is it impossible to give a thorough explanation.

They have constantly residing at Rome a *General*, to whom they all yield implicit obedience: this man makes choice of certain fathers who, from the assistance they continually render him, are called *Assistants*. There is at least one of these assistants to every nation, from which he derives his name and title: thus, one is called the *Assistant of Spain*, another the *Assistant of France*, a third the *Assistant of Italy*, or of any other province or kingdom. It is the business of each of these individuals to inform the father-general of all the political events that occur in that province or realm of which he is the *assistant;* his information is derived from correspondents residing in the principal cities of that province or kingdom; these correspondents, after acquainting themselves with the state, quality, nature, inclination, and intention of the princes, give notice, every post, to the *assistants* of all events that have recently taken place. These give information to the father-general, who calls all the *assistants* together and holds a council with them: they then anatomize the whole universe, setting forth the interests and designs of all the Christian princes: this done, they consult together upon all the matters of which they have been recently advised by their correspondents, and, after examining them and balancing one thing against another, promptly decide on supporting the interests of one prince and opposing those of another, according as best suits their own convenience and private ends; and as mere spectators of a game see better than the persons actually engaged in it what turn it is likely to take, so do these fathers, with the interests of all the princes before their eyes, know well how to observe conditions, time, and place, and how to apply the means calculated to improve the affairs of a prince, from whom they know they can obtain an advantage.

I must observe, secondly, that it is downright wicked of monks, who have retired from the world for the special purpose of attending to the care of their own and their neighbours' souls, to meddle so much with affairs of state; and that they should meddle with them with such objects as they have in view is a serious evil, which needs to be reformed, in consideration of the bad consequences that result from such conduct as theirs.

These fathers confess a great part of the Catholic states, and, in order to get access to the higher classes, they refuse to admit poor people to their confessionaries, and very frequently confess princes themselves. By this means they easily fathom all the designs and resolutions of both princes and subjects, and immediately give information of them either to their general or their *assistant* at Rome. Now, with but a moderate share of caution, they will find out what injury they can do to this or that prince, when thereto moved by their own interest, which is the final object to which all their actions are directed.

Now, for the preservation of a state it follows as a natural and inseparable accident, that if this man be not watched, that man is necessarily ruined; and it is on this account that princes are so very severe with those who discover their secrets and punish them as though they were their own and their country's enemies: on the other hand, when one prince understands and knows the intentions of another, he behaves with greater caution, and thus advances his own interests; and this is the reason why ambassadors usually spend no slight sums of money on spies, and, for all that, are generally deceived in the accounts and informations given them: but the fathers of the Company, by means of the confessors and consultations holden with their correspondents who reside in all the principal cities of Christendom, and also by means of other dependents of theirs (of whom I shall speak by-and-by), are accurately and minutely informed of all the points discussed and determined in the most secret councils, and are almost as well as, if not better, acquainted than the princes themselves, with the state of their revenues, their expenditure, and even their designs; and this knowledge is acquired at no heavier cost than the postage of their letters, which, *according to the statements of the postmasters,* amounts to sixty, seventy, and oftentimes a hundred escudos a post. Thus do they become acquainted with the concerns of princes, whose good qualities they underrate, and those whom they wish to make odious to other princes they deprive of their reputation, and, in a word, cause rebellions and outbreaks in the lands of those princes; which they have the more effectual means of doing owing to their knowledge of the inmost secrets of the hearts of the subjects, through the medium of confessions, whereby they can tell who is well-affected to the prince, and who is dissatisfied and displeased with him: thus, by the accounts of political affairs which they receive, they are easily enabled to sow discord among princes and raise suspicion and jealousy in their minds. So, by their acquaintance with the feelings of the subjects, they have no difficulty in raising tumults and setting the people at variance with their prince, and exciting in their minds a contempt for his person. This forces upon us the conclusion, that it is contrary to the interests of a state for the prince to confess (much less allow this to be done by any of his confidants, domestics, secretaries, councillors, or chief ministers,) to persons who endeavour to pry so eagerly into matters of state and employ their knowledge of them as the key to obtain the favor of princes; for in these days there is no lack of monks whose lives and whose learning are by no means inferior to what these fathers can boast of, and on whose services greater reliance can be placed; for the persons of whom I speak neither understand nor attend to any thing else but the care of souls and of their monasteries.

For the clearer understanding of what I have said and am about to say, it is well to know that there are four classes of Jesuits. The first consists of secular persons of both sexes, who are styled *blind obedience;* for in all their actions they are ruled by the council of the Company, whose orders and mandates they are ready to obey. These are most frequently gentlemen and persons of rank, widows, citizens, and mercers; of whom, as of fruitful plants, these fathers annually reap

INSTRUCTION FOR PRINCES. 251

abundant fruits of gold and silver. To this belong those women commonly called *teatinas*, who are persuaded by the fathers to contemn the world, and then those worthies get possession of their jewels, dresses, furniture, and finally, good fat incomes.

The second class consists solely of men, some of whom are priests and some laymen, who, though they lead a secular life, and generally obtain pensions, dignities, and incomes of other kinds, have vowed to receive the habit of the Company whensoever the general may order them to take it; hence they are called *Jesuits in voto:* the fathers make great use of their services to support the fabric of their monarchy, for they have these men stationed in all kingdoms and provinces, and about the courts of all princes and grandees, for the purpose of employing them in the manner that will be stated in the seventh paragraph after this.

To the third class belong those who live in monasteries, whether priests or laymen, and who, not having as yet professed, may be ejected from them at the will of the father-general, but cannot leave them of their own accord. As these persons neither hold offices nor employments worth mentioning, they usually pay a simple obedience to the orders of their superiors.

The fourth class of Jesuits consists of the *politicians*, in whom the government of their order is vested: these are the persons who, when tempted by the devil with the same temptation to which Christ was subjected in the wilderness (*Hæc omnia tibi dabo, &c.*), have accepted the conditions offered them, and now labour to make their order a perfect monarchy, which begins at Rome, to which city nearly all the affairs of Christendom are referred, and at which resides the head of these *politicians*, who with a large body of the same order act as generals: these men, informed by their spies of all the more weighty and important matters discussed at the Court of Rome, after examining into them and first deciding what game it will best suit their own interests to play, take care to attend daily the houses of the cardinals, ambassadors, and prelates, before whom they adroitly introduce the subject which is under discussion or which they know will shortly be discussed, and represent it to them in the light that they think the strongest, or in the form which they imagine will be most conducive to their own benefit—and, in general, they so alter the aspect of affairs as (according to their own expression) to make black appear white; for the first accounts received, particularly when they come from religious persons,[1] usually make a strong impression on the minds of the hearers: hence it is that very important negotiations respecting the affairs of princes and other exalted personages, when carried on at Rome through the medium of ambassadors, have often failed in meeting with the expected result, the council having been prejudiced by the interested statements of these fathers, who have contrived that discredit should be thrown upon the accounts given by the ambassadors

[1] That is to say, members of religious orders or communities.—*Translator*.

and other agents. Of this same artifice, which they employ at Rome with the prelates and cardinals, they avail themselves in their private conferences with other princes and the Jesuits of the second class, and so we may conclude that most of the negotiations in which Christendom is concerned pass through their hands, and none of them succeed save those to which these fathers raise no opposition. Great, indeed, is the cunning of these fathers, in fact it is almost impenetrable, and therefore cannot be made thoroughly manifest; but any prince who takes warning from my observations may get a tolerably clear knowledge of it, as by them he will be enabled to reflect on things past and thereby understand the truth of my words, and by calling to mind their artful ways in the management of former transactions, he will discover much more than can be stated here. The fathers do not rest satisfied with employing these secret artifices for the purpose of insinuating themselves into all secular matters, though they believe them to be the only means of acquiring their universal monarchy. The jurisdiction they desire to have they some years ago solicited of his Holiness Gregory the Thirteenth, whom they entreated to favor their views, representing to him and persuading him that it was for the good of the Church that they had made this application to him, and begging of him, whenever he sent a legate or apostolical minister, to require that person to take some father of the Company with him as his companion or confidant, by whose counsel all the actions of such legate or apostolical minister were to be guided.

It is by this contrivance, as well as by their acquaintance with political affairs, that these fathers, or at least the leading members of their body, have gained the friendship of many spiritual and temporal princes, whom they have persuaded that they (the Jesuits) have said or done many things to their advantage. From this have resulted two serious evils: the first is that, abusing the friendship and goodness of princes, they have not hesitated to disgust many private families, both rich and noble, by usurping (if I may be allowed thus to express myself) the estates of widows, and causing the greatest misery to parents by bringing over to their profession the persons who appear to them the most clever of those that go to pursue their studies with them: and it often happens, when these students chance to prove ignorant or to become ill, that, under some fair pretext, the fathers turn them out of doors, but retain their property (for at the time of their profession they were compelled to make those fathers their heirs), while they utterly exclude the poor from their studies, in violation of the aforesaid St. Ignatius's orders, and in opposition to the intentions of the persons by whom revenues have been left to them for this express purpose, such benefactors supposing that their bequests would be properly applied to the benefit of the community at large, and the public be the gainers thereby.

The second evil is, that these fathers have a singularly artful way of proclaiming to the world what intimate friendship they have with princes, pourtraying it much greater than it really is, in order to make all the ministers of the latter friendly to themselves, and to force those ministers to urge their claims before them (the Jesuits) as a matter of favor and not of right; nay, they have been known to boast publicly at Rome that it was in their power to make cardinals, nuncios, lieutenant-governors, and other officers; and some of them have positively asserted that their general is more powerful than the Supreme Pontiff; and others have said that it is a better thing to belong to that order which can create cardinals than to be a cardinal: all these things have been said publicly by them; in fact, there is no one familiarly acquainted with these fathers, to whom they have not made such or similar statements.

Relying upon the effects of their political intrigues, they have the affrontery to say that they can raise up or cast down whomsoever they please, and, by using the cover or cloak of religion, they not unfrequently carry their point. When they recommend any one to a prince, they do not pick out the most meritorious person, but, on the contrary, more generally oppose the man who is such, when they know him to be a person in whom they cannot place the utmost confidence; and they are in the constant habit of bringing forward men who are likely to be of use to themselves, without caring whether so-and-so be well-affected to the prince, whether he be a deserving man or capable of rendering a satisfactory account of the office or place of trust committed to him: hence it is that the prince is always living in a state of alarm, and the disposition of the people is manifested by discontent and outbreaks.

As the boatswain, when he sees that he has a favorable opportunity,[2] gives a whistle to the galley-slaves, who pull hard all and speed the galley on, so do these fathers, with the general and assistants at Rome, during the quiet of the siesta, conclude that the appointment of some individual to this or that office or post of honour, will turn to their own account, and then the father-general advises the brethren who reside at other places; on which the whole fraternity act with unanimity, all of them pulling together and exerting themselves to the utmost, nearly at the same moment, to obtain for their favourite the appointment they wish him to get. And very ungrateful would that individual be, who, while under such obligations to these fathers, should 'refuse to gratify, as well as assist them, whensoever they might need his services, with the same zeal as they had displayed in his behalf. And as this dependent or these dependents (for the Jesuit fathers have many such) are thus placed under greater obligations to them than to the prince from whom they have received that office or dignity, so do they serve them with greater love and affection than the prince himself. Thus it is that these temporal sovereigns become embayed; for supposing themselves to have found a faithful servant, they have, in reality, appointed a spy selected by those fathers, of whose services the latter

[2] *Tiempo*, which also signifies *weather*, and may, perhaps, here be used in this sense.—*Translator.*

often avail themselves to the injury of the very prince who aggrandized their own nominee. I could produce clear examples in confirmation of all that I have hitherto advanced, though it is sufficiently confirmed by experience and general opinion; but that I may not excite too much odium against myself, I shall avoid descending to particular cases, concluding, as I do, that the probable reason why these fathers usually style their order a great monarchy, is because they imagine and believe that they have princes and ministers under their thumb: indeed, it was but a short time ago that one of the gravest of these fathers, speaking in public in the name of his order to a Serene Highness, commenced his address with these arrogant words, which originated, no doubt, in his notions of their monarchy: *Our Company has always had a good understanding with your Serene Highness.*

These fathers strive, with all their might and main, to persuade the world it is owing to their countenance and support that all persons have been any wise favoured by a prince, and in this way they obtain more sway over the minds of the people than the princes themselves. Now this is a very serious evil; for it never can be beneficial to a state that monks so ambitious and so political should rule the minds of those ministers who can be guilty of treason or raise a commotion, whenever they have the inclination to do so: nor is it consistent with the security of a state that these fathers of the Company should be enabled (through the medium of ministers dependent upon them) to introduce and place in the service of princes, in the capacity of councillors and secretaries, any of those *Jesuits in voto,* of whom I have previously spoken, and who afterwards get the prince to employ one of these fathers as his confessor or preacher; and when they have succeeded in this, then all these men acting in concert serve as spies for the father-general, whom they furnish with a detailed account of every thing that is discussed, even in the most secret councils: thus are the intentions of the prince made known and his most important secrets discovered, while he is unable to detect the delinquent, and generally allows his suspicions to fall on the most innocent.

As subjects are, generally, by nature inclined to follow the example of their prince, so do these men who yield obedience to the father-general, on seeing that he pays the greatest attention to political affairs and thereby endeavours to aggrandize the Company, apply their minds to the same thing; they make use of the prince's relations, from whom they try to get information respecting the state of his heart and to worm out his most secret designs, for the purpose of communicating every thing to the assistant of Rome or the father-general; by this they hope to win his favor and obtain some office or post of honor which they would not have acquired by any other means, for it is not the practice of the fathers to confer offices and places of trust upon great men, but upon those whom they know to be well qualified to assist in raising the Company to that pitch of aggrandisement to which they aspire, the acquisition of which they consider a sufficient ground for their interference in secular matters.

Now, as by working the still such water is distilled and drawn from various herbs as will have the effect of curing and healing a dangerous ulcer; and as bees gather honey from different kinds of flowers; so, from the punctual accounts which the fathers receive respecting the interests of all princes and all the events that occur in every state, do these men, by force of deduction, come to a conclusion as to what will help them to cure the almost incurable ulcer of desire to aggrandise themselves,[2] and extract a certain knowledge which is of peculiar service to them, whereby, to the benefit of one and to the injury of another, but more frequently to the injury of the one than to the benefit of the other, they gain their end. Besides this they are in the habit of keeping in suspense the hopes of princes whose designs they have penetrated, telling them that they have taken measures to insure the success of their designs and the realisation of their hopes; but when they have secured their own interest, considering that the excessive elevation of those princes might, some day, prove prejudicial or hurtful to them, like lawyers with suits, they defer the business in hand, and, afterwards, with marvellous

[2] This sentence is not very clear; this, however, I take to be the writer's meaning; "Since the Jesuits aspire to a universal monarchy, they employ any means (however unscrupulous) which they think calculated to assist them in gaining their object, supposing that if they succeed in obtaining it, all their desires will be satisfied, whereas they are ignorant of the insatiable nature of ambition."— *Translator.*

dexterity and artifice turning over a new leaf, totally undo and destroy the whole of the business which they had begun.

The commencement and conclusion of the league of France by these fathers, and its subsequent abandonment and rejection by them when they saw that Henry the Fourth's affairs were in a more flourishing condition; the gift of England so repeatedly made to the Spaniards by these fathers, and a hundred other similar cases, so fully confirm what I have advanced in this discourse of mine, that no additional proof of my statement is necessary.

From what has been said, it follows that the Company have not a good and right understanding with any prince spiritual or temporal, but make such use of him as suits their own convenience: on the other hand, it follows that no prince, much less any private gentleman, can rely on them; for as these fathers show themselves equally well affected to all, becoming Spaniards to Spaniards, Frenchmen to Frenchmen, and acting in the same way towards persons of other nations, when occasion requires it; they evidently have an eye to their own interests alone, and care not whether they injure this or that man: it is on this account that enterprises and negotiations with which these fathers have mixed themselves up, have seldom been successful, for they have no mind to render any further help and assistance to any one than it is to their own advantage to afford; and in this they are very cunning, for some of them pretend to be partizans of the Spanish crown, some of the French, some of the Emperor, and some of other princes whose countenance and support they desire to have. And when one of these princes makes a Jesuit his confidant, the latter writes to his general an account of the business which is to be discussed, and waits for an answer from that functionary, in order to see whether the instructions sent by him are in accordance with the will and intentions of the prince by whom the matter was entrusted to him; for, provided the Company be served, little does he care for the interests of the prince.

Besides this, as these fathers are acquainted with the interests of all princes and are informed of almost everything that is discussed in their most secret councils, those who pretend to be partizans or confidants of Spain propose to the king and his chief ministers some very important conditions and considerations of state that have been sent to them from Rome by some of those fathers that are styled politicians. The like conduct is observed in France by those who profess devotion and attachment to that crown, and the same rule applies to the rest of them; hence it is that princes become so suspicious of each other that not one of them will trust another; and this diffidence of theirs is in the highest degree prejudicial to the tranquillity, the public peace, and the general welfare of Christendom, inasmuch as it raises obstacles to the conclusion of a league against the common enemy, and renders it difficult to secure a lasting peace between Christian princes.

It must be admitted that the eyes of the world have

been so opened to their subtle discussions on matters of state, that now, to the great injury of the church, no other subjects are regarded or attended to: it is in these scales that every one weighs his actions, and the worst of all is that the heretics have learnt the tricks of these fathers, and are now employing them to the serious injury of us with those princes by whom they are protected; so that when these heretics first became somewhat acquainted with literature, from which it was hoped that they would one day learn the error of their ways, they have instead thereof become atheists and politicians whom it is next to impossible to convert, unless God miraculously interpose in their behalf.

Here, in order to show the cunning of the Jesuits and their way of winning over to their side and catching hold of princes, I must not omit to state, that some years ago a father assistant of England, named Personio,[4] wrote a book against the king of Scotland's succession to the throne of England, and another father, named Cristonio,[5] with others of the same order, in a printed book of theirs defended the king of Scotland's title to that crown, in opposition to the opinion of the said father Personio, with whom they pretended to dis-

[4] The individual here called Personio was one Parsons or Persons: in 1594 he published, under the name of R. Doleman, *A Conference about the next succession to the Crown of England*. It is clear from the preface of this work that it was for the *first time published in* 1594. In the last paragraph but one of this *Instruction*, Pope Urban the Seventh, who *died in* 1590, is spoken of as a person *still living*. Hence it follows that the *Instruction* is a forgery.—*Translator*.

[5] Chricton (?) a Scotch Jesuit.—*Translator*.

agree, carrying on their controversy with particular artfulness and with the concurrence of their general; it being their object to gain access to the person that succeeded to the crown, whoever he might be, and to find means through his assistance to aggrandize their order and benefit themselves: hence it is quite clear that princes are the object of all the actions and determinations of these fathers, and consequently their common saying that their order is a great monarchy is verified.

Though our experience of infinite cases that have happened proves as clear as the daylight that these fathers, in obliging or disobliging a prince, are actuated entirely by motives of self-interest, it will nevertheless appear from what I am about to state, that there is no person in the world whom they ought to obey more readily than the Supreme Pontiff, both out of regard to their being Christians themselves, and also out of respect to the solemn vow of obedience to him which they take: and yet, when the Supreme Pontiff Pius the Fifth (of whom it is impossible to speak too highly), enlightened by the Holy Spirit, desired to reform these fathers and compel them to act up to their professions, as other religious communities do, they would not obey him, because they thought that such obedience would be prejudicial to their interests; on the contrary, some few who obeyed the Supreme Pontiff and made their professions were by the rest of the fathers contemptuously called *Quintinos*, and not one of these has hitherto succeeded in obtaining a benefice. In like manner did they oppose the glorious St. Charles, Archbishop of Milan, who, as legate *à latere* of his Holiness, desired to bring them to a religious discipline. But are they who disobey the sacred canons less disobedient to his decrees?—they who make a gainful traffic in pearls, rubies, and diamonds brought from the Indies? for it is an established fact, that most of the precious pearls sold at Venice belong to these fathers—a fact which has been ascertained from the brokers whom they have employed and do still employ.

That these fathers do not obey the Supreme Pontiff is well known to some of their Company who were summoned from Rome and prosecuted on this account: but in order to avoid introducing the name of any prince to whom this treatise of mine may not be very acceptable, I shall withhold names and dwell no longer upon this topic. I am anxious to be of service to all men, and do not wish to offend any one, for it is not my design in this place to inveigh against these fathers (whom, in other respects, I regard and esteem), but only to give a brief account of their manners and customs.

Now it occasionally happens, be it observed, that a person afflicted with a dangerous malady complains so piteously that his cry reaches the heavens, though he is ignorant of the origin and cause of his malady: thus does all the world complain of these fathers, one because he is persecuted by them, another because his confidence has been betrayed by them; and the evil continues, while men are unable to discover and get at the root of it, namely the desire and intent of these fathers to aggrandize themselves; out of respect for which desire they care not whether they displease this or that man the most, whether they deceive princes, whether by their cunning they deprive widows of their estates, whether they ruin noble families, or whether, as generally happens, they are the cause of those suspicions and disgusts that arise between Christian princes, through their own determination to meddle and insinuate themselves into the principal negotiations that are carried on. Now, as in the economy of nature it would be very inconvenient that the part last formed should first attract and carry off purer blood than the vital parts of the frame for the purpose of serving as an instrument to the inferior parts, inasmuch as it would be exhausted thereby; so is it a contradiction to the natural state of things that the order of these fathers, which was instituted in the Church for the purpose of eradicating heresies and bringing sinners to repentance, should attract and bring over to itself the most weighty and the most important concerns of princes and prelates, withdrawing thereby the vital spirits of their interests and appropriating them all to themselves: for by this means public as well as private peace is interrupted, and many persons worthy of promotion are passed over, while others who ought to be passed over are promoted, to say nothing of a thousand other inconveniences resulting therefrom.

I might adduce numerous instances from experience to show how great is the ambition of these fathers to aggrandize themselves, but shall content myself with proving them by the words of Personio, one of the gravest of these fathers, written in a book of his composed in English and entituled "*The Reformation of England*,"[5] where, after having spoken very ill of Cardinal Paul, a prelate who, as well for his exemplary virtue as for his services to the Church, deserves to be holden in everlasting remembrance; and, after having noted certain defects and blemishes in the Council of Trent, he finally concluded that whensoever England should turn to the true Catholic faith, it would then be convenient to reduce her to the form and condition of the primitive Church, by putting all ecclesiastical property into a common fund, and entrusting the care and administration of it to seven sages that belong to the Company, to distribute them in such a way as should seem to them the most suitable: nor will he allow, nay, he forbids under heavy penalties, the return of any monk to England, of what order soever he be, without the licence of these fathers, with the design and purpose of preventing all but themselves from gaining a living by collecting alms. But as self-conceit blinds a man's

[5] "Next followes his *Booke of Reformation*, which under Reformation, was *Father Parsons Babell*, that is, his Castle in the aire, wherein he prescribes Rules to all Estats: here you see, he is no changeling, the same man that he was before; or rather grown more audacious and impudent, and wel he might, considering that these orders were begunne in their deepe *Iesuiticall Court of Parliament at Stix in Phlegeton*, and suggested thence into *Father Parsons* sconce, being ended and compiled into a full and complete volume, by him and his *Generall*, intituled, *The High Court of Reformation for England*."—*Life of Father Parsons*, by Thomas James, *Oxford*, 1612. —Translator.

eyes, and, however wise he be, makes him do very unwise things, what this father goes on to state is thoroughly ridiculous. Whenever England, says he, is reduced to the true faith, it is not expedient that the Pope should, for five years at least, interfere with the titles or patronage of ecclesiastical benefices in that kingdom, but that every thing should be in the hands of those seven sages, who will bestow those benefices in such a manner as they may think most conducive to the interests of the Church, with the design and purpose of obtaining, after the expiration of the five years (through the medium of their devices of which they have an abundant stock), a prorogation of the same privilege for five years more, and of continuing the prorogation for such a length of time as eventually to exclude his Holiness from England. Who doth not now see pourtrayed, as in a picture, the covetousness and ambition of the Jesuits, and their eagerness to become monarchs? who is not acquainted with the great cunning wherewith they advance their own interests, and knows not how little regard they have for the welfare or the misfortunes of all others besides?

But in the time of Gregory the Thirteenth they begged and pressed him to give and invest them with all the parish churches at Rome, in order that their monarchy might commence in that city; and though they could not obtain this at Rome, they have obtained it in England, where of late they have had *an archpriest, a Jesuit in voto,* elected; who, instead of protecting the clergy, hunts all the priests that are not dependents of his, like a rabid wolf, reducing them to a state of despair, and prohibiting them under heavy penalties from conversing together; so that now nearly all the English Clergy are *Jesuits in voto,* nor is any one admitted at the English Colleges that hath not previously promised to become a Jesuit. Thus, were that kingdom to return to the ancient and true faith, England would become a Jesuitical monarchy; for all the ecclesiastical revenues, all the abbeys, and all the other dignities would be conferred upon Jesuits.

This is certain (and I say it with tears in my eyes) that very few heretics are now converted: this observation applies with peculiar force to England, where, as I said before, not one of the old clergy, who did very good service, is left: this must be attributed to these fathers, who pay greater attention to, and care more about, their own interests than the souls of men; besides which the heretics themselves know how the Jesuits oppress the Catholic priests and with what artifice they proceed, and hate them so mortally that numbers refuse to be converted, because they do not choose to be tyrannized over by those fathers. I here omit many things respecting their pretensions to other people's estates, which they show their eagerness to possess, as well as to aggrandize themselves; I also omit a good deal about their way of gaining a prince's favor, by persuading him that they have the people at their disposal, and can make them well-affected to his person: and now leaving it to every one to consider whether what I have just said be clear and palpable,

I shall conclude this discourse with four brief observations.

Observation the first.—Men of such haughty spirit and of such high notions are always in want of changes and ever on the look out for them and bringing them about; for it is by new commotions that they usually gain their ends, for which they open a way with the arms of their industry and their arts, in which we have seen them to be so well practised; for to a prince who loves and is anxious for the peace and security of his dominions, these fathers not only cannot be of service, but may do him harm by causing tumults and placing his state in jeopardy, if, when he has any of them residing in it, he do not favor them, or, if when he favors them, he allow himself to be governed by their counsels.

Observation the second.—If these fathers, who have no temporal jurisdiction, cause the world such frequent and such serious inquietude, what would be the consequence if one of them were elected Pope? Why, the first thing he would do would be to fill the College of Cardinals with men of his order, and perpetuate the Pontificate among its members; on which they, governed by self-interest, protected and supported by the Pope, might endanger the states of many princes, particularly those of their nearest neighbours.

Observation the third.—They would exert themselves to the utmost to obtain from the Pope the grant of some city or of some temporal jurisdiction, which they would employ as a means to establish other claims which could not be maintained without injuring other princes.

Observation the fourth.—As soon as the College should be remodelled and filled up by these fathers, all the patrimony of Christ would be in their hands; and as a dropsical man, the more he drinks the thirstier he becomes, so would these men, by increasing in covetousness in proportion to their increase in grandeur, be the cause of a thousand disturbances. And since there is nothing more subject to change than the affairs of states, these fathers are now striving harder than ever, and with all their might and main, and with all their cunning, to procure changes in order that they may be the better enabled to introduce their scheme of government: meanwhile they now go looking about for the eldest son of some prince, and try to bring him over to their order, and induce him to endow them with his dominions,—and they would actually have succeeded in this design of theirs, had not some persons got wind of their artful intentions and opposed them. In the case above mentioned, they would have had no difficulty in lording it over the ecclesiastical staff; and as they are sagacious men and know what they are about, they would attempt to set up a thousand claims for the purpose of extending their authority, and would not want means to gain their end; and even supposing this were attended with no other result than the alarms and suspicions in which princes would live, and particularly those nearest to them, this would be an inconvenience of no trifling consideration.

INSTRUCTION FOR PRINCES. 271

It is necessary for the preservation of the public peace and for the tranquillity of every prince's dominions, for the increase of the Church and for the good of the world, that his Holiness, Urban the Seventh, with the aid of other Christian princes, should put a bridle in the mouth of this Company, which now conducts itself in so disorderly a manner, provided we would not see the same thing happen to them that happened in olden time to those members of the family of Dabius (in whose steps these fathers appear to be treading), who were destroyed by the Emperor Claudius.

When ordered to write and express my opinion respecting the best measure to be adopted for regulating the conduct of these fathers (without giving offence to them or injuring them, but, on the contrary, conferring upon them an important benefit, for I am anxious to make them monarchs of souls which are Christ's real treasure, and not of this world and of its concerns which are mere rubbish), I promise to do so with all charity and with all the ability which it shall please the Divine Majesty to give me.—*Unum pro cunctis sufficiat opus.*

Letter written from Antwerp to King Philip the Second, on the eighteenth of February, 1571, by Benito Arias Montano.

To *His Royal Catholic Majesty:*

Bound as a loyal servant by Christian simplicity and the tie of an affectionate service to all things pertaining to God and to your Majesty, and to your unfettered rule over the commonwealths subject to your Majesty; I, in consideration of this, declare that one of the commands which your Majesty should be particular in giving to the governor and ministers of those states and to their successors is, that they should not encumber themselves with any of the Teatinos, nor allow any of those persons to meddle with politics; nor should they advance any of them to situations in those states to which any such authority or profit is annexed as will raise them above their present station, and your Majesty should give special orders that no governor employ any of them as his preacher or confessor; for, before God and my conscience, I know that the governor does all he can do for the service of God and your Majesty, as well as for the free administration of good government in those states: and your Majesty may rest assured that there are few persons in Spain not belonging to the Company that have had more frequent opportunities of becoming acquainted with the aim and object, with the cleverness and the powerful influence the fathers exert to gain their point (I avoid speaking of private matters), than I have; and my knowledge of these things is derived, not from one, but fifteen years' acquaintance with the Jesuits.

I have heard that the Duke of Alva was somewhat lukewarm about the claims they tried to establish in his time, and believe that he had lawsuits with some of them about matters pertaining to your Majesty's service, of which they bitterly complained (first in secret, and afterwards openly), and now they triumph at the news of the new governor's appointment, and boast that they do and shall enjoy greater authority and higher privileges than they can even desire or demand; for, to adopt their own language, he is a creature of theirs, and I hear that they intend to exert every means in their power to carry whatever they propose and approve. I determined, as in duty bound, to inform your Majesty of this in a private letter I sent by Gaztelú, who is ignorant of its contents; for I am fully aware that they have spies stationed everywhere to inform them of all your affairs as well as other people's; I also know how hostile they are to all persons invested with the slightest authority, when they chance to hear that those ministers have, against their (the Jesuits') will, had anything to do with your Majesty's affairs; nor am I ignorant of the mischief which their secret hostility may do those persons. As the introduction of private matters in this letter would only tire your Majesty, whom it is my sole aim and object to please, I omit every thing calculated to offend your royal person and dignity. God grant your Majesty a happy life, and prolong it many years for the glory of His holy name.—Antwerp, Feb. 18th. Your Majesty's chaplain and servant, *Benito Montano*, kisses your royal feet.

Notices of Árias Montano.

Now that we have seen the severe judgment passed on the Jesuits by Árias Montano, it will not be out of the way to transfer to this place a passage from a work not published[1] [*till the end of the last century.— Translator*] entituled, *Memoirs of events relating to this Royal Monastery of San Lorenzo, from the laying of its first stone on the 23rd of April, 1563, when the first monks came to it, till its completion, and down to the year 1591, with the principal events that occurred in Spain and other countries in those times, written by Fray Juan de San Jerónimo, who was at the Escurial the whole time of its building, and was entrusted by Philip the Second with the account-book of all the expenses laid out on the works. Juan de San Jerónimo died in the year* 1591.

Patris Josephi de Sigüenza: Continuation of these Memoirs, down to the following year 1592, *written by the same Sigüenza.*

" On the 1st of March, 1577, by command of our lord the King, Dr. Benedicto Árias Montano, Chaplain to His Majesty and prelate (comendador) of the order of Santiago, came to this monastery to inspect, expurge, and put in order the Royal Library of San Lorenzo, being a man well fitted for so important an undertaking and so high a trust. Now, these were the doctor's qualifications: in the first place, he was a learned clerk

---

[1] It was published in the library of the Rabbins by José Rodriguez de Castro.

and a great divine; he was familiar with all the sciences and deeply acquainted with the Hebrew, Chaldaic, Greek, Latin, Syriac, Arabic, German, French, Flemish, Italian, Portuguese, and Castilian languages, all of which he knew and understood as well as if he had been brought up in the countries where they are spoken. This doctor was the person who, at the command of His Majesty King Philip, our Lord, went to Flanders to superintend the printing of the Royal Bible of five languages at Antwerp by Plantinus the printer, as may be seen by referring to the book and the prefaces he wrote to it while there.

"This doctor was a native of Frejenal near Seville[2]: so abstemious was he that he only took one meal every twenty-four hours, and even then he did not eat meat or fish, but only vegetables and fruits and the liquor of the olla whether it were oil or gravy: he slept on hard boards, on which he laid a mat and a Bernia blanket: in humility he surpassed all who were acquainted with him: so affable was he that he made every one regard him with affection and love; the learned courted his friendship, and the gentry were edified by him; officers, architects, painters, and men of talent found something to learn of him: the said doctor was ten months at this house, expurging the library and making the Greek and Latin catalogues

[2] The author of these memoirs must have been wool-gathering when he wrote these words. Frejenal, though in Andalusia, *is on the very borders of Estramadura*, and not within *a hundred miles of Seville!—Translator.*]

in it: he divided the books into sixty-four classes, keeping the printed works separate from the manuscripts: he ordered Roman statues and portraits of Supreme Pontiffs, Emperors, Kings, and learned persons to be placed in the library.

At the beginning of September in the aforesaid year '79,[3] Dr. Árias Montano came to this house to inspect the library, by command of His Majesty, who assigned him the house of Santoyo for his residence."[4]

[3] This should be '77, which is the year mentioned at the commencement of the last paragraph but one. The error appears to have escaped the notice of Don Adolfo de Castro, who has copied this document *verbatim* from the Biblioteca de los Rabinos Españoles. —*Translator.*]

[4] Árias Montano died at Seville in 1598, aged 71. Notas literarias de Pellicer, par° 4to., printed in the Biblioteca de los Rabinos Españoles.—*Translator.*

THE END.

LIBRARY OF DAVIDSON COLLEGE